CHOSEN
(KOREA)
SEA
Shanghai
EAST CHINA
SEA
PACIFIC OCEAN
(Formosa)
Philippine Is.
Legend
Railroads
Provincial Bounderies
FIRST TRIP
2nd "
3rd "
4th "
Dotted area indicates extent of Japanese penetration.

TWIN STARS OF CHINA

The five boys, typical of the New China, who accompanied the author on his last trip across North China. From left to right: Auyang (dramatist), Liu (novelist), King (journalist), Lin San (poet), and Wang Yang (photographer).

TWIN STARS OF CHINA

A Behind-the-Scenes Story of China's Valiant Struggle for Existence by a U. S. Marine who Lived & Moved with the People

By

EVANS FORDYCE CARLSON

ILLUSTRATED FROM PHOTOGRAPHS
TAKEN BY THE AUTHOR

Foreign Languages Press

First published by Dodd, Mead and Company, New York, USA, 1940.

Home Page:
http://www.flp.com.cn
E-mail Addresses:
info@flp.com.cn
sales@flp.com.cn

ISBN 7-119-03478-2

Foreign Languages Press, Beijing, 2003

Published by Foreign Languages Press
24 Baiwanzhuang Road, Beijing 100037, China

Printed in the People's Republic of China

PREFACE

Huang Hua

It is a great honor for me to write a preface for the new, PFS (China Society for People's Friendship Studies) 50-book series under the general title of ***Light on China.*** All these books were written in English by journalistic and other eyewitnesses of the events described. I have read many of them over the seven decades since my student days at Yenching University. With some of the outstanding authors in this series I have ties of personal friendship, mutual regard, and warm memories dating from before the Chinese people's Liberation in 1949.

Looking back and forward, I am convinced that China is pursuing the right course in building a strong and prosperous country in a rapidly changing world with its complex and sometimes volatile developments.

The books in this series cover a span of some 150 years, from the mid 19th to the early 21st century. The numerous events in China, the sufferings and struggles of the Chinese people, their history and culture, and their dreams and aspirations were written by foreign observers animated by the spirit of friendship, equality and cooperation. Owing to copyright matters and other difficulties, not all eligible books have as yet been included.

The founder of the first Chinese republic, Dr. Sun Yat-sen wrote in his Testament in 1925, "For forty years I have devoted myself to the cause of the people's revolution with but one end in view: the elevation of China to a position of freedom and equality among the nations. My experiences during those forty years have convinced me that to attain this goal we must bring about an awakening of our own people and ally ourselves in common struggle with those people of the world who regard us as equals."

Chairman Mao Zedong declared, at the triumphal founding of the People's Republic in 1949, "The Chinese people have stood up." Today, having passed its 53rd anniversary, we see the vast forward strides that have been taken, and note that many more remain to be made.

Many foreign observers have traced and reported the real historical movement of modern China, that is: from humiliation — through struggle — to victory. Seeking understanding and friendship with the Chinese people, their insight and perspective were in basic harmony with the real developments in China. But there have been others who viewed China and the Chinese people through glasses tinted by hostile prejudice or ignorance and have invariably made irrelevant observations that could not stand the test of time. This needs to be better understood by young people and students, at home and abroad. The PFS series ***Light on China*** can help them gain an overview of what went before, is happening now, and will emerge in the future.

Young students in China can additionally benefit from these works by seeing how foreign journalists and authors use fluent English to record and present historical, philosophical, and socio-political issues and choices in China. For millions of students in China, English has become a compulsory second language. These texts will also have many-sided usefulness in conveying knowledge of our country to other peoples.

Students abroad, on their part, may be helped by the example of warm, direct accounts and impressions of China presented by their elders in the language that most readily reaches them.

Above all, this timely and needed series should help build bridges of friendship and mutual understanding. Good books long out of print will be brought back to strengthen the edifice.

My hearty thanks and congratulations go first to ex-Premier Zhu Rongji, who has been an effective supporter of this new, PFS series. They go to all engaged in this worthy project, the Foreign Languages Press, our China Society for People's Friendship Studies, and others who have given their efforts and cooperation.

Chairman Mao Zedong has written: "So many deeds cry out to be done, and always urgently. The world rolls on, time presses. Ten thousand years are too long. Seize the day, seize the hour."

The hour has come for making these books available to young people in China and abroad whose destiny is to build a better world together. Let this series add a small brick to that structure.

Beijing, Autumn 2003

TO THE MEMORY OF MY MOTHER,
WHO BEQUEATHED TO HER CHILDREN A RICH
LOVE FOR MANKIND
REGARDLESS OF RACE, CREED OR COLOR

TABLE OF CONTENTS

INTRODUCTION

DURING the past two decades the nations of the world have been gradually moving into one or the other of two antipodal camps. The people of one group of states believe that progress, happiness and the economic well-being of the individual can be best realized through the practice of Democracy. They concede that certain adjustments are still necessary in order that all may enjoy social, economic and political equality, but they contend that these adjustments can be made within the democratic framework—a framework which affords a wide range of individual freedom. In the opposing camp are those states whose leaders have set up a totalitarian government, or where the control of national affairs is in the hands of a military autarchy. Here individual freedom is sacrificed to the state, and to the whims of the privileged group which controls the state.

The struggle between these two camps entered the violent stage in 1931, when Japan invaded Manchuria. It was continued with Italy's invasion of Ethiopia, in the face of the objections of the democratic states. This was followed by the rise of Franco in Spain, and by Germany's excursions into Austria, Czecho-Slovakia and Poland. In Asia the struggle was broadened and intensified by Japan's attempt to conquer China; and in Europe this phase has its counterpart in the bitter battles of 1940.

It is essential that we of the Western Hemisphere recognize this struggle for what it is: a world-wide attempt of the totalitarian states to extend their power and to crush the democratic ideal. The war in Europe and the war in Asia are part and parcel of the same struggle. Both Germany and Japan plan not only to set up super-states in Europe and Asia, respectively, but to extend their control to the Western Hemisphere as well.

This book is about the war in China. My acquaintance with China dates from the rise of the Kuomintang Party in 1927. When the present conflict began, in 1937, I had just returned to China for the third time, and during the succeeding eighteen months I was fortunate in being able to accompany China's armies as an observer for the U.S. Navy Department. In this book I have attempted to tell the story of these wanderings, which took me over the length and breadth of China, much of the distance on foot and horseback. What I saw and heard I have undertaken to record and to interpret in the light of my previous study and observation of Far Eastern history.

As I moved about the country I tried to realize four or five objectives. Any enterprise, if it is to be successful, must be led by men of integrity. Therefore, I sought to meet and study as many as possible of China's leaders. I was particularly interested in China's Communist Party, for it seemed to possess characteristics quite different from the type of doctrine which we have come to associate with Russia. As a military man I sought to observe and analyze the strategy and tactics employed in this war. And finally, in order to understand the customs and practices of the people, as well as to comprehend the military operations, it was necessary to know the geography of the country.

Some Americans have been amused at Chinese statements that they are fighting the battle of democracy in Asia. And yet, to those of us who have watched this struggle at close range, the Chinese claim is by no means fantastic. If China goes down to defeat, Japan will be on the road to becoming the greatest of world empires. Those who are familiar with the Japanese military mind, that mind which is obsessed by the concept of Divine Mission to carry the Japanese brand of culture to the four corners of the world, have no illusions about the manner in which she would utilize her power.

It is an anachronism to continue to regard China as a vast but weak nation. For the past decade China has been marching forward, and since the present struggle began, in 1937, China's entire social and economic order has undergone radical changes. This nation, with a civilization five thousand years old, is destined to become a world power in her own right, and if she retains her independence she will become a democratic stronghold in Asia.

Chinese place names are confusing to the Westerner, and so I have attempted to draw an analogy between the geography of China and North America. Let us assume that Nanking is located at Washington, D.C. Then Shanghai would be in the vicinity of Norfolk, Virginia, and Peip'ing would lie three hundred miles northwest of Ottawa, Canada. The Yangtze river would rise in the Rocky Mountains, somewhere on the Utah-Colorado border, and flow southeast and east by way of Tulsa, Oklahoma (which would correspond to Chungking), Lexington, Kentucky (the location of Hankow), and past Washington, D.C. (Nanking).

The Peip'ing-Hankow railroad would cross the east-west Lunghai line at Lansing, Michigan (Chengchow), and the Tientsin-Pukow railroad would intersect the Lunghai road at Erie, Pennsylvania (Hsuchowfu). Sian would correspond to Dubuque, Iowa; T'aiyuanfu, the capital of Shansi, to Marquette, Michigan; and the Wu T'ai mountains of northeast Shansi would occupy what is eastern Lake Superior. Moving to the southwest, Kunming, the capital of Yunnan, would correspond to San Angelo, Texas, and Haiphong, Indo-China, would be about where Brownsville, Texas stands. These locations are approximate, of course.

This book would not have been written but for the urging and encouragement of kind friends, whose interest and assistance I gratefully acknowledge. For the use of the first person I apologize to the reader. It is not pleasant to write of one's personal feelings and experiences, and I have done so only because I believe that I was privileged to witness events which are little known, and which have considerable historical significance. If this book possesses any merit, it lies in the honesty with which I have attempted to portray the people and events I observed.

Finally, I wish to acknowledge, with appreciation, the courtesy of the publishers of *Asia*, *Amerasia* and *Pacific Affairs* magazines, and of the International Secretariat of the Institute of Pacific Relations, for permission to rearrange here some of the material which was first used by them.

Plymouth, Connecticut,

June 1, 1940

ILLUSTRATIONS

TWIN STARS OF CHINA

CHAPTER I
SHANGHAI, 1937: JAPAN UNDERESTIMATES A NATION

I

BRILLIANT sunlight suffused the Yangtze estuary on this mid-August morning of 1937 as the *S.S. President McKinley* steamed slowly towards the Whangpoo river and Shanghai. It brought into sharp relief the green of the fields off to the west, a welcome contrast to the foul yellow of the intervening water. And it played about the decks and superstructures of the grim vessels of war which flanked our course, now and then finding a polished surface on which its rays seemed to bounce and wink impishly at us.

The war vessels rode at anchor, and each flew at its stern the flag of the Rising Sun of Japan. Squat destroyers bobbed jauntily behind sleek light cruisers, and up ahead the bulky superstructures of heavy cruisers lurched ponderously back and forth across the flawless sky. Decks were cleared for action and guns pointed menacingly towards the western shore.

As the *McKinley* turned into the Whangpoo, off Woosung, two divisions of light bombing planes rumbled overhead, their lower wings also bearing the red emblems of the Rising Sun. Presently they strung out into single file and the leader dove swiftly towards the dome of the administration building of the new Chinese Civic Center of Greater Shanghai, followed in column by his five companions. Small puffs of smoke drifted up from the dome, showing that the bombs had hit their mark. It seemed unreal, but we were witnessing war— the opening stage of Japan's effort to dominate the Chinese people.

When I had sailed from Seattle three weeks before it had not been with the expectation of attending a war, though all who had lived in the Orient during the past decade realized that ultimately China and Japan must fight, for no nation can, with either honor or safety, permit repeated invasions of its sovereignty. My object was to undertake the formal study of the Chinese language. But, "there's a Divinity that shapes our ends, rough-hew them how we will," and by the time the *President McKinley* had docked at Yokohama fighting had commenced at Shanghai.

Destiny had taken a hand in the direction of my affairs, and although I did not know it, there would be no poring over ideographs in a language school at Peip'ing for me. Instead I would tramp the hinterland of China during the next eighteen months, accompanying the armies as an official observer for the United States Navy, and witnessing at first hand China's efforts to preserve her independence.

The great ship dropped anchor a mile above Woosung. Although there was a full passenger list, only a handful of people descended with me to the tender for debarkation at Shanghai. This was no place for tourists, or even for businessmen whose affairs could be postponed to more peaceful times. Turning out from the side of the ship the tender headed up-stream for the eight-mile run to the Customs Jetty, and I settled back to reflect on the panorama of changes that had occurred in China since my first arrival ten years before.

I had come out then with a regiment of Marines, sent to protect the lives and interests of Americans against the Kuomintang armies of Chiang Kai-shek which were moving up from the south. In the interim these armies had eliminated the old provincial war-lords, and China had been unified under a government established by the Kuomintang Party (Nationalist—or Party of the People). The national capital had been shifted from Peip'ing, in the north, to Nanking, on the Yangtze.

A split in the Party had occurred at this time, the Communist elements being purged. These had organized a Red army and a Soviet area, in which agrarian reforms were stressed, and for nine years a bitter civil war had been fought which had only ended the preceding December in a truce. This was followed by the formation of a united front against the increasing encroachments of Japan.

During these ten years China had become stronger, despite internal friction. Communications had been improved, laws were revised, education was advanced, and China had developed a self-respect and a national pride which caused her leaders to insist that she be treated as an equal by the nations of the West. The period when Americans, Japanese and Europeans could enjoy special privileges here was fast ebbing. The businessmen of the West were already preparing to revise their methods of dealing with the East. But from across the China Sea an arrogant Japan viewed with increasing perturbation the signs of China's growing strength. A strong China had no place in her plans for a New Order in East Asia.

In September, 1931, Japan had tested the reaction of Western Powers to her program of expansion by conquest. Her armies invaded Manchuria, and the puppet state of Manchoukuo was set up. Encouraged by the patent reluctance of the Powers to oppose her, Japan undertook, in 1933, the conquest of Jehol, in Inner Mongolia.

These invasions of China's sovereignty aroused the ire of her people and accelerated the growth of a latent spirit of nationalism. National Salvation societies sprang up throughout the country, personal and political antagonisms were laid aside, and the nation settled down to prepare for the test of strength which now seemed inevitable. When, on the seventh of July, a Japanese army detachment in North China had attempted to dictate to a Chinese garrison at Lukouchiao, the Chinese government challenged its authority. The time for the test of strength had arrived.

As I mentally reviewed this series of events the tender sped past the warehouses of the Yangtzepoo district of Shanghai, which extend for five miles along the north bank of the Whangpoo, made the turn to the south at the Garden Bridge, and came to rest at the Jetty, on the west bank. Here the Bund presented an unfamiliar sight. Absent were the usual milling crowds of coolies, merchants and hucksters. Absent also was the heavy traffic of motor cars, tram-cars, brokers' wagons, bicycles and rickshas. Even the faces of the lofty hotels and office buildings bore an unfamiliar expression, for their lower windows were barricaded and their doorways were sheltered with walls of sand bags, stacked like cord wood. Across the way the Palace Hotel showed a ragged hole in its roof where a bomb had entered.

Jim Mills, veteran roving correspondent of the Associated Press, had joined me at Kobe, and now we asked each other what we should do.

"I suggest that we look up Morris Harris first," said Jim, "and find out from him what the score is."

This was a good idea, and we started for the Cable building. Harris was an old friend of both of us. For ten years he had presided over the Associated Press bureau here in Shanghai, and there was little he didn't know about current affairs.

"You've come to a hot spot," smiled Harris. "You're smack in the middle of a war."

Then he proceeded to give us an outline of recent developments. "Ten days ago a clash occurred out near Hungjao airdrome (five miles west of the Settlement) between an officer and a seaman of the Japanese Naval Landing Force and a Chinese sentry. Since then Japan has poured naval re-enforcements into the Landing Party, and the Chinese have brought several army divisions down from Nanking. Fighting broke out four days ago, and last Saturday Chinese planes accidentally dropped bombs here in the International Settlement, damaging the Cathay and Palace hotels, and severing water mains on Avenue Edward VII, on the French Concession boundary. Nearly two thousand casualties resulted, including several foreigners. Foreign consuls have advised evacuation of women and children, and of those businessmen whose presence is not essential here. The battle line right now extends from the Settlement boundary on Soochow Creek, north through Hongkew for two miles, then bends east and southeast through the Yangtzepoo district."

It looked very much like the war we had been so long expecting, for the Nanking government had given every indication of resisting.

At Harris' suggestion we arranged for rooms at the American Club. When that was done I went out to call on Admiral Harry E. Yarnell, the Commander-in-Chief of our Asiatic Fleet.

In the Whangpoo river, off the Bund, towered the flagships of the fleets of America, Britain and France, while below, and around the bend, lay the Japanese armored cruiser, *Idzumo*, with the flag of Vice Admiral Hasegawa flying at the main. Above the foreign warships, and opposite the south boundary of the French concession, the Chinese had sunk steamers and sea-going junks to form a boom which barred the movement of ships up-stream.

A boat took me to the *U.S.S. Augusta*, which was moored at the head of the column of foreign war vessels, and I was ushered into the cabin of the Commander-in-Chief. I found a quiet, mild appearing man whose kindly, weather-beaten face scarcely suggested his sixty-odd years. During the eventful weeks to come I was to discover that behind the quiet reserve was a discerning and discriminating mind, and that these calm, penetrating eyes sheltered a firm resolve not to yield an inch to any attempt of Japanese military or naval officials to trespass on American rights.

"It seems to me," remarked the Admiral, "that you could be more useful here than in Peip'ing right now. Do you know anything about the language?"

I informed him that I had studied it for two years while on duty at Peip'ing in 1933-35.

It was finally settled that I would be attached to the office of the Naval Attaché at Shanghai, a decision in which the Ambassador concurred.

That night an incident occurred which was one of many that would try the Admiral's patience and test his spirit during the succeeding months. A Japanese destroyer moved up-stream and dropped anchor scarcely three hundred yards off the bow of the *Augusta*. All through the night it bombarded Chinese positions on Pootung, south and east of the Whangpoo. The proximity of the destroyer to the *Augusta* prevented the Chinese from replying to the fire. The following morning Admiral Yarnell despatched a sharp note to the Japanese naval commander, and the episode was not repeated. But others equally trying were to follow.

On shore, business was virtually at a standstill. The younger businessmen were on duty with the Shanghai Volunteer Corps, which was assisting British and American units to guard the borders of the Settlement. The Japanese had already occupied the Hongkew and Yangtzepoo districts of the Settlement, north of Soochow Creek, but the officials of the neutral Powers here were determined that the troops of both belligerents would be kept out of the foreign districts to the south. The battle lines lay to the north of these foreign districts, but that did not prevent them from being visited by stray shells and bullets. During the three succeeding months there was never a moment when any part of Shanghai was free of the sound of gun fire and exploding shells.

At the American Consulate-General I found efficient and bespectacled Clarence Gauss, the Consul-General, calmly directing the mass of additional administrative work which the hostilities had thrown on his office. Women members of the secretarial staff had been evacuated, and Mr. Gauss and his consuls were doing most of their own typing.

It was fortunate that Clarence Gauss should have held this post at this critical time, for he was ideally equipped, by virtue of his long years of consular and diplomatic service in the Far East, to handle the multitude of delicate problems which arose. Every morning throughout the battle he met in his office with Admiral Yarnell and Colonel Charles F. B. Price, the brilliant commander of the Fourth U. S. Marines. Together this distinguished triumvirate ironed out current problems and prepared plans for such emergencies as could be foreseen. No note of friction marred the cooperation of these three, and it was due largely to their sound judgment and ceaseless vigilance that no overt act or diplomatic blunder endangered America's neutrality here during the battle.

II

My colleague at Shanghai was Major Edward Hagen, of the U. S. Marines, a loyal and faithful friend. Hagen had his regular duties as Assistant Naval

Attaché to perform, and it was decided that I would concern myself with the belligerent armies, principally the Chinese.

I had participated in wars before, but this was the first one I had observed officially from the side lines. The first question was, "How should I go about it"? A war has to be seen to be observed, I argued, and to see it one has to get out to the front where the fighting is going on. I applied for a designation as an official observer, and Generalissimo Chiang Kai-shek would have none of it. Such designations weren't being issued.

The days were slipping by and I was seeing only what could be seen from the roof tops of buildings on the perimeter of the International Settlement, opposite the Chinese right flank. Finally, I analyzed the objections of the Chinese to the presence of foreign observers with the army in this manner: First, they probably felt that a Western observer would ridicule the methods and equipment of their armies; and, second, Chinese commanders were probably reluctant to assume responsibility for the safety of observers. They simply didn't want to be bothered.

The attitude of the Chinese was understandable, for in the past Westerners had shown little willingness to understand the Chinese way of life, much less their way of waging war. I decided to disabuse their minds of these prejudices, and to attempt to secure a pass from competent authority which would be honored by the sentries. Armed with this authority I could sally forth into the battle lines without burdening the commanders with a sense of responsibility for my safety.

With the aid of old Chinese friends I secured the pass I sought. Now I could get out into the fields to the north and west of the city, where the battle was in progress.

Parts of two Japanese divisions had landed, by this time, along the south bank of the Yangtze, between Woosung and Liuho, a distance of twenty miles, thereby relieving the pressure on their naval landing force, which had begun the fighting at Shanghai. During the 1912 battle here this maneuver had brought about the capitulation of the Chinese defenders, whose left flank was exposed. But now the Chinese left flank extended beyond Liuho, and the invaders were compelled to resort to frontal attacks in order to gain ground.

One day I decided to try my pass. Moving west through the residential section of the Settlement, I passed the British defense works on the west boundary and turned north into the battle area. Across the fields from the rural districts columns of coolies padded their way towards the city, loads of fresh vegetables suspended from their shoulder poles. They appeared oblivious of the Japanese planes which droned overhead until one swooped low to strafe the ground. Then they would drop their burdens and crouch in ditches, or behind grave mounds, which dotted the plain. This custom of burying the dead above ground possessed advantages.

A sentry stopped me, as I approached the system of trenches, and inquired for my hu-chao. A glance at my yellow-bound passport was sufficient, and he waved me on. It worked, and I was elated.

Artillery fire from both sides was sporadic, but hardly a Chinese soldier was visible above the surface. The army had dug in. Here and there a reenforced concrete machine-gun position was manned by sharp-eyed men from Kiangsu and Anhwei provinces. They gazed at me wonderingly as I approached. "How are you, lao hsiang (fellow countrymen)," I asked cheerily, "using the form of address popular in rural China?" They grinned broadly, said they were well and wanted to know how I was. There is something about the atmosphere of a battle field which invariably invokes a feeling of brotherhood among men. Doubtless these men thought I was a crazy foreigner to be risking my life out here in a war that was not my own, but it was my life—and anyway, we might all be dead at the next minute. We were brothers sharing a common danger.

These soldiers wore the thin cotton uniform of horizon blue, though I met some units that wore the olive drab. Legs were usually encased in wrap puttees similar in color to trousers and tunic. Their rifles were of various makes—German, Russian, Czecho-Slovakian. Non-commissioned officers of the higher ratings, and officers, carried the heavy German Mauser pistol, encased in a wooden holster which could be slipped on to the pistol as a stock.

On this day there was little activity. The trenches were much the same as those soldiers dig in Western countries, so I turned into a communication trench which led to the rear. A man in the uniform of a private addressed me in perfect English.

"You are an American ?" he asked.

"Indeed I am," I replied. "Where did you learn your English?"

"In America," he replied, amused at my surprise. "I graduated from one of your universities, and then returned to China to teach. But now our country needs men to fight for her, and I am here doing my bit."

Never before had I heard of a college man being in the ranks of the Chinese army. For centuries the proverb, "as you would not use good iron to make a nail, so you would not use a good man to make a soldier," had reflected the low regard of the Chinese people for military men.

"Are there many of your sort in the army now?" I inquired.

"Yes, many," he assured me. "The spirit of nationalism is wide spread, and the people are becoming increasingly conscious of their united strength. It was the students of schools and universities who for years kept alive the idea of nationalism, and who pressed for resistance to Japanese demands. Now our work is bearing fruit. Our people are coming to realize that if the nation is to survive, all must subordinate their personal ambitions and work for the common welfare."

Just how extensive was this consciousness of national welfare, I wondered, and as I continued towards the rear I queried soldiers and coolies.

"What are you fighting for?" I asked a perspiring coolie, who rested beside his shoulder pole, with its double-ended load of cooked rice.

"National salvation," he replied without hesitation.

"But what is national salvation?"

He turned this question over in his mind for a moment, and then replied slowly: "The enemy wants to take our homes from us. If we work together we can defeat him."

It was as simple as that to him. His home was in danger, and if it was to be saved he and others like him must work together. In my years in China I had never before seen anything like it. I wondered if the Japanese realized the extent and quality of this spirit.

Emerging from the communication trench I came to a narrow footpath which skirted a truck garden. Coolies padded towards the front, caldrons of steaming rice, or boxes of ammunition, suspended from shoulder poles. Walking wounded meandered towards the rear, or rested against the broad bosoms of the grave mounds. Overhead whined the shells of a Japanese battery which was seeking the range of a small village a half mile ahead. It is curious how quickly the ear attunes itself to the sound of swishing shells, determining with remarkable accuracy their direction and probable point of impact. Aerial bombs are different. They always sound the same—as though they are coming directly at you.

At the village I found the company kitchens installed in mud-walled houses. The local populace had evacuated, leaving the soldiers in full possession. Three gaping holes in the walls showed that not all the Japanese shells had gone amiss. But the cooks appeared unperturbed.

"What do people eat in your country?" one of them asked curiously.

"Meat. potatoes, peas, corn," I told him.

"No rice?"

"Yes, a little rice," I replied. "But more often we use it as dessert."

Rice as a sweet dish! That was beyond him.

"How can you walk in those heavy shoes?" he asked, curiously.

I compared my stout leather walking boots with the thin multistitched cotton cloth shoes which clad his own feet.

"I'm used to them," I replied. "Besides, they protect my feet from the mud and the stones."

"I take mine off in the mud," he said, a little disdainfully, as he moved off to tend his fire.

Not all the soldiers were so articulate, but all were ready with a smile or a joke when approached in a friendly manner. Moreover, they possessed a native intelligence which enabled them to grasp an idea quickly. It was only a little more than a decade ago that the Chinese soldier was little more than a piece of merchandise who worked and fought in proportion to his rate of pay.

In the interim political training under the tutelage of the Kuomintang had developed in him a degree of social consciousness and a sense of responsibility to the nation.

I pondered over this revelation as I worked my way back to the city. The war would be long, I ruminated, if Japan persisted in her attempt to conquer these people.

III

Major Hagen and I were sitting at lunch with Admiral Yarnell and his Chief of Staff, Captain McConnell, on the *Augusta*, one day late in August. Suddenly we were startled by the unmistakable whistle of some kind of missile, close aboard.

"Are those fellows firing over us?" exclaimed the Admiral, as he left his chair and went to the porthole to look for the point of explosion.

He referred to the possibility that Japanese naval vessels, from their positions down the Whangpoo, might be firing over the *Augusta*.

But no explosion sounded, and somewhat mystified the Admiral returned to his seat. Hardly had he sat down when a terrific detonation shook the ship. From my position, facing the Customs Jetty, I could see smoke and debris boiling out of the canyon that was Nanking Road.

The telephone rang and the Naval Purchasing Officer, who had offices ashore, reported that a large bomb had passed through three concrete floors of the Navy warehouse, and come to rest on the ground floor without exploding. This was the bomb which we had heard. Another had fallen a few minutes later into Nanking Road, near the Sincere department store, one of the city's busy intersections.

Hastily finishing our lunch, Hagen and I departed for the scene of the explosion. The police and fire departments of the Settlement had already removed most of the wounded, and the bodies of two hundred dead were being loaded into trucks.

The bomb had struck a balcony railing outside the second floor of the Sincere store, and fragments had damaged every building in the intersection, while the concussion broke windows blocks away.

This was the last of the aerial bombs to drop within the foreign settlements, but each day saw literally tons of bombs dropped on the Chinese district of Chapel, joining the Settlement on the north, where the Chinese right flank was deeply entrenched. The Japanese had the air to themselves during daylight hours, and from sunup to sundown their planes ferried bombs from the landing field at Point Island, five miles down the Whangpoo, to the Chinese positions in Chapel. It seemed impossible that men could continue to live under such a deluge of death, but they did. The Chinese had dug bombproofs, and when the Japanese infantry attacked they were invariably met with vicious machine-gun and rifle fire. The defenders refused to be budged from this key position.

Both sides continued to pour re-enforcements into the areas behind the lines. By the 13th of September the Japanese had succeeded in landing nearly fifty thousand troops, and had made some progress inland over towards Liuho, nearly twenty miles to the north. This placed the Chinese troops which had been resisting nearer to Shanghai in a salient, and one night General Chang Chih-chung, the Chinese commander, straightened out his line by evacuating this salient. The battle continued for over a month along the new line.

Early one evening the Chinese launched a co-ordinated counter-offensive along their right flank, and a squadron of planes came down from Nanking to assist. I was listening to the rising crescendo of battle from the vantage point of the Yu Ya Ching road bridge when I noticed a Chinese plane flying low overhead with its running lights on. What, I thought, could be the reason for this gross indiscretion? Later in the evening I learned the story.

It seemed that one plane had fallen behind, and as it neared the city the pilot spotted a squadron of Japanese planes which was returning from a bombing mission. The enemy planes had turned on their running lights so as to identify them to their own anti-aircraft batteries. With quick resourcefulness the Chinese turned on his lights and followed the Japanese to their landing field. As the last plane alighted he swept over the field and released his bombs in tandem, destroying seven enemy planes.

Chinese planes were never particularly effective at Shanghai, but they worried the Japanese, and caused them to expend an excessive quantity of ammunition. After the first few days the Chinese confined their air operations to night raids, the raiders coming singly, or by pairs, at irregular intervals during the night. The approach of one plane was the signal for Japanese anti-aircraft guns, both land and ship based, to cut loose. It was a spectacular pyrotechnic display, but seldom resulted in bringing down a plane. Sometimes Chinese cunning made their adversary appear ridiculous.

There was the night, for example, when two Chinese planes approached the city from the west. One landed at the Hungjao airdrome, west of the foreign areas, and the pilot accelerated his motor, the sound being picked up by the Japanese sound-range instruments. Every anti-aircraft gun they had was directed to the west, the fire passing over the foreign settlements, and occasional unexploded shells dropped in them with disastrous effect. In the meantime the second plane made a long detour to the south and approached the Japanese positions from that direction undetected until it loosed its bombs and was off.

On another night I heard a plane coming down the Whangpoo river, flying low. It was after midnight, and there had been several previous raids. Perhaps this was the reason the Japanese held their fire until the plane was over the foreign flagships. Then they let go, but the plane was underneath the trajectories of the guns. Continuing on its course, it released its bombs over the Japanese Consulate-General, reversed its course, and returned up-stream, still flying under the trajectories.

Out to the north the battle continued day and night, with the lines seesawing back and forth. The superiority of the Japanese in artillery and in the air began to tell, though, and inch by inch the center of the Chinese line gave way. The tenacity of the defenders was almost beyond belief, but their casualties mounted to the fifty thousand mark, and continued up. How long could they continue to hold? This was the question which was on the lips of all in the city. But out behind the lines fresh troops continued to arrive. They were not the hand-picked veterans who had been trained in the German supervised training centers at Nanking, for these already constituted the backbone of the defense. They came from the provinces, men full of enthusiasm and fired with the spirit of national salvation, but lacking in experience and training. They came up to the front eager and vibrant; and in a few days they, too, lay still on the brown autumn soil, or were jogged back to hospitals at night in brush-covered trucks, over the freshly built roads.

IV

One of my Chinese secret service friends was going to Nanking, about 170 miles north-west by automobile. Would I like to accompany him? Of course. I had long wanted to see what the lines of communication looked like. And the trip would also afford an opportunity to see Ambassador Johnson and other friends at the Embassy.

My friend was typical of the wealthy merchant class. It was close to midnight when we motored, without lights, past the successive sentry lines. The countersign consisted of two words, my friend using one, and the sentry replying with the other.

A network of new roads had been constructed back of the battle position, and incessant rains had reduced them to the consistency of glue at some points. After a few miles we found ourselves hopelessly mired in the middle of a column of trucks which were in the same predicament. My friend had no solution for the situation, and as dawn approached his agitation visibly increased.

"The Japanese planes will be here at dawn," he groaned. "We ought to go back to Shanghai."

But there was no turning back—or going forward without much digging and padding of the road.

A short, wiry soldier, obviously from some province of the south, sauntered along. My companion hailed him. He strolled casually around the car, regarding its mired wheels with seeming indifference. Then, without losing his air of nonchalance, he left us and moved off towards a small village which was beginning to show signs of life.

Half an hour passed. A hubbub arose from the village, and presently a curious caravan issued forth. As it wound towards us over a tortuous path we saw that it consisted of fifty-odd villagers, each bent low under a load of straw. At the head of the column was the short soldier.

Without a word to us he jacked up the rear wheels, injecting armfuls of straw beneath. The balance he directed to be distributed over an improvised road bed, around the trucks ahead. The villagers, laughing and joking as they sloshed through the mud, virtually lifted the car onto the new road bed, and we were off. Such is the initiative and ingenuity of the Chinese soldier.

The rest of the trip was covered before night. During the next eight hours four flights of Japanese planes passed overhead. They flew at twelve to fifteen thousand feet altitude and obviously had more important business than the strafing of a lone passenger car.

At T'angshan, on the outskirts of Nanking, a policeman stopped us.

"Pull over to the side of the road under that tree," he directed. "The air alarm just sounded."

In a few minutes a flight of thirty planes approached from the east and divided into two squadrons, one continuing to the central part of Nanking, and the other swinging north towards the river. For the next ten minutes the sound of dull explosions reached our ears.

A siren sounded the end of the raid, and we proceeded. In Nanking we found that the city had been subjected to a series of raids throughout the day. The electric light plant had been struck, and one of the largest hospitals was a shambles.

Many old friends were at the Embassy. The offices resembled a military headquarters, with maps on the walls and a press of business that kept everyone moving. The feminine members of the staff had been evacuated, throwing the stenographic work onto the already overworked administrative staff.

Captain Frank Roberts, the Assistant Military Attaché, invited me to share his home during my stay, and we spent half the night exchanging impressions. Quiet, studious and efficient, he would have much preferred to be observing on the front, but he was the type of officer who tried to get the most out of the job at hand. When the opportunity came for him to test his mettle, he was prepared. It was Roberts who took charge of the survivors of the *U.S.S. Panay*, after she had been bombed, guided them to safety and made contact with the authorities.

The Ambassador, Nelson Trusler Johnson, was easily the mainspring of the Embassy, not only because he was chief of the mission, but because of his buoyant personality and his ability to inspire his staff and give them confidence. In appearance he was a bit on the heavy side, and his reddish hair had become thin on top. But it was his hearty, jovial manner and his consideration for his fellowmen which drew people to him. He has been in and out of China for thirty years, speaks the language, can quote Chinese classics by the yard, and knows the culture, history and customs of the country. These accomplishments have enabled him to guide the affairs of this nation in China, as chief of mission, since 1930 with a deftness and understanding which is given to few diplomats.

At this time he was passing through an extremely awkward period. A few days before the Japanese had threatened to initiate unrestricted bombing in Nanking, and foreigners were warned to depart. The Ambassador issued the customary warning to Americans to leave the threatened area, and on the 20th of September he removed the Embassy staff to the *U.S.S. Luzon*, an American gunboat which lay in the river. The move was in accordance with the established policy of avoiding incidents by keeping out of the way, when it can be done without loss of dignity and without impairing the functions of the mission. Other Embassies took similar precautions, but apparently Mr. Johnson was the only chief of mission formally to advise the Chinese Foreign Office of his action.

When the news reached the United States the following day a storm of protest swept the country. It was directed for the most part against the Japanese for making it necessary for the Embassy to move, but the Ambassador came in for considerable criticism. On the following day, the attack having failed to materialize, he returned to the Nanking offices, but the controversy raged at home for days.

I mention this incident only because I was on the ground a few days after it happened, and because I have known the Ambassador for years, and feel that the criticism he drew at this time was unjust. He possesses a high sense of duty, and would never utter a word in his own defense. I have been in aerial raids with him both at Nanking and later, at Hankow, and his good humor and serenity of spirit were always an inspiration to those who were with him.

Sharing Mr. Johnson's office at this time was gentle, scholarly Willys Peck, the Counsellor of Embassy. A master of the nuances of the Chinese language, no foreign service officer is more highly regarded in China. Also on the staff were George Atcheson and Hall Paxton, who went through the *Panay* bombing later, and Douglas Jenkins, Jr., whose next duty was at Warsaw, Poland, where he learned even more about war.

Air raids were a daily occurrence during these three days. Dugouts had been constructed throughout the city, and the populace was well drilled in their use. The first alarm, the scream of a siren, usually gave twenty minutes warning, and immediately the people would commence to dog-trot through the streets to their allotted shelter. In ten minutes the streets would be clear. At the Embassy the staff usually assembled on top of the dugout, a good vantage point from which to observe the air duels and bombing.

General Chang Hui-chang accompanied my Chinese friend and me on the return trip to Shanghai. I had known him ten years before, when he had gained the title of the Chinese "Lindbergh" by making a tour of China in a Ryan monoplane. Now he was on his way to the Chungsan district of Kwangtung province (near Canton), to become governor of that area.

On the road General Chang amused himself—and us—by attempting to identify the native provinces of the troops we passed, simply by examining their appearance. His accuracy was amazing.

Now we had more time to observe activities along the countryside. At each village young men were being taught the elements of military evolutions. New roads were being built, and a steady stream of supplies was moving towards Shanghai by trucks, by trains, and by boats over the intricate system of canals.

At Soochow we passed the newly constructed system of defenses, the third that lay behind Shanghai. Here also was the headquarters of General Ku Chu-t'ung, Commander-in-Chief of the Shanghai area.

East of Soochow we were in the district where the American, Frederick Townsend Ward, won fame with his Ever Victorious Army during the Taip'ing rebellion, just before our Civil War. Ward's fame remains undiminished in China, though abroad the name of Chinese Gordon, the British officer who succeeded him when he was killed, is better known.

Night was falling as we again approached the Shanghai battle front. Troops filled the roads, as they moved up to relieve their comrades in the trenches. Presently the rumble of the battle reached our ears. Trucks camouflaged with branches of foliage and bearing wounded from the battle field squeezed their way into the line of troops and traffic which choked the road. In the darkness this could have been an army on the march in any country, were it not for the coolies who padded silently past us, their burdens of food, kitchen gear or munitions swinging rhythmically from shoulder poles. At a snail's pace we inched along until we reached the sentry line on the outskirts of Hungjao, five miles west of Shanghai.

There was something depressing about the bright lights of the city as we motored through the streets of the International Settlement. Probably it was the suddenness with which we had emerged from the somber atmosphere behind the front. Back there men were plodding and sweating, suffering and dying; here people seemed so free of care, so oblivious of the pain and struggle which was little more than a stone's throw away. Neon signs announced the latest cinema attractions. Speeding taxicabs bore gay dinner parties to night clubs. Only the ragged refugees, huddled in cheerless groups along the sidewalks, suggested the note of tragedy which harmonized with the battle which raged without.

V

As the battle moved into the third month the Japanese high command showed signs of increasing annoyance. Plans for winding up the China "incident" in three months had definitely met a reversal. There had been a few local gains, but the general resistance of the Chinese seemed to be gaining in strength, rather than otherwise. Even more serious from the Japanese standpoint was the fact that the Chinese success at Shanghai had given courage to the whole nation. Perhaps the invincible Japanese army was not so invincible. The high command addressed itself to a re-shaping of its policy.

Back in August the Japanese premier, Prince Konoye, had made the astounding statement that "Japan's one course is to beat China to her knees so that she may no longer have the spirit to fight." Now the Commander-in-Chief of the Japanese forces at Shanghai, General Iwane Matsui, came out with the equally startling statement that the main objective of his army was "to scourge the Chinese government and army." Such language implied a particularly virulent type of arrogance on the part of the spokesman. And it reflected a sharp change in Japan's objectives in China.

In July the Japanese had sought merely to gain control of the five northern provinces of Hopei, Shansi, Shantung, Chahar and Suiyuan. Now it was proposed to destroy the Chinese government. The conquest of China was to begin immediately, instead of being attempted in piece-meal fashion. The Russian campaign, so long dreamed of by the Kwangtung army of Manchuria, must wait.

Re-enforcements began to arrive on the Shanghai front. The invading army grew to eighty thousand. Heavy artillery supplemented the light and medium artillery which was already pounding the lines. Tazang, a small village northwest of Chapel, became the focal point of attack. With business-like persistency the Japanese army settled down to the task of blasting its way through Tazang—an operation which, if successful, would compel the retirement of the Chinese right flank from Chapel.

One Sunday morning late in October General Matsui, the Japanese commander, issued an official statement that the Chinese army was retiring all along the line. I had heard of no such movement, and a telephone conversation with American and British observers, who were able to see the Chinese lines from their observation posts, elicited the information that the situation was normal.

Commanders-in-Chief do not issue official statements without good reason. Something was in the wind, and I decided to go out and have a look around. Thinking that he might like to go along, I telephoned John B. Powell, publisher of the *China Weekly Review*, who was always ready for an expedition which offered a whiff of adventure, or a good story.

"Let's take my car and ride out behind the lines," he suggested.

In a few minutes we were off.

J. B. is more than a magazine publisher in Shanghai; he is an institution. For over twenty years he has been here, editing newspapers, publishing the *Review*, and pinch hitting for the homeside papers, when they needed an extra correspondent. A steady plugger for justice and the truth, and a fearless exposer of corruption and shady dealing, he has defeated more than one attempt to muzzle him—and even to kill him.

We headed out along the south bank of Soochow Creek, west of the Settlement, where the Chinese had already constructed reserve positions. It was an exhilarating October day. Over to the north the usual artillery duel was in progress, and the situation appeared to be normal. Boats glided silently on the creek, sculled by perspiring boatmen, those outbound crowded with refugees, and the inbound ones loaded with coal or munitions. Here and there women stood knee-deep in the water, scrubbing clothes on stones worn smooth by their ancestors.

This peaceful scene was suddenly shattered by the siren-like scream of a dive bomber, followed by another and another. The sky that but a moment ago had been clear was now teeming with planes. We had calmly motored into a hornet's nest. Attack planes strafed the ground, light bombers dove here and there, and high overhead twin-motored Heinkels droned ominously.

The craft on the creek were already securing to the banks, the occupants seeking such shelter as was available. It was no time for motoring, and we parked near a small factory which flew a German flag, and mounted to the roof.

The significance of General Matsui's statement was now apparent. He hoped to accelerate the retirement of the Chinese right flank by paralyzing communications and breaking up reserves behind that flank with a smashing air attack.

Up ahead the road crossed to the north bank of Soochow Creek. Three heavy bombs had just been dropped in the vicinity of the bridge, and we decided to walk up and see if any damage had been done. We were still two hundred yards short of the bridge when the drone of heavy engines told that the Heinkels were overhead. As we glanced aloft six bombs flashed in the sunlight as they left the three huge monoplanes. For the moment our interest was academic, but this Olympian attitude underwent a swift change when the sickening swish-wish of the descending bombs reached our ears. I flung myself in a convenient ditch, and J. B. dived in another direction. Deafening concussions followed.

Looking up rather gingerly, I spied J. B.'s head protruding from a post hole a dozen feet ahead.

"They missed the bridge again," he grinned.

The bombs had struck a newly constructed trench system, fortunately unoccupied, half way between us and the bridge.

It was two hours before we could return to the car. Moving from depression to depression, we inched our way back, while the bombardment continued. We blessed the Chinese for burying their dead above ground, for occasionally the grave mounds provided protection from strafing planes. Chinese soldiers had the same idea, and sometimes we shared the same mound, working around its base so as to keep the attacking plane on the far side.

The attack ceased as abruptly as it had begun, and we returned to the city.

Three days later the Chinese evacuated Chapei and placed their right flank along the south bank of Soochow Creek, so that it was still hinged, on the Settlement, though now it rested on the West boundary instead of the North.

A widely publicized feature of the retirement was the refusal of a battalion of five hundred men of the 88th Division to evacuate a warehouse near Yu Ya Ching road. It was a heroic gesture, for the battalion was immediately surrounded by the enemy and subjected to a severe bombardment, but it had no military value, and in four days the men surrendered to the International Settlement authorities and were interned.

VI

The battle at Shanghai might have continued for months if it had not been for a piece of gross negligence of the Chinese in relaxing their vigil along the north shore of Hangchow Bay. Despite the withdrawal of the Chinese right flank to Soochow Creek, the lines were holding well, and two prepared positions, at Tsingpu and Soochow, contained strong defensive works which could have been effectively utilized if further retirements became advisable. But on the fifth of November came the news that the Japanese had landed a brigade on the north coast of Hangchow Bay, opposite the Tsinpu line.

It later developed that General Chang Fa-kwei, who commanded this defense area, had been shifted to command the Shanghai Front. There had been a miscarriage of orders and the Manchurian troops which were ordered to relieve General Chang's forces failed to arrive before the others had departed. The omnipresent Japanese intelligence service conveyed the news swiftly to the High Command, and the landing was made almost without opposition.

A general Chinese retirement was now imperative, for the enemy was now in a position to cut the lines of communication. On the night of the 8th-9th of November the bulk of the Chinese army silently evacuated its positions on the Shanghai front, and retired towards Soochow.

It was inevitable that the retirement, under these circumstances, should be attended with much disorder. Three hundred thousand troops were crowded into the narrow peninsula between the Yangtze and the Whangpoo rivers, which is only forty to fifty miles wide. Chinese staff officers had not had the experience or the training to enable them to move this large body of troops in a systematic manner, especially when it was necessary to fight delaying actions on the front and on one flank as well. Both the Tsinpu and Soochow positions were given up, and preparations were made to defend the national capital at Nanking.

The Naval Attaché, Commander Overesch, had come down from Peip'ing a few days before the battle ended, and he joined me in inspection trips along the front. We were both impressed by the high spirit of the troops and the business-like way in which they resisted the Japanese attacks. Machine guns, trench mortars, and guns of twenty, thirty-seven and seventy-five millimeters were used effectively and in accordance with recognized tactical and technical principals. China's deficiency was in the quantity of these weapons which were available, and she was miserably handicapped by her inferiority in the air. Spirit, flesh and blood could not indefinitely prevail in the face of superior fire power in a pitched battle.

As the Japanese troops worked around the west and south boundaries of the Settlement and French Concession they discovered that between five and six thousand Chinese troops had been left in the native city south of the Concession. Soon it became apparent that these troops intended to resist, though their cause was hopeless. Perhaps they had been inspired by the example of the battalion which had remained in the warehouse when Chapel was evacuated.

The main resistance was made along the bank of a canal which extends south from the French Concession boundary. Overesch, Hagen and I watched the sharp, uneven engagement from an adjacent building. The Chinese entrenched themselves on the east bank, machine guns being their heaviest weapons. The Japanese rolled tanks up to the west bank, and used thirty-seven millimeter guns at a range of sixty yards. Dive bombers and artillery added to the Japanese striking power. Yet the Chinese held out for an hour and a half.

Finally a Chinese soldier, bearing a wounded man on his back, waded into the creek which separated the defenders from the French Concession. Slipping, sliding, and paying not the slightest attention to the bullets which splashed around him, he moved steadily ahead, and eventually gained the opposite bank, where the friendly hands of French soldiers hauled both to safety. His success was the signal for his comrades to follow suit. Crowding into the creek, they scaled the bank, threw down their arms, and were interned by the French. Firing ceased, and all resistance appeared to have collapsed.

I returned to the International Settlement for a bite of food, and found a message from Edgar Snow, who had just come down from north China. Going around to his hotel I found Malcomb McDonald, long-time correspondent in China of the *London Times* with him. I was full of the exciting drama I had just witnessed, and insisted on showing them the set-up, so we went together to the scene of the recent engagement.

McDonald, an enigmatic Scot, had been only mildly interested in my account of the affair, but when he saw how close the opposing forces had been to each other, and how clearly observers had been able to see the clash, he sensed the power of the drama that had been enacted here.

"Where are the Chinese now?" he inquired eagerly.

"Those who didn't surrender retired to the east," I replied. "I don't believe there will be further resistance, though."

However, Mac insisted on trying to find them, and so we moved east to Avenue Dubail, which ends at the boundary of the Chinese native city. At this southern terminus stands the French Concession power plant, and in one corner of the compound a water tower rises to a height of sixty or seventy feet. About five feet below the tank is a platform, and on the ground, at the base of the supporting structure, is another platform, five or six feet in height. We mounted the latter so as to see over the wall to the south, and simultaneously firing began. With their backs to the wall, seven or eight hundred Chinese soldiers were resisting the advance of Japanese infantrymen from the south.

The Chinese were in the open, while their adversaries were able to use the cover of buildings. The whole affair was senseless, but this fact did not detract from the valor of the Chinese. The engagement continued briskly for several minutes. Suddenly we became aware of pieces of cement which were falling from the water tank. Looking up we were amazed to see a steady stream of machine gun fire bearing on the side of the tank.

The fire was too protracted not to have been deliberate, and we speculated as to the reason for this violation of the integrity of the French Concession. Circling the base of the structure and looking aloft I saw feet protruding over the edge of the upper platform, at the rear. The toes were down, indicating that the owners were flat on their stomachs; and the shoes were those of Westerners. Who were these people, and what were they doing in that exposed position?

Firing continued for twenty minutes, the machine-gun fire playing against the side of the tank like a stream of water from a hose. Suddenly the Chinese wheeled about and dashed for the wall. Scrambling over, they made their way through the maze of barbed wire into the arms of the waiting French troops, threw down their weapons, and surrendered.

It was about this time that we noticed blood dripping from the upper platform. Looking up, I saw that the toes remained motionless, so I ascended the ladder, determined to solve the mystery. When I emerged on to the platform seven prostrate forms lay before me, heads buried in their arms. So motionless were they that I thought they were dead. I spoke, and one man slowly raised his head, his face pale and drawn.

"Are the Japanese here?" he whispered. "Have they come in?"

I reassured him, saying that the Chinese troops had surrendered to the French, and that he could get up now.

He rose and joined me, and five of his companions pulled themselves gingerly to their feet and descended the ladder without a word. One form lay in a pool of blood, and we bent over him.

"He is dead," murmured my companion.

"Who is he?" I inquired.

"I don't know," he replied. "We were observing the battle from here when the machine gun commenced firing on the tank. Bullets ricocheted over this platform, and we lay down. He tried to climb into the cylinder there, which leads to the heart of the tank, but was hit in the leg, so he lay down beside us. Later he raised up to see what was going on below, and a bullet caught him over the eye."

I asked my companion for his own name, and he dove into a pocket and produced a visiting card. "I am Doctor Richer," he said.

It was hardly the place to be exchanging visiting cards, but this regard for convention could not be ignored, and I handed him my own.

Feet descended from the hollow center of the tank, and a blond-headed young man joined us. With visible agitation he bent over the prostrate form.

"Do you know him?" I asked.

"Yes, he's my boss, Pembroke Stephens, of the *London Daily Telegraph.*"

Now I recalled having seen Stephens behind the Chinese lines on various occasions. He had appeared to be a lonely man, always keeping to himself, and we had never met, except casually as observers of the tragic drama of war. Now he was a victim of this drama—the last foreign casualty of the battle of Shanghai.

The reason for the deliberate firing on the water tank was never satisfactorily explained. The rumor which persisted in Shanghai was that Stephens had incurred the ill-will of a Japanese journalist by his pungent indictment of the invasion, and his frank support of the Chinese cause, and that this journalist was with the machine gun section which did the shooting.

VII

Two important conclusions could be drawn from the battle of Shanghai: (1) China was determined to fight for her independence, and her army possessed the ability to absorb, as well as give, a terrific amount of punishment; and (2) the Japanese military machine, which had been regarded as formidable since its victory over Russia in 1904-05, was revealed as a third-rate army, when judged by European standards.

The Chinese army had never been rated very high by foreign military men, both because of its inferior organization, training and equipment, and because of the reputation of its leaders for selling out to their opponents in the civil wars. The tenacity of the Chinese resistance here amazed foreign observers, and the failure of any important leader to sell out restored confidence in Chinese integrity. Civil war was one thing, but a threat to national independence was quite another. For years the people of this vast nation had been developing a national consciousness, and this development was now reaching fruition.

It was this spirit of nationalism which the Japanese leaders had failed to understand. When they commenced the invasion they thought China would fall apart and become a dozen quarreling cliques, as had happened at times during the civil wars. But their invasion had encountered racial and national solidarity. The people were aroused, and they were prepared to sacrifice homes, ambition, even life, for the preservation of the integrity of their China.

And what of the Japanese army? It was not that the men lacked courage, for no man is braver on the field of battle than the Japanese. It was, rather, that the leaders lacked initiative and resourcefulness, and that the army had been trained to fight by rote. Everything was done according to formula, and when the formula didn't work there was no alternative.

Take the conduct of an offensive, for example. The accepted formula was for the infantry to advance after the way had been paved by preliminary aerial and artillery bombardments. When the infantry ran into resistance they sat down and waited for the artillery to blast a path. But the Chinese had protective shelters, and when the artillery fire lifted, their troops poured forth to repel the attackers.

Another Japanese weakness was the apparent inability of their artillery to lay down a creeping barrage. The only time during the battle that I saw a barrage that could be called "creeping" was during the Tazang offensive. And here the barrage was invariably six and seven hundred yards in advance of the infantry, affording ample time for the defenders to man their positions.

The inferiority of the Japanese infantry in hand-to-hand combat was also a surprise, for bayonet training has long been a favorite exercise. But in this type of fighting the Chinese were distinctly superior.

When the battle ended the Japanese had about 90,000 men engaged, while the total number of Chinese troops was about 300,000. Japanese casualties had aggregated about 40,000, of whom nearly half had been killed or seriously wounded. China's killed and wounded had run well over the hundred thousand mark.

The toll among Chinese civilians had also been high, an estimated 20,000 being killed or injured, while tens of thousands more were rendered homeless.

In the foreign areas of the city the damage to foreign property, as a result of fire and bombardment, was about $100,000,000.

It was towards the end of the battle here at Shanghai that reports began to trickle in from the north about small victories which were being won in Shansi province by China's Eighth Route Army. This was the old Red Army of civil war days, and it had developed what was known as the Partisan type of warfare. Guerrilla tactics and strong popular support were said to be basic elements in this type of resistance.

As I pondered these reports I began to see how the strong spirit of unity and nationalism, which was sweeping the country, could be translated into a formidable form of resistance. Perhaps the leaders in the north were doing this—using Chinese initiative and ingenuity to neutralize the Japanese superiority in fire power and mechanized equipment. If so, and if they succeeded, this would change the entire aspect of the war.

I determined to see what I could do about going north and examining at first hand the methods and doctrines of the Eighth Route Army.

CHAPTER II

CHINA MOVES WEST

I

THE battle at Shanghai had shown that the Chinese armies lacked the equipment, training and organization to defeat the Japanese in the positional type of warfare. However, both the armies and the civil populace had displayed a will-to-endure hardship and a will-to-co-operate in the cause of national salvation. If this spirit was nation wide and intelligently directed, the advantage which the Japanese enjoyed in modern military equipment and organization could be neutralized. As an official observer I felt that this possibility should be investigated, and as an individual I was interested in the democratic characteristics of the methods which these reports from the north suggested were being used.

Edgar Snow was the first Occidental to visit the Chinese Communist area in Shensi province. In the summer of 1936, with extraordinary daring, he had run the Kuomintang blockade and spent four months with this unique group. His reports provided the first authentic information of the objectives and accomplishments of these men and women who had been isolated from the outside world for nine years.

I had known Ed since he first came to China in 1928, and I had a high regard for his honesty, courage and intelligence. Towards the end of the Shanghai battle I discussed with him the possibility of being admitted into the area controlled by the Eighth Route Army.

"I believe," he assured me, "that the army leaders would welcome your inspection of their organization."

"What sort of men are they?" I asked, inquisitively.

A far-away look came into Ed's eyes. "They're different," he said slowly. "They're humble, earnest men, scrupulously honest in word and action. Take the Chinese habit of trying to 'save face,' for example. They endeavor to conquer it by inviting criticism and by severely criticizing themselves. Evasion and procrastination are their arch-enemies. And they deal promptly and vigorously with current problems."

This sounded a bit Utopian, but I had great confidence in Ed's integrity. These men must possess unusual qualities to merit such high praise. My interest grew.

When I explained to Commander Overesch my belief that the methods employed by the Eighth Route Army seemed likely to affect vitally the broad problem of China's resistance, he grasped the significance of a strong People's Movement, and authorized me to proceed into the interior to make observations.

The Eighth Route Army was operating in Shansi province, nearly a thousand miles to the northwest, as the crow flies. The most likely place from which to gain entrance was at Sian, the city in Shensi province where Generalissimo Chiang Kai-shek had been kidnaped in December of the preceding year. But first it was necessary to obtain a passport from the Generalissimo, and to reach him at his headquarters at Nanking it was now necessary to skirt the right flank of the Japanese armies, which lay between Shanghai and Nanking, by moving to the north bank of the Yangtze river and traveling over the canal system there.

Perhaps a brief analogy between the geography of China and that of the United States would aid in clarifying the distances involved. The area of China, excluding Manchuria, is about equal to that of the United States, but it is four to five hundred miles wider from north to south, while the distance from Turkestan on the west to the tip of the Shantung peninsula is about 2,

700 miles. From Shanghai the coast recedes to the north and south, so that Peip'ing is actually three hundred miles west of Shanghai.

If we should assume that Nanking corresponds geographically to Washington, D. C., then Shanghai would be somewhere in the vicinity of Norfolk, Virginia, and Peip'ing would be in Canada, about three hundred miles northwest of Ottawa. The Yangtze river would rise in the Rocky Mountains, and flow east, passing Tulsa, Oklahoma, which would correspond to Chungking, and Lexington, Kentucky, which would be the location of Hankow. Sian and Dubuque, Iowa, would occupy the same relative positions; Chengchow, where the Peip'ing-Hankow railroad crosses the east-west Lunghai line, would correspond to Lansing, Michigan; and the Wu T'ai mountains, an important guerrilla base in Shansi, would be in the eastern part of Lake Superior. Moving from Shanghai to Nanking by the north bank of the Yangtze meant that I had to cross from Norfolk to the Maryland shore in order to avoid the Japanese army, which lay between Norfolk and Washington.

It was the middle of November when I scurried around the stores of Shanghai purchasing equipment. I would probably be in the field with the army during the winter months, and heavy clothing would be needed. A sheepskin-lined coat and a pair of stout hiking boots were my first purchases. Next I got a suitable sleeping bag and a haversack. The latter could be slung over my shoulder, and would carry those articles which I wished to have with me on the march. I would drink only boiled water, so I purchased a small tea-kettle. Chop sticks, a rice bowl, an enamel cup and a wash basin completed my gear. I planned to live as nearly as possible like the Chinese, and would eat their type of food.

On the 19th of November, a week after the battle had ended, I was on board the *S.S. Hsin Pekin* with a ticket to Nantungchow, a city on the north bank of the Yangtze and about fifty miles up the river. A cold clammy rain fell. The ship should have sailed at eight o'clock, but it was already nine and the donkey engines still whirred and cargo booms clanged as nets of fresh cabbage were lifted from the holds of the ship and dumped onto the slimy wharf of the French Bund. Over on the wharf small boys in tattered garments loitered around the edge of the growing pile of cabbage, deft fingers snatching the loose leaves whenever the dock foreman was preoccupied. At the south end of the Bund a huge iron gate separated the French Concession from the native city. Behind the gate a Japanese cavalryman, looking a bit incongruous on his tall, rangy horse, seemed to symbolize the recent conquest of the city. Beyond him the smoke of a score of fires suggested the price of the conquest.

I examined my surroundings. On the upper deck with me was "Silent Jim" Norris, a salesman of American airplanes. There were also two White Russians and two men who appeared to be Turks from Turkestan. The deck below was jammed with Chinese refugees, their meager household effects tied in blankets and quilts. They were part of the thousands who had sought the relative security of the foreign areas as the battle approached their homes in the adjacent countryside. Now they were heading for free China, commencing a trip which would take them a thousand or more miles into the interior. Behind lay their homes, burned or occupied by the enemy; ahead lay they knew not what, but they were determined to start life anew somewhere in those vast areas of the west where they could still be governed by their own people.

The whistle warned that at last the hold was clear of cabbage. The bow of the ship swung out from the dock and was caught by the current. Soon we were heading down stream past the French, British and American cruisers, which I would not see again for a year.

Rounding the bend to the east at the Garden Bridge, we slipped rapidly down the Whangpoo, dodging sampans, barges, coal-burning tugs and Japanese destroyers. The Yangtzepoo district on the north, and the Pootung district on the south, presented pathetic spectacles. What had once been solid factories and warehouses were now charred skeletons of characterless brick and stone. The one-time proud and bustling commercial metropolis of Shanghai had been reduced to a minor trading center whose continued existence rested on Japanese sufferance. Only the Japanese hospital ships along the foreshore showed signs of activity as stretcher bearers brought aboard a new cargo of wounded.

II

"Silent Jim" Norris was a garrulous soul who had come out to China five years ago to fly mail planes up the Yangtze to Hankow and Chungking, across the mountains into the northwest, and to the old imperial capital at Peip'ing, as China expanded her commercial air lines. Now he hoped to sell planes to the Nanking government. He was an entertaining traveling companion, for he had a seemingly limitless fund of stories, and he never complained about the physical difficulties of travel. It was Jim who broke the ice with the two Turks.

The elder, Sabri, was a government official in Sinkiang, the Chinese province of Central Asia which is sometimes known as Turkestan. He was also a member of the Central Executive Committee of the Nanking government, a fact which won the co-operation of local officials when we landed at Nantungchow. His son, Arthur, was a student and spoke English fluently.

We found Nantungchow overrun with refugees who were endeavoring to work their way westward over the system of canals which lies like a pattern of lace along the north bank of the Yangtze, there being no roads here worthy of the name. Nine thousand of them had arrived this same evening, coming by steamer, sampan and barge. Theirs was a sorry plight, for they had little or no money and depended on the benevolence of the local populace for food and lodging. Mostly they slept out of doors, huddled in cheerless groups on the leeward side of buildings.

We boarded a canal boat on the following morning, one of six which were to be towed by a steamer. Our destination was K'owan, seventy miles to the west, where we hoped to be able to find a river boat which would take us across the Yangtze to Chingkiang. There we would again be in Chinese-controlled territory, and could take a train for Nanking.

By this time we had made the acquaintance of the two White Russians, who we found were on their way to guard a foreign-owned factory near Chingkiang.

Boarding the boat, we seated ourselves on the backless benches, each stowing his luggage underneath. The refugees were not far behind. They surged aboard, crowding every available nook. When the seats and passageway were filled they lay down under the benches, and between them. These people were the lao pai hsing (literally "one hundred old names," a term used to describe the civilian population collectively), and it was they who were bearing the brunt of the war. But neither here nor later did I ever hear any suggestion from them that their government should compromise with the enemy. They wanted their children to be free men and women.

For the next two days and nights we moved at a snail's pace. Food was a problem, for the cooking facilities were limited. The Russians had brought some black bread which they shared with us. Other than this we subsisted on peanuts and tea. The Chinese fared no better.

Seated in front of me was a young Chinese whose intelligent eyes and long artistic fingers attracted my attention.

He smiled at me cordially and inquired if I was going far.

"Nanking, Hankow—perhaps farther," I replied cautiously. It was unwise to be too explicit about one's business until the political convictions of the acquaintance were known.

"I'm going to Sian," he confided, his eager face alight with anticipation.

"Really? I hope to go there, too." I felt more confident now.

His black eyes searched my face swiftly.

"You, too?" he exclaimed softly. "Are you also going to Yenan?"

Yenan was the headquarters of the Communist Party in north Shensi.

"I hope to."

"How wonderful! Have you been there before? Tell me about Yenan."

"I don't know much about it," I replied. "That is why I want to go there. But you, why are you going?"

Generalissimo Chiang Kai-shek, leader of the Republic of China, and the symbol of unity to the Chinese people. *Photograph taken at Hankow, towards the close of the battle.*

"I hope to be accepted in one of the training schools for leaders," he said. "I had a good job in the office of a foreign broker, but I gave it up because it seemed to me that I should help defend my country. In Shanghai we hear that the Eighth Route Army leaders are honest and that they are working to improve the welfare of the people. They say that these leaders know how to defeat the Japanese. They lead them into traps, and then attack them from the rear."

"Are there many men from Shanghai who have gone to the Eighth Route Army?" I asked.

"Yes, many. Most of the younger men go there—and the women, too."

I did not see this young man after we left the ship, but he was the first of hundreds I was to encounter during succeeding months who were drawn north to the Eighth Route Army from all of the provinces of China. Invariably they were attracted by reports of the integrity of the army leaders. Here was hope that officials would use their official positions to advance the interests of the people, rather than to enhance their private fortunes. Young China was thinking in terms of democratic government and of equality of opportunity and a higher standard of living for all.

Around me mothers nursed their babies, men talked in low tones as they sucked their water pipes (a tobacco pipe with a water-cooled bowl), and the older children clambered over the grown-ups as they sought greater freedom of movement outside. From time to time an itinerant actor or musician gave an impromptu entertainment, which was received with boisterous applause.

One of these Jim Norris dubbed the "slap-slap-boom-boom" man. He skillfully manipulated two pieces of bamboo lath, about four feet in length, in the fingers of his left hand, while under his left arm was tucked the barrel of a bamboo tube, about nine inches in diameter, with a snake skin drawn taut over the forward end. As he sang improvised ballads about members of his audience and the events of the trip, he punctuated his song with slaps of the lath or by rapping sharply on the snake skin covered tube.

Another clever performer imitated with great fidelity the songs of birds and the cries of babies of various years of age. The latter caused the mothers to go into paroxysms of laughter.

We were wedged so tightly into the compartment that it was difficult to get out, so Jim made a deal with the slap-slap-boom-boom man to bring us tea at ten cents per pot. Thereafter we referred to him as the "i-mao-chien" man (i-mao-chien being ten cents in the Chinese language). The refugees caught on, and soon the passengers were calling him "i-mao-chien," amid roars of laughter.

The general spirit of levity and good will was infectious. Jim and I decided that we should contribute to the entertainment, and we sought a song which was familiar to us as well as to the Turks and the White Russians. Finally we hit on "The Volga Boatman," which we sang, each in his own tongue. If any racial prejudice had survived the preceding hours of the trip, this demolished the last vestige. Thenceforth we were human beings sharing the same vicissitudes and moved by the same stimuli. Cold and hunger, exaltation and bereavement were known to all of us, and within each glowed a spark called brotherly love which needed only a word of sympathy and understanding to fan it into a flame.

It was three o'clock in the morning of the third day when we arrived at the end of the canal trip. A fifteen-mile walk still lay ahead before we would reach K'owan, but we could not start until half-past five because the city gates here did not open until then. Along with the Turks and the Russians, Jim and I repaired to an Inn where the cook, an early riser, prepared for us a bowl of piping hot noodles.

That afternoon a strange caravan wound its way into K'owan. Some walked, some rode in rickshas, and some even managed to ride rented bicycles. Jim and I walked, our duffle bags and bedding rolls piled in a ricksha.

Two ships lay in the cove off K'owan. One carried the house flag of Butterfield and Swire, while the other bore the colors of Jardine, Matheson Company. Both flew the British flag at the stern. We had visions of steaming in comfort to Nanking, for the boom which the Chinese had placed in the Yangtze river to keep Japanese warships from moving up-stream was now to the east of us at Kiangyin. We went out to the *Pao An*, the Jardine ship, which was both loading and unloading. But the Captain informed us that he had just received orders to remain at K'owan as a depot ship, to care for British travelers who were moving upriver by the canal route. He would, however, be glad to provide us with a meal before we continued our journey.

What a meal! As we were finishing it a small steamer cruised past. Just arrived from Chingkiang, it would return immediately, we were informed. A sampan, hurriedly hailed, conveyed us to the steamer, and within the hour we were en route to Chingkiang, which was reached shortly after nightfall.

At the railway station stood a train made up mostly of coal cars, bound for Nanking, so some soldiers said. We threw our baggage over the side of a car and distributed ourselves on top of it, not too uncomfortable. After five hours of waiting we were told that the train would not go to Nanking, and transferred our luggage to a passenger coach of another train already loaded with soldiers. Squeezing ourselves into the vestibule we sat on our bags, thinking we were lucky to occupy this last surviving corner of space. What errant optimism! Just before the train departed another group of soldiers arrived. Apparently they were just from the front, for they manifested the reckless boisterousness which characterizes men who have lately been released from the gates of hell. They wedged themselves into the vestibule, and we finished the trip with soldiers draped over, behind and around us.

III

Nanking already had the appearance of a city of the dead. Streets which were ordinarily teeming with people were all but deserted. Military trucks loaded with impedimenta sped to the Bund, on the south bank of the Yangtze, and returned empty for further loads. Air raid sirens still warned of the impending arrival of Japanese planes, as they had when I was here in September, but now the few people who responded sauntered listlessly to the underground shelters. The Japanese armies were approaching the capital, and the government was moving west.

The retirement of the Chinese armies from the narrow tongue of land between the Yangtze and Whangpoo, where had been fought the battle of Shanghai, had almost become a rout. Chinese staff officers lacked the training to move successfully three hundred thousand troops in that most difficult of military operations, a withdrawal. Furthermore, the Japanese landing on the north side of Hangchow Bay had threatened the south flank of the strong defensive position in the vicinity of Soochow, making it untenable. Nanking was protected by a line of defenses which extended from Chingkiang through Kuyung, forty miles to the southeast, and thence to the Yangtze again east of Wuhu. But if this line was penetrated the defending Chinese troops would be caught in a cul-de-sac with the Yangtze, half a mile wide, at their backs. Chiang Kai-shek must be prepared to sacrifice any troops he might employ for the defense of the city itself.

Not even a ricksha was to be found in the vicinity of the railroad station when we arrived. In a few moments, however, a light Ford truck drove up and in the front seat were two men who looked as though they might be Americans. Jim recognized them. One was an aviation-engine expert named Lancaster; the other was Andrus, a communications specialist. Both were employed by the Chinese Aviation Commission. They offered to take us to the hotel.

"The Generalissimo and Madame Chiang Kai-shek are still here," Andrus informed us, "but Julius Barr is standing by to pilot them away at a moment's notice." Barr was the pilot of the Generalissimo's private plane.

W. H. Donald, the Generalissimo's Australian adviser, was also here, they said. But most of the Embassies had moved to Hankow, which would be the new location of the government.

There was no difficulty in securing a room at the Metropolitan Hotel. This beautiful structure was almost devoid of guests.

I found that Donald was living out on Purple Mountain, near the Generalissimo's home, and arranged to see him.

As I rode out the Chungsan road old memories flooded my mind. In

June, 1929, I had attended the State Burial of Doctor Sun Yat-sen here, and had marched in the funeral procession along this same road to the mausoleum on Purple Mountain. Then the Kuomintang Party had just been establishing the new government here, after its armies had succeeded in uniting China by eliminating the rule of provincial war-lords. Hundreds of thousands of people had lined the sides of the road to pay homage to the father of the revolution, their hearts filled with hope for the future. Now the road was devoid of all but military traffic. Ragged holes in the magnificent new government buildings bore mute evidence of China's tragedy. Many homes were piles of rubble. And on the sidewalks in front of the stores stood stacks of merchandise which the remaining merchants hoped might be transported into the interior. Only the dome of the mausoleum, high on the mountain side, remained intact—a challenge to the Sons of Han to fulfill the faith of their revered leader by uniting to throw out the invader and re-establish their independence.

Donald had become something of a legend in China. For years he had been an unofficial adviser to some Chinese official. Before coming to the entourage of Chiang Kai-shek he had been with young Marshal Chang Hsueh-liang, of Manchuria. It was said that he knew more than any foreigner of the inner forces which had been instrumental in shaping the destinies of the Chinese Republic. He knew hardly a word of Chinese, and he never ate Chinese food when he could help it, yet he was highly regarded for his integrity and his unswerving loyalty to the person he happened to be serving.

This was my first meeting with him. I found a husky, well-built man of medium height who, I thought, was probably in his late fifties. His frank, kindly face was deeply lined, and his hair was almost gray. He listened intently as I explained my plan for going to the northwest, and my hope of obtaining permission from the Generalissimo to make the trip.

"You know," he said, "that travel in the interior is difficult at this time. The government can hardly assume responsibility for your safety."

"Yes, I know," I assured him. "All I wish is a passport which will identify me to the military authorities. I assume full responsibility for my safety."

He finally agreed to present my request to the Generalissimo, and to let me know his decision.

With a feeling of confidence, I left him and drove to the American Embassy.

"Welcome to our beleaguered city," smiled George Atcheson, who had become the senior official at the Embassy. "How about remaining in Nanking for Thanksgiving and sharing a turkey with us—if we can find a turkey?"

"Glad to," I responded, "if I can't get away for the northwest before Thursday."

A score of other Americans were still in the city, engaged mostly in missionary, medical or educational work. George Fitch, the local representative of the. Y.M.C.A., was living at the home of Colonel J. L. Huang, I learned, and Jim Norris and I went over to see him.

The house we entered had the air of a college fraternity house, except that all present but George Fitch were Chinese. J. L. Huang was easily the leader of this interesting ménage. Fat and jolly, he had at one time been a Y. M.C.A. secretary. Of recent years he had functioned as Secretary of the New Life Movement, which was started in 1934 to revive the old Chinese virtues of courtesy, justice, integrity and self-respect. Concurrently he had held the post of Secretary of the Officers' Moral Endeavor Society, which sought to improve the moral fiber of the corps of officers. Now he was director of a new organization called the War Area Service Corps. The other Chinese present were his assistants.

Theodore Tu was a talented musician who was responsible for the development of mass singing in the army. Sam Mei had been born in the United States, and held a degree in engineering from an American university. Jack Young was another American-born Chinese. Jack was something of an explorer, having made several expeditions into Central Asia, one of them with Colonel Theodore Roosevelt, junior, when the latter went in search of the giant panda. The other member of the group was Chuk, the

Generalissimo's official photographer.

All of these men spoke English as fluently as they did their mother tongue. During the coming months I was to meet them in various parts of China performing special missions for the Generalissimo. Some would be engaged in providing mobile motion-picture units for the benefit of the troops at the front. Others would guide groups of foreign journalists, present bonuses to wounded soldiers, or establish guest houses for the Russian aviators who were already beginning to arrive.

Now they gave themselves over to relaxation. We spent the evening talking, joking and singing songs of America as well as of China.

George Fitch was exceedingly popular with this group. He was a man of deep spiritual conviction whose influence among Chinese was extensive. While his official job was to direct the affairs of the Y.M.C.A. here, he had been an unofficial adviser for the New Life Movement. In the weeks to come he was to remain in Nanking through the Japanese occupation. He would see the wholesale slaughter of Chinese men and the raping of countless women by the victorious Japanese, and he would then go forth to tell the world of the ruthlessness of the Japanese invasion. Now, however, he was engaged in co-operating with other foreigners in attempting to establish a Safety Zone which it was hoped would be respected by the invaders, and would provide security for women and children when the city finally capitulated.

It was a memorable evening. Here was a group of Chinese who had been educated in the West, and who had the confidence of the head of their nation. They understood Chinese psychology and they knew the psychology of the West as well. They were professing Christians, men of deep faith, and earnest in their desire to mold their China into a nation which would be a strong moral force in world affairs. The potential constructive force of such a group was measureless provided its members could subordinate themselves to the task of enhancing the welfare of the common man.

The following day J. L. Huang took me over to see General T'ang Sheng-chi, who had been designated to command the troops which were to defend the city.

General T'ang was an officer of the old school who went in for military trappings and surrounded himself with a large and elegantly attired staff. He was rated as an able military man, having been an army leader for nearly thirty years. His record of loyalty to the government was not entirely clear, however, for in 1930 he had allied himself with General Feng Yu-hsiang against the Generalissimo. The following year he was pardoned and restored to military command. I found him to be affable and cordial as he talked of his plans for the defense of the city.

"I intend to defend Nanking to the last man," he assured me. "The Japanese may eventually capture the city, but they will pay a heavy price for it."

Then he proceeded to discuss the technique of street fighting. His whole conversation was devoted to the defense measures which he proposed to employ within the city, and said nothing of making a stand outside the city.

When I left General T'ang I felt that the capitulation of Nanking was not far off, for once the Japanese were inside the walls with their tanks and other mechanized equipment, the city would be theirs.

On Thanksgiving Day Donald sent over my military pass, an imposing document fourteen inches long by sixteen inches in width. At the bottom was the great red seal of the Military Affairs Commission.

I had already inquired about boats bound for Hankow and had learned that no schedules were being maintained. Boats loaded at Nanking and proceeded as quickly as possible to Hankow, where they unloaded and sped back for a new cargo. One of the Jardine, Matheson boats was due to arrive on the following day. In the afternoon I went over to the Embassy to have Thanksgiving dinner with George Atcheson.

Colonel Claire Chennault, who heads the American aviation advisers, was at the Embassy. Chennault had retired from the Air Corps of the American army a few years before. Shortly before the beginning of the present conflict he had taken over the Chinese aviation training school, which was started in 1932 by Colonel Jack Jouett. His school at Hangchow had been bombed on the first day of the war, and he had moved it to Nanking. Now he was taking it up river to Hankow. He was a tall, spare figure of a man who had been a crack pursuit pilot in the American army, and whose mastery of air tactics and strategy had already proved to be of tremendous value to the Chinese.

George's cook had managed to find a goose instead of a turkey, in the confusion that was Nanking. Captain Frank Roberts, Captain James McHugh, respectively Assistant Military and Naval Attachés, and Hall Paxton, Second Secretary of the Embassy, drifted in, and we addressed ourselves to Thanksgiving dinner under conditions which we would long remember. In the midst of it the air alarm sounded, and we repaired to the roof of the Embassy dugout, to watch the raid.

Yates McDaniel, of the *Associated Press*, Tillman Durdin, of the *New York Times*, Weldon James, of the *United Press*, and Malcomb McDonald, of the *London Times* (only recently with me at Shanghai), joined the group.

This raid was significant for the type of bombs which were dropped. Previously the bombs had been of the heavy type, the explosive action sending fragments and debris up in a sort of parabola; these bombs seemed to be of the light fragmentation type, and the explosive action was lateral. Apparently they were designed for use against personnel. The Japanese were anticipating the early occupation of the city and did not desire to cause more destruction of buildings than was necessary.

The following evening J. L. Huang informed me by telephone that the *Tuck Wo*, one of the Jardine steamers, was arriving, and would return upriver in a few hours. I hurried to the Bund with my bags.

Here was a scene of great confusion. Along the river bank, looking like a fantastic dike, stood a huge mound of goods awaiting shipment. Military impedimenta of all types were mingled with household effects of thousands of refugees. The latter hovered in groups over fires which they had made of odd bits of wood while they awaited an opportunity to leave the city. They cared not whither they went: up the river to Hankow, or across the river to the terminus of the rail line which led to the north. On all sides wounded lay on improvised stretchers, only their gaunt, strained faces suggesting the pain of wounds which were concealed by bandages on legs, arms, heads and abdomens.

Andrus and Lancaster, the aviation specialists, joined me on the Bund. Jim Norris was staying. I would miss his happy-go-lucky companionship.

The ship was anchored five miles up the river, and we boarded a ferry for the trip. Steaming past the American gunboat *Panay* and numerous native river craft we headed west to share the life of Free China. Off to the south the crenelated walls of the city faded into the night. What stories those walls could tell. Within them a Chinese had set up the capital of the first Ming Dynasty. Here had been signed, nearly a century ago, the first of the unequal treaties with the powers of the West. Still later these walls had been held by the Taipings, fanatical rebels from the south, and they, too, had made it their capital. Soon they would be guarded by the soldiers of a foreign empire. This, I felt, would be but another transitional stage in China's development. Her people were moving west, but they would return a stronger and more vital people. Those walls would one day enclose the capital of a China which would be a world power.

IV

A crowded boat was no novelty now. Every inch of space of the *Tuck Wo* was occupied. However, as we proceeded upriver we began to drop off passengers at the various ports. On the morning of the third day we sighted Hankow, on the north bank. Along the Bund lay the imposing European-style buildings of the foreign settlements. Across the river was the twin city of Wuchang, the yards of the Canton-Wuchang railway in the foreground. Steaming past the *U.S.S. Luzon*, flagship of our Yangtze patrol, we tied up at a pier opposite the Custom House.

Lancaster and Andrus went off to look for their respective wives, who had preceded them, while I went over to the Asiatic Petroleum Corporation building, where was located the American Consulate General.

Here Ambassador Johnson had taken up temporary quarters. Here also was quiet and gracious Paul Josselyn, the Consul-General.

"Where do you think you're going?" inquired the Ambassador.

"Up to the Eighth Route Army, I hope," I replied.

"Well, take care of yourself," he cautioned. "Don't take unnecessary chances." He sent me off with a fatherly pat on the back.

At the *U.S.S. Luzon* Rear Admiral Marquadt, commander of the Yangtze patrol, was equally cordial and solicitous.

"If you need any medical supplies," he told me, "go down to the sick bay and the doctor will fix you up."

I accepted his offer and selected a small assortment of medicines and disinfectants such as iodine, mercurochrome mercurio-sulphur ointment, quinine, aspirin, bismuth, paragoric and boric acid powder. These, with a few bandages and some adhesive tape, I had found from experience to be most useful in the field.

There was no further reason to tarry in Hankow, so I went to the station to see what could be done about passage to the north. Conditions were much the same as had prevailed at Nanking. No schedules were being maintained, refugees were everywhere, and no one knew when a train would leave for the north. Most of the rail service was being used to transport equipment and supplies from Pukow (opposite Nanking), trains moving north from that point to Hsuchowfu, then west on the Lunghai road to Chengchow, and south to Hankow.

I deposited my luggage on the platform among the refugees, and draped myself on top of it to wait for the next train. Six hours later one arrived. Before it had come to rest men, women and children were clamoring for admission. I wedged myself into the passageway of a second class coach and again sat on my luggage. In an hour we were under way for the north.

Now I was getting into the real China, away from the areas of foreign influence. We passed over rolling country and on the following morning we came to the great wheat growing plains of Honan. From time to time we were shunted on to a side track to make way for southbound trains, piled high with miscellaneous equipment. Motor cars stood amid airplane engines, bamboo telegraph poles and household effects. Here and there on the open flat cars soldiers and their wives or sweethearts sought shelter from the sharp December wind in the maze of paraphernalia.

At Chengchow a train was preparing to depart for the west and Sian, my destination. There was the usual struggle for a place in a passageway. Soldiers bound for regiments which were defending the line of the Yellow River flooded the cars. By midnight we were off.

The plains gave way to loess soil through which streams had cut deep gorges. The roads along the way were sunk beneath the surface, years of pounding by wooden-wheeled ox carts having pulverized the soil. From the car windows I could see caves in the sides of hills and valleys. This loess country was famous for its cave dwellers.

At Sanchow we came within sight of the Yellow River. It lay to the north, below the city, in a huge canyon a mile in width. We remained within sight of the river until we reached T'ungkwan, where it flows down from the north and bends sharply to the east. Here it was possible to cross to Fenglingtu, on the Shansi side, and entrain on the narrow gauge T'ungp'u railroad for points in the interior of Shansi, which, according to our geographical analogy, would correspond to the eastern Wisconsin-Lake Michigan-Lake Superior area.

Sian lay nearly a hundred miles farther west, and we arrived there in the evening. Here at last was peace. The city had not yet suffered the ravages of war. And here, in the heart of the northwest, a guest house was maintained by the China Travel Service, with running water and modern sanitation. I was to appreciate this guest house more fully when I returned here after months of primitive living in the north.

The following morning I presented myself at the office of Lin Tso-han, the local representative of the Eighth Route Army. Mr. Lin was at Yenan, headquarters of the Communist Party in northern Shensi, but Wu Yuen-fu received me and heard my request.

The office was plainly furnished with a table and a few chairs. On the wall hung large pen sketches of Karl Marx, Sun Yat-sen, Chiang Kai-shek, Mao Tse-tung (political leader of the Party), and Chu Teh, the commander of the army.

There was a candor and an alertness in Mr. Wu's face which I was to learn to associate with all men of his faith.

"I'll have to send your request to Chairman Mao Tse-tung, at Yenan," he informed me. "It may be a few days before we receive a reply."

My next call was on General Chiang T'ing-wen, the Governor of Shensi. General Chiang was said to be a relative of the Generalissimo's, and was deeply in his confidence. He was known as a man of iron will, and was anti-communistic in his sentiments.

A secretary accompanied me to the General's residence, and a tall man of imposing dignity entered the reception room. In appearance he bore a strong resemblance to certain types of our American Indians. But it was his small, artistic hands which fascinated me.

"You have come a long way, Ts'an Tsan (attaché)," he welcomed me. "I hope that you are comfortable here in our northwest."

I assured him that I was, and then told him of the object of my trip. He nodded his head, and I suspected that he had been advised in advance of my mission.

"The Eighth Route Army is now operating against the Japanese in Shansi, where they recently won an important victory."

He then proceeded to outline the situation in the north. The Japanese had occupied the railway from Peip'ing to Paot'o, in Inner Mongolia. They had also moved south from Peip'ing along the railroad towards Hankow, but had not yet reached the Yellow River. In eastern Hopei a Japanese column had occupied the railway south from Tientsin to the Shantung border. In Shansi the invaders had entered from the north, along the T'ungp'u road, and from the east along the Ch'engt'ai railroad, to occupy the provincial capital of T'aiyuanfu.

The General discussed in considerable detail his own defense measures along the Yellow River. I left him with a respect for his ability, and with the feeling that though his attitude and thought pattern suggested a tendency to be dictatorial, he was a man of intelligence who was amenable to reason.

V

The days passed without word from Mao Tse-tung. I was beginning to think that my mission was in vain. In the meantime there was ample opportunity to observe the life of the community.

Many Russian fliers and planes had assembled here, and J. L. Huang had established a guest house for the accommodation of Russian personnel. Here the young pilots and mechanics of the Soviet Union could relax in an environment that was made as homelike as possible; and here they could find food to which they were accustomed.

Three universities which had formerly been in the Tientsin-Peip'ing area, were now here. Each morning I saw the students tramping through the streets in formation as they prepared themselves for the time when they would have to penetrate even further into the interior. They were eager, bright-eyed young men and women, and as they swung along in unison they sang the new patriotic songs. Their physical director was Mr. Ben Shaberg, a graduate of the University of Missouri, who had come out a year ago to join the faculty of Peking Normal University.

At the China Inland Mission I found Mr. and Mrs. Swenson, who had spent twenty-five years in China, mostly in Kansu province. Mr. and Mrs. Burdett were at the British mission, and at the British missionary hospital were Doctor Clow, Doctor Ruth Tait and Miss Nettin. Doctor Clow's mother was in T'aiyuanfu, now occupied by the Japanese, and he gave me a letter to her which I was later able to deliver through the good offices of a Chinese guerrilla leader.

On the streets of Sian I saw an exceptionally large number of soldiers with one or both legs amputated. My conclusion was that the local hospitals must specialize in this type of wound, but Doctor Clow informed me that such was not the case. The reason was that the local hospitals lacked the equipment with which to treat serious wounds of the extremities, and amputation was the only safe alternative.

Few of the seriously wounded cases got back to Sian, I was told. Doctor Clow's hospital was filled to overflowing, and the hospital received seventy cents (Chinese currency) a day for each patient. Later I was to learn that the International Red Cross Committee at Hankow had subsidized the mission hospitals in order to enable them to care for the wounded. This subsidy proved a boon to many such hospitals which had previously been operating in the "red."

It was the 10th of December when authority finally arrived from Mao Tse-tung for me to proceed to the army in Shansi. I was about to sit down to lunch at the Guest House when an orderly from the Sian office of the army dashed in and informed me that I was wanted at the office immediately. As I approached another soldier ran out and told me to continue on to the railway station where an officer was waiting to accompany me.

"Look here," I remonstrated, "I haven't my equipment with me." I had visions of spending the winter in the sub-zero weather of Shansi without sleeping bag or a change of clothing.

He shrugged his shoulders and said "pu yao chin (it doesn't make any difference)," but I was adamant on this point. I wasn't going to allow myself to be stampeded into launching on an expedition without reasonable preparation, so I turned about and retraced my steps to the Guest House. As I was closing and strapping my gear a young officer with a sleeve badge bearing the caption "8 R A" entered, a mischievous smile playing at the corners of his sensitive mouth.

"There's another train at four o'clock," he reassured me. "You see, we try to be prompt in executing orders. When the order from Comrade Mao arrived I knew that a train was due to leave in a few minutes, and I thought we might take it."

I chuckled at this example of zeal. Here was young China trying so hard to break away from the old habit of procrastination that I was to be rushed off on an all-winter expedition without my luggage. Well, it was a healthy sign, and I would have preferred to leave my equipment rather than suppress it.

At four we boarded a train for T'ungkwan, accompanied by a patrol of eight men, each armed with a Thompson submachine gun of Chinese manufacture. The Great Adventure had begun.

CHAPTER III

THE EIGHTH ROUTE ARMY

I

A TRIP in a New York subway express during the rush hour is a joy ride compared to travel in the third-class coach of a Chinese train in war time. The car in which we traveled to T'ungkwan was literally crammed with humanity.

The Chinese are essentially individualists. Centuries of struggle for existence have developed in each man, woman and child the habit of looking out for himself. This urge of the individual is universally recognized, a fact which explains the tolerance with which inconvenience is accepted when it is occasioned by an individual who is attempting to gain an advantage for himself. At one station, for example, a man thrust a huge chest through a window of the car into the laps of protesting passengers. This was followed by five large bundles. There was a good deal of heated joshing about it, but the chest went into the aisle, where it became the seat for half a dozen people, and the bundles remained where they had come to rest.

At T'ungkwan (corresponding to Madison, Wisconsin) we detrained and made our way past the long line of itinerant food vendors and purveyors of boiled drinking water to a group of mud-walled buildings which served as the local office of the Eighth Route Army. Here we would spend the night, and I was shown a bench on which to lay out my sleeping bag.

T'ungkwan stands on a bluff seventy to eighty feet above the Yellow

River. On the heights across the river is the village of Fenglingtu, southern terminus of the narrow gauge T'ung-P'u railroad, which extends north for two hundred and ninety miles to T'aiyuanfu, capital of Shansi province, now held by the Japanese. To the west of Fenglingtu the Yellow River flows from the north, bending sharply to the east around the foot of the heights on which the village rests. The Wei and the Lo rivers come from the west to drain their waters into the Yellow near the bend.

The military importance of T'ungkwan is obvious, for it commands the approach to Sian from the north and east. Within a few months the Japanese army would seize the heights of Fenglingtu, but this would be the extent of its penetration in this direction. It was not prepared to make the sacrifices which a crossing here would have entailed.

On the following day we descended the bluff and embarked on a river junk for the half-mile trip across the swift-flowing current. The south bank was strewn with machinery which had been hastily removed from the arsenal at T'aiyuanfu. This would be reassembled at some point in the south, and soon the lathes would again be turning out munitions for China's armies.

A dilapidated motor-bus awaited us at Fenglingtu, for trains were not running at night in Shansi. We fortified ourselves with a bowl of noodles apiece, while men, women and children stood around and gazed curiously at this ruddy-faced foreigner who handled his chop sticks so clumsily.

"Tsou pa (let's go) !" cried the bus driver. We packed ourselves into the bus, and were off in a cloud of dust for the north. I still had no idea what our destination was to be. Indeed, during the next three months I seldom knew where the night would find me. There was nothing to do but accept events as they developed.

Late on the following morning we sighted the heavy walls of what appeared to be a hsien city (county seat). "Linfeng," explained the officer in charge.

Linfeng was the new provisional capital of the province, and we had come one hundred and thirty miles. Here was located the government of the aging Governor, General Yen Hsi-shan.

We drew up with a flourish before the gateway of a large stone building and bright-faced soldiers whose arm badges bore the legend of the Eighth Route Army greeted us vociferously. Evidently several were old friends of some of the members of my guard, for they flung their arms around each other in fraternal embraces, shouting "huan yin, t'ung chih (welcome, comrade)."

I was cordially received by the commander of this supply base of the army, General Yang Li-san. In a few moments I had washed and was partaking of a meal of bean sprouts, rice and chicken—a feast in this part of the country.

But this was not to be the end of the day's journey. General Yang interrogated me concerning the reasons why I wished to visit the army. I was the first official of a foreign government to come here, and I could see that there was some apprehension as to my motives. However, at noon I was informed that I would be sent by mule back to the leaders' training school which lay to the northwest across the Fen river. An hour later I was jogging along with one soldier as companion and guide. Towards evening we arrived at a small village tucked in the foothills of a mountain range which extended to the north.

The atmosphere here fairly sparkled with cordiality and comradeship. All except the older men and women, and the children, wore the horizon-blue uniform of the army. Girls whose ages ranged from eighteen to twenty-five years, their blue forage caps pulled down over black, severely plain bobbed hair, mingled freely with young men of corresponding ages. Everyone in the town seemed to be on excellent terms with everyone else.

I was conducted to the office of the Commandant of the school, General P'eng Hseuh-feng, a wiry, dynamic individual of forty-five. Another inquisition followed. Apparently satisfied with the candor of my replies, General P'eng proceeded to explain the object of the school.

These young men and women were being trained for leadership in the Partisan forces, he said. Partisans he described as being volunteers who entered military service for the period of the emergency. They were organized into companies and battalions which operated for the most part in the areas where they had been recruited and where they were thoroughly familiar with the terrain.

Four student companies made up the school, three of men and one of women. The course covered a period of nine weeks, and graduates went out to organize Partisans in areas behind the Japanese lines. Sixty percent of the instruction was in military tactics and technique, with especial emphasis on the tactics of guerrilla operations. The remainder was devoted to political subjects, the students being taught the fundamentals of representative government, how to organize civil communities, and the ethics of personal and group conduct.

On the following day General P'eng (who, I found, was known simply as "Comrade") accompanied me on a tour of the class rooms and living quarters. Students sat on low stools which they carried with them from room to room. Textbooks consisted of mimeographed pamphlets. Instruction was conducted in a manner reminiscent of classes in American universities, students taking voluminous notes, and the instructor illustrating his lecture with diagrams on a blackboard.

The living quarters of the students were immaculate. Students were assigned to rooms by squads of eleven and twelve each. A Chinese sleeping room in north China has a raised platform, called a k'ang, which extends across one end of the room, and serves as a bed. The base of the platform is enclosed, and the interior lined with stone and mud so as to provide a fire box. Sleeping on a k'ang is like sleeping on a stove. The fire is stoked from one end (sometimes outside the house), and the degree of warmth received by the sleeper depends on the distance he is from the fire box end. The center of the k'ang is the preferred position.

In these rooms space on the k'ang was allotted each member of the squad. During the day blankets were folded neatly at the head of each student's space. Field equipment was arranged uniformly on pegs along an adjacent wall. Even tooth brushes and towels had a specified location. The quarters of no Western army could have been more military in appearance.

In the evening the students gathered in groups around charcoal braziers to discuss cultural topics in which they were interested. One group consisted of budding poets, while another concerned itself with drawing and painting.

Others studied music, literature or handicrafts. By ten o'clock they were tucked in for the night, for the new day began before daylight.

Mountain climbing, I was told, was an essential part of each student's training. On the following morning I joined one company on its pre-breakfast run. It formed before daylight and headed for the slopes behind the town. After fifteen minutes of climbing we came to a series of terraces, which extended for a mile up the mountain.

The student captain formed the men in a skirmish line, with five to ten paces between individuals.

"When I give the signal," he said, "I want to see who can be the first to reach the top terrace (a mile distant)."

He blew a whistle and we were off, shouting, laughing, scampering across the narrow plateaus and scaling the banks of the terraces. In a few minutes all were assembled on the upper level, puffing and blowing, but glowing with vitality.

They formed a circle and sang the rousing songs of new China, their voices swelling into the gray valley below where the thin line of the Fen river was faintly visible.

Would I sing them an American song? No, but I would play one on my harmonica. Adjusting the instrument to my lips, I swung into the stirring strains of the Marine Corps Hymn, "From the Halls of Montezuma to the shores of Tripoli." Soon they were humming it. As they formed up and started down the slope in column of twos their voices continued to carry the air of this marching song of the American Marines.

Comrade P'eng had news for me. Nanking had fallen and an American gunboat, the *Panay*, had been sunk by Japanese bombs. Details were lacking and I pondered the significance of this last item. Had any of my friends of the Embassy been aboard? And what of the reaction in the United States? The sinking of the *Maine*, in 1898, had precipitated a war. Would this result in hostilities with Japan? In the absence of further information I decided to continue my trip.

"You may go to the headquarters of the army today, if you wish," Comrade P'eng informed me. This was encouraging, for I was beginning to chafe at the delay.

Headquarters lay twenty miles to the north. A captured Japanese horse, a long gangling animal, was saddled in my honor. By noon we were on the way—Liu, my youthful bodyguard, a packer, and a pack animal with my traveling gear.

Towards evening we entered an innocuous-looking village and followed a sheaf of telephone wires to a compound which was obviously the nerve center of a large organization.

I tied my horse to a convenient post and turned to survey my surroundings. Approaching me was a stocky man, of medium height, who wore the plain horizon-blue uniform of a private soldier. His bronzed, weather-beaten face was wreathed in a warm smile of welcome, and his outstretched hand sought my own. Intuitively I realized that here was Chu Teh, the famed commander of the Eighth Route Army. And intuitively I felt that I had found a warm and generous friend.

II

No photograph of Chu Teh does him justice, for no still picture portrays the facial animation in which is reflected something of his kindly and sympathetic personality. During the coming months I was to learn that Chu Teh was loved by every man in his army. Mention of his name was sufficient to bring a soft light into the eyes of his hardy campaigners. "Chu Teh? Ahhh, Chu Teh!" They would linger over the words, the intonation of their voices conveying adoration. He was the man who had led them in a thousand battles. He shared their hardships and their provender. And from him there was always a kindly word for all who approached, no matter how trying the circumstances.

I could understand this feeling, for after a few hours in his presence I, too, was conscious of a feeling of confidence in him. There was a certain nobility

The "Brains" of the Eighth Route Army. Left to right: Jen Peh-hsi, Political Director; Chu Teh, the Commander-in-Chief (sometimes known as the Chinese Napoleon), and Tso Chuan, the Acting Chief of Staff.

Part of the city of Pao Teh, on the Yellow River in Northwest Shansi.The city was burned by the Japanese. Note the proximity of the burned area to the Norwegian mission (white building in center of picture).

of character about him which set him apart. He was so utterly selfless, so kind, so patient and yet so profound in his judgments. He constantly invited criticism and spoke disparagingly of his own accomplishments. But his analysis of a military situation was incisive and revealing.

This was the man who had once been an opium-smoking militarist, and who, at forty, had reformed and determined to dedicate his life to raising his people out of their social and economic despair. This was the man who had led the former Red Army from Kiangsi province in the south on a six-thousand-mile trek into the northwest, despite the opposition of the combined armies of the Central Government.

In later weeks as I tramped the mountain trails with his men I reflected deeply on my impressions of this extraordinary individual. I concluded that he possessed three outstanding characteristics, and these I translated into terms of American personalities. He had, I felt, the kindliness of a Robert E. Lee, the humility of an Abraham Lincoln, and the tenacity of a U. S. Grant.

At this first meeting he led me through the courtyard of a typical Chinese dwelling (rooms built around a central court) to his headquarters. It was a simply furnished room, with a sleeping k'ang in an alcove at one end. The walls were papered with maps of the Shansi-Hopei region. Here we chatted for a few moments in Chinese until an interpreter arrived. The latter proved to be an old acquaintance, Tsou Li Po.

Li Po, as I soon came to know him, was a young intellectual of twenty-six years of age who had graduated from a Shanghai university. I had met him first in Sian, when he was en route to the army to gather material for a book. He was a sensitive chap, warm hearted and intellectually honest. A strong attachment developed between us, and when I departed for a tour of the battle area ten days later, Li Po accompanied me as interpreter.

"You are the first foreign military officer to visit our army, Ts'an Tsan," said Chu Teh. "We are glad to have you here, but just what would you like to see?"

"I would like," I replied, hopefully, "to live with your troops on the march in the battle area."

Chu Teh smiled tolerantly, and I continued.

"You see, we hear stories of the so-called partisan tactics which your army is using so effectively against the Japanese. I, as a military man, am interested in knowing about the methods which comprise these tactics. And I would like to know something of the doctrines which govern the conduct of the men of your army."

Chu Teh had been scrutinizing my face carefully as I talked. Now he pushed back the blue forage cap from his forehead with a gesture of decision.

"Good," he ejaculated softly. "Tomorrow I will call a meeting of my staff and you can ask them all the questions you wish. The trip with the army we'll discuss later. Now let's have some food."

He led the way across the courtyard, where four youthful bodyguards stood at ease, thumbs tucked in broad leather belts from which hung Mauser pistols, a two-handed broad sword slung across the back of each. A round table occupied the center of the room we entered, and at one end three men stood talking.

"This is the Political Director, Comrade Jen Peh-hsi," said Chu Teh, introducing a short man of slender figure, about whose face was a bird-like alertness.

The bearing of the next man suggested long military training, and I judged him to be about thirty years of age. "Comrade Tso Ch'uan, the acting Chief of Staff," explained Chu Teh. The third member of the group was a tall, muscular Korean who was introduced as Tsai Ch'ien, Director of the Enemy Works Department (army intelligence).

There were firm handshakes all around, and we sat down on backless stools and addressed ourselves to a meal of rice, cabbage soup and eggs.

"Pu yao k'e ch'i (don't stand on ceremony)," counseled Comrade Jen. "We can't entertain you in the grand manner, but you are welcome to share what we have."

The manner of these men was friendly and uninhibited, and already I felt thoroughly at home. The term "pu yao k'e ch'i" appeared to be the watch word of the army. It implied a desire for directness in speech and action, a desire to avoid the superficial politeness which has been so much a part of

Chinese official etiquette since the days of Confucius. No orthodox Chinese official, for example, would have come out to greet me in the spontaneous manner of Chu Teh. Instead I would have been received by ceremonious secretaries and ushered into the presence of the Great One with pompous unctuousness. There would have followed twenty minutes of tea sipping, as we sat stiffly on the edges of our chairs and exchanged meaningless platitudes. But here was an ease of manner and an absence of reserve which was refreshingly genuine.

"Would you like to see a basket ball game?" asked Chu Teh as we finished the meal.

He led the way to a field outside the village where two soldier teams were battling for supremacy. Here was a scene that could have been duplicated in any American village. Each team had its section of rooters, and hoots and shouts rent the air as the ball moved up and down the court. Presently a figure in olive drab uniform joined us, and I recognized with a shock that the face above the trim tunic was that of a Westerner.

"Here is a fellow-countryman of yours, Ts'an Tsan," said Chu Teh. "This is Comrade Smedley."

Agnes Smedley! For years I had heard of this gallant woman who had dedicated her life to aiding the cause of oppressed people in Asia. I had read her autobiographical book, *Daughter of Earth*, and I knew also that during the years when the Red Army was being pursued by the troops of the Central Government she had risked her life to give aid to that army. How, I wondered, would she regard my presence here?

"I'm glad to meet you, Miss Smedley," I told her with sincerity.

"Well, you've met me," she cracked back, and there was a touch of belligerency in her voice. But there was also in it a quality which suggested deep emotional feeling. This quality, I was to find, dominated her character. Suffering touched her deeply, and she constantly sought to alleviate it. When the suffering was obviously the result of domination or exploitation her wrath knew no bounds, and the offenders felt the lash of her vitriolic tongue and pen.

She looked a little grim in her military uniform, and her face bore the marks of suffering. But it was a strong face, with determined chin and deep-set, intelligent eyes. Her hair was dark brown and severely bobbed. No vanity about this lady, I thought. Absolute honesty in thought, speech and action was written all over her.

She walked back with Chu Teh and me to my living quarters, a room in the home of a merchant. Here I found that a bodyguard and an orderly had been assigned to me. Lo, the bodyguard, was a strapping fellow of eighteen years who had joined the Red Army from his home in Hupeh eight years before. Chang, the orderly, was thirteen, and came from Szechuan.

We sat around a charcoal fire and talked, while Chang brought peanuts, roasted chestnuts and tea.

"Tell me something about your organization, Commander Chu," I suggested.

"We Communists," Chu Teh began, "are not as ferocious as we are sometimes painted. In the past our aim has been to emancipate the Chinese peasant, who was kept hopelessly in debt by the landlords, and whose standards of living were little better than that of an animal. China is rich in natural resources, and there is ample here to provide all with a decent living if the products of the country are equitably distributed. What we desire is the establishment of a real democracy, with our party participating on a basis of equality with the Kuomintang. But right now all of the energies of the nation must be centered on the task of defeating Japan, for the Japanese would make vassals of us."

"Tell him how the army came to Shansi," suggested Agnes Smedley.

A boyish grin expanded over Chu Teh's face.

"Arrangements for the Red Army to be incorporated into the Central Government forces as the Eighth Route Army were not completed until late in August. But we moved swiftly, and by the first of September our 115th Division had crossed the Yellow River near Hotsin into Shansi. The 120th and the 129th Divisions followed soon after.

"The Japanese had occupied Tat'ung, in north Shansi, and were proceeding south along the Tung P'u railroad. Another column, consisting of part of the Japanese 5th Division, was moving overland from the northeast Shansi border towards the P'inghsing pass of the Great Wall. Shansi provincial troops were resisting the southward thrust from Tat'ung, so it was decided to send the 115th Division to the Wu T'ai mountain area in the northeast. I established my headquarters at Lan Ju Sen, and the 115th Division moved to the south side of the P'inghsing pass without the Japanese becoming cognizant of its presence. Nieh Yong-sen, the vice-commander, was in charge.

"The terrain in that area is extremely rugged. The road over which the Japanese column must come was an old trail, sunk beneath the floor of the valley. On both sides rose hills of moderate size.

"Eight Shansi regiments were also present under the command of General Sun Chu. It was decided that we would wait until the Japanese were well within the pass, then attack with the Shansi regiments moving from the west towards the enemy, while our division moved in from the south flank and from the rear.

"At seven o'clock on the morning of the 25th of September the Japanese brigade entered the pass. An hour later the Shansi troops had still made no move to attack and Nieh sent a messenger to inquire if any change of plan had occurred. Sun Chu replied in the negative. Nieh decided that immediate action was imperative if the advantages of surprise and position were to be utilized. Two regiments struck the enemy's flank, and two battalions enveloped his rear. The Japanese were caught in a trap and a thousand were slain in the sunken road. Most important, though, was the capture of the brigade headquarters by the battalions which attacked the rear, for the field orders and records were taken, though the General escaped.

"In this engagement we captured blankets, overcoats, munitions and food which were badly needed by our troops. The Japanese officers had been contemptuous of our military ability, for otherwise they would not have been caught unawares. Now they are more careful." Chu Teh chuckled quietly as he completed the narrative.

"He hasn't told you quite all," supplemented Agnes. "He hasn't told about the march down here from Wu T'ai. I made that march with the army. I'll never forget it.

"Another Japanese column had broken into Shansi from the east, along the Ch'eng T'ai railroad. We raced down from the north, making forty and fifty miles a day in order to cross the railroad ahead of the Japanese. Our rear guard engaged the enemy and held them back until the last of our pack train cleared the railroad. But we had been unable to carry sufficient food for the trip, and the area through which we marched had been stripped by the armies which had preceded us. I'll never forget the gaunt, determined faces of our men as they hitched their belts a little tighter and plodded off on another day's march of fifty miles. And the wounded," her voice filled with pathos; "there were no anesthetics for them, and few bandages. The peasants improvised stretchers of blankets and old doors and carried them with the army."

It was getting late, and my guests rose to go.

"I'll send for you at about eleven o'clock tomorrow," was Chu Teh's parting word.

"And I'll send you some coffee for your breakfast," added Agnes. "I'm just up the street in the next block."

Chang, the orderly, and Lo, the bodyguard, hovered about solicitously. They epitomized the spirit of this army: friendly, self-reliant and democratic.

"Off to bed with you, comrades," I admonished them. "Don't worry about me. I can take care of myself." They grinned delightedly at my use of the term "comrade." Well, it was a comradely atmosphere and no one could have resisted its infectious appeal.

"See you tomorrow, comrade," they replied gleefully. "May you sleep well."

III

Day was breaking when I was awakened by a battery of trumpeters practising calls at the edge of the village. I lay quiet for a few moments listening to the sounds of life around me. In the next room the two boys were conversing in low tones. Outside whistles sounded amid the muffled tread of marching feet. In the distance a group was singing one of the familiar marching songs. The army believed in making good use of the daylight hours.

The door opened gently and Chang's inquiring face appeared. It expanded into a smile when he saw that I was awake.

"K'ai fan (food is prepared)," he announced. "And here is hot water for your shave." A basin of steaming water was followed by a bowl of millet, fried eggs and tea.

The two boys stood around examining with intense curiosity my sleeping bag, watch and shoes, as I busied myself with the routine of washing and eating.

The boys informed me they were called "hsiao kwei" in the army. It meant "little devil." Lo had run away from home because he wanted adventure, and Chang had been placed in the army by his father, who couldn't afford to support him. Some boys came into the army as young as eight years, they said. They began as orderlies for commanders of regiments and higher units. Later they were promoted to the status of bodyguard. Those who studied and otherwise proved their ability to lead could become squad and platoon leaders. One former hisao kwei was now a regimental commander.

An hour later they left me. They had to go to school, they said. School consisted of lessons in character writing and lectures on the ethics of personal conduct.

Agnes Smedley and Li Po, the interpreter, came in.

"Here's some coffee," said Agnes, "and I've also brought some honey. It's a great delicacy here. I found it in an apothecary shop in Hungt'ung."

Li Po had some hsiao bings, a hard round biscuit made of wheat flour. We sliced and toasted them over the charcoal fire, while Agnes boiled some coffee.

"You must go to Wu T'ai," ruminated Agnes, cocking her feet up on the side of the earthen stove, while she munched a hsiao bing contentedly. "They're doing great things up there. It's a mountainous area, you know, and completely surrounded by the Japanese. Chu Teh left Nieh Yong-sen up there to organize the area for resistance, and he has set up a representative government.

It's a pure democracy, and they're experimenting with new ideas, political, social and economic, trying to find a formula which will effectively serve the interests of all the people."

"I want to go to Wu T'ai, too," chimed in Li Po. "If you do go, how about taking me along as interpreter?"

"That's a promise, Li Po," I assured him.

A hsiao kwei entered and informed me that Chu Teh was awaiting me in his office.

If the Japanese had bombed the headquarters of the Eighth Route Army that day they would have decimated the high command, for assembled there were the members of the staff I had met the preceding day, P'eng Teh-hwai, the vice commander, Lin Piao, the brilliant commander of the 115th Division, and Chu Teh.

P'eng Teh-hwai was the tough member of the command group. He was equally as democratic as Chu, but he realized that a certain measure of iron has to be injected into leadership if discipline is to be assured. And he was willing to provide that measure. But his heart was with the down-trodden peasant, and part of his own self-discipline was to eat a bowl of millet, the peasant food, with each meal.

Lin Piao was the most youthful of the commanders, being only twenty-eight years of age. An industrious student, he was also an intuitive leader, and his brilliant record of victories had won him the command of the First Front Army, which had recently become the 115th Division. He held concurrently the post of President of the Military Academy at Yenan, the Communist headquarters in Shensi.

"First," said Chu Teh, "would you be willing to give us an analysis of the political situation throughout the world? We are so isolated here that we have few opportunities to learn about what is going on abroad."

I launched into a rough description of the political forces at work in Europe and America, as well as in Asia. Each man took notes as I talked.

Their questions indicated how amazingly well they were informed. What would the British do if Germany invaded Czecho-Slovakia? Why were the democratic nations not helping the Spanish government to overthrow Franco? Why did not America move to compel Japan to respect her commitments under the Nine Power Treaty?

"Now it's your turn," smiled Chu Teh. "Fire ahead with your questions." He called a hsiao kwei and told him to bring peanuts, pears and tea.

"Let's start with military operations," I suggested. "What is the fundamental basis of your plan for resisting the Japanese invasion?"

They looked at each other quizzically, and then broke into roars of laughter. I saw the humor of the situation. Here was an army which was fighting for the life of the nation, and I was asking for the plan by which they hoped to defeat the enemy.

Chu Teh essayed a reply. "We can't, of course, reveal the location of our troops or the plans for immediate operations, but our basic idea is this:

"We believe that China can best offset the superiority which Japan enjoys in modern military equipment and organization by developing a form of resistance which will include the entire populace. This means that every man, woman and child must become imbued with the determination to continue resistance regardless of the bitterness of the hardships or the length of the struggle. There must be an economic plan which will enable districts of ten or twelve counties to be relatively self-sufficient, for communications are poor, and some districts will be isolated by the Japanese. This is the first part of our plan. Japan does not have enough soldiers to occupy all of our country. She will try to control us by political means. But if our people are determined to remain independent, and if they are willing to make sacrifices in order that their children may enjoy freedom and a larger measure of happiness, Japan can never accomplish her purpose."

He paused to shell some peanuts, and Tso Ch'uan took up the conversation.

"The work of indoctrinating the people with the determination to resist," he said, "is conducted by the political department of the army. Comrade Jen Peh-hsi will tell you of that later.

"Now, about the military aspect of the plan." He sketched rapidly on a sheet of paper a rough outline of Shansi province, putting in the T'ung P'u railroad from north to south through the center of the province, and the Ch'eng T'ai railroad from T'aiyuanfu east to the Peip'ing-Hankow line.

"The Japanese occupy the T'ung P'u road as far south as T'aiyuanfu (Marquette, Michigan) and the Ch'eng T'ai road (running east from Marquette to Sault St. Marie) as well. We have placed our troops so as to besiege these lines of communication. North of T'aiyuanfu we have placed a division to the west of the road and another to the east. A third division operates south of the Ch'eng T'ai. The country is rugged, but our men are accustomed to mountain climbing. They can march sixty and seventy miles a day, if necessary. The Japanese cannot do over twenty, for they carry heavy equipment and take artillery with them. Our men move in mobile units which seldom exceed six hundred men in strength. Each unit carries its own radio plant, so that its movements can be co-ordinated by the division commander. These units are constantly raiding the Japanese lines of communication, attacking garrisons and ambushing columns on the march. The people help to keep us informed of the movements of the enemy. Superior information, mobility and a determination to prevail are our chief assets."

I regarded this group with admiration. Here were men who were not waiting for others to solve their problems for them. They were taking the tools at hand and using their energy and intelligence to fashion these tools for the accomplishment of the task which lay before them. Men with such determination, such magnificent spirit, could not be crushed.

"What about the work of the political department?" I asked Jen Peh-hsi.

"Let's take that up tomorrow," he suggested. "Dinner is ready now."

I looked at my watch and saw that we had talked for five consecutive hours.

IV

Ting Ling's War Area Dramatic Troupe was giving a performance that evening. Ting Ling was a young woman of Thirty years whose patriotic stories and plays had deeply stirred her countrymen. Her liberal views had brought about her arrest a few years before, and she was released from prison at Nanking only a short time before the commencement of the present conflict.

The performance was to be held in the village theater, an open air affair which consisted of a stage which faced a large open court. When Agnes, Li Po and I arrived the court was already filled with townspeople and men of the army. On the platform a young man in uniform was leading the crowd in singing one of the new patriotic songs:

"We have no food, we have no clothes;
The enemy will send them to us.
We have no rifles, we have no artillery;
The enemy will make them for us.
Here we were born and here we were raised,
Every inch of the soil is ours;
Whoever tries to take it from us,
Him will we fight to the end."

The voices romped through these lines of the Song of the Partisans with a vigor and feeling that carried conviction. In my future wanderings I was to hear them over and over again, for songs such as this had spread through the interior of the country like flame before a stiff breeze, but always they would be associated in my mind with these earnest men and women here at the headquarters of the army.

Chu Teh entered and sat beside me on the bench, taking one of my hands in both of his in a gesture of affection. But he could not sit still for long, and soon he was wandering through the crowd, stopping at every step to chat with someone, or stooping to raise a child in his arms and chuck it under the chin. The atmosphere was pungent with good-will, tolerance and fellowship.

Ting Ling stepped out on the platform, a striking figure in the olive drab of a captured Japanese overcoat. In simple unaffected manner she described the significance of the scenes which were to follow.

The first depicted the capture of Lukouchiao by the Japanese, the act which precipitated the war. Next came a scene which portrayed the conversion of a tyrannical Chinese officer of the old school to the quiet, self-effacing leadership of a man who was beloved by his men. The final scene emphasized the value of co-operation in resisting the Japanese incursions. It introduced a peasant family which was interested only in its own affairs and felt that the war was none of its concern. Japanese soldiers arrived, killed the father, raped the daughters and forced the sons to work for them. One of the sons had a friend among the guerrillas, and from him he learned how the Japanese could be defeated if all Chinese co-operated. He exhorted the other members of his family to resist. One night a daughter stabbed her Japanese assailant to death with a butcher knife. The brothers killed two other Japanese who were living at the house, seized their arms, and the family escaped to the guerrilla area.

These scenes were enacted with a fidelity which was not lost on the spectators. The latter responded by punctuating the dramatic climaxes with shouts of "Ta tao Jih Pen chu I (Down with Japanese imperialism)."

By nine o'clock the performance was over. As the crowd dispersed the expression of grim resolution on the faces of men and women showed that the theme of the plays had made a deep impression.

The following morning Jen Peh-hsi came early to my room.

"We can talk here today," he greeted me. "I'll explain our political work to you.

"Political work," he commenced, "is the life line of the army and the heart and soul of our resistance to the invasion. Our weapons are antiquated and inferior, but we can compensate for this handicap by emphasizing political indoctrination. Both the soldiers and the people must know why China is fighting Japan. They must learn how to co-operate, how to live together harmoniously and how to defeat the invaders. The work is divided into three parts: (1) Education within the army, (2) work among the civil populace, and (3) work among the enemy.

"The object of the first part of the program is to develop a strong, well integrated army whose morale is high, and whose conduct is exemplary. The company is the educational unit, and there is a trained political leader in each company. Daily classes are conducted for those who cannot read or write, for soldiers must be literate. When units are on the march lesson papers are pinned to the back of the cap of the man ahead, so that the soldier may study as he walks. By lectures, cartoons, plays and games we endeavor to instil in each man the principles of honesty, truthfulness, humility and co-operation.

"Leaders," he continued, "are in daily intimate contact with their men. In fact, there are no social barriers within the army. Leaders are men who have given convincing proof of their ability to lead. Their authority is respected by all, for their ability and knowledge inspire confidence. But they are comrades as well, and when they are off duty they are on an equal social basis with their followers, whom we term 'fighters.'

"Before troops go into battle a meeting is held and the leader explains the reason for the engagement. The relative strength of the opposing forces is outlined, and the probable results of victory as well as the consequences of defeat are explained. After the battle another meeting is held to discuss our mistakes, for only by knowing our mistakes can we hope to correct them and enrich our experience.

"An army must have certain regulations to guide the conduct of its personnel. We have eleven simple rules. The three major ones are:

1) Execute the anti-Japanese patriotic principles;

2) Execute the instructions of leaders;

3) Don't take the smallest thing from the people.

"Then there are the eight minor rules:

1) Soldiers must ask permission before entering a house. Before leaving, the occupants must be thanked for their hospitality, and they must be asked if they are satisfied with the condition of the house.

2) Keep the house clean.

3) Speak kindly to the people.

4) Pay for all you use, at the market price.

5) Return all borrowed articles.

6) Pay for all things which are broken or destroyed.

7) Never commit a nuisance (dig latrines).

8) Do not kill or mistreat prisoners.

"Some of these rules might seem unnecessary to a Westerner, but in China armies had acquired the habit of mistreating the civil populace and taking from them what they wished. Many of the rules sought to correct this condition. An army which followed these precepts was bound to inspire the confidence of the people."

"I begin to see," I interjected, "why you also carry out political work among the people. You want to raise their conduct and morale to the standard you have developed in the army."

"Yes," replied Comrade Jen. "The army might be compared to fish, and the people to the water through which we move. The water must be cleared of obstructions, and the temperature must be conducive to the efficient movement of the fish. The people, too, must learn why we fight Japan and how they can aid in stemming the invasion. They must learn how to govern themselves and how to live together in harmony. We attempt to accomplish this purpose through the medium of mass meetings, wall newspapers, propaganda plays and through the use of slogans.

"If we remain in a locality, the people are organized into societies in order to better complete their education. Usually this organizational work is carried out within the hsien (county) under the supervision of the Magistrate, who is the chief civil official of the hsien. In each village there will be a society for the merchants, one for the women, another for the children, and one each for the workers and the peasants. Membership is entirely voluntary, but the advantages of joining are urged upon the people. These societies then become the basic units for instruction. Schools are set up for the older people as well as for the children, so that all may learn to read and write. They are taught how to conduct meetings and how to select their village and county officials. If the people are to discharge the obligations of citizenship, they should also have a voice in the direction of their own affairs."

Truth, idealism and sound wisdom were embraced by these words. If this program was actually practised, then I had stumbled on to Utopia. The prospect was thrilling.

"How about your work among the Japanese?" I inquired.

"Our idea," replied Jen Peh-hsi, "is that the Japanese military leaders are oppressors. Their troops have been misguided and deceived by malicious lies. Our purpose is to break their mass solidarity by causing the soldiers to think and act individually. We believe that there are great possibilities here. Among the Japanese troops there are Koreans, Manchurians, Mongolians and Formosans, so we use all of these languages in preparing our propaganda. We have a special corps of trained men and women who insinuate themselves into the Japanese garrisons and leave these tracts for the men to read. We also require that each fighter of our army memorize certain phrases in the Japanese language so that he can shout them if he comes within earshot of the enemy. Examples of these phrases are: 'Lay down your rifles; we will not kill you,' 'Do not shoot your Chinese brothers,' and 'Demand to be sent home—Japanese soldiers are our brothers.'

"We also make a point of treating Japanese captives well. They usually have the freedom of the village in which they are located. Some of these we send back to the Japanese army in the hope that they will find an opportunity to tell their comrades how well they have been treated.

"The results of this work among the enemy are slow in developing, but we feel that if we keep at it persistently it will bear fruit in the long run."

The hsiao kweis had brought in food, and it was time to bring another day's conversation to an end. Moreover, I needed time in which to mull over and absorb the astounding picture that had been presented to me.

V

The sharp, bright days of December passed quickly in this friendly atmosphere. Agnes and I hiked a good deal around the countryside, sometimes towards the mountains of the west, and at other times along the Fen river. I gained a deep respect for the courage and fortitude of this extraordinary woman who had forsaken the comforts of what we regard as civilization for a primitive life among an alien people. Now in her middle forties, her one desire was to remain with these people who were making such a valiant effort to realize the ideals for which she had consistently fought.

On one occasion we made a trip to Hungt'ung, which lay eight miles to the east, to visit a British missionary family. Mr. and Mrs. Trudinger had served the China Inland Mission for forty years. They represented the better type of missionary, the type which accepts the Chinese as equals, and they were greatly excited by what we had to tell them about the character of the Eighth Route Army. As we were leaving, Mr. Trudinger asked whether Chu Teh would accept a copy of the *Bible*. I thought he would, so the good missionary inscribed his personal copy of the Chinese version to Chu Teh, and requested that we present it to him. Chu Teh received it gravely and the next day he brought around a book which he requested that we present to Mr. Trudinger in his name. The title was: *An Analysis of Fascism*.

I was eager to get out into the field with the army in order to see how these plans of the army leaders were working in practice. One evening at dinner I broached the matter again to Chu Teh. His hesitation convinced me that he was concerned for my safety, as Chiang Kai-shek had been when I attempted to secure permission to visit the fighting areas around Shanghai. I determined to allay his fears.

That night I addressed a letter to Ambassador Johnson in Hankow. "I am going to the front," I wrote, "at my own request, and considerably against the advice of Commander Chu Teh. If I should be wounded or killed I want it distinctly understood that no blame is to devolve on the Eighth Route Army or on the Chinese government."

The following morning I took this letter, unsealed, to Chu Teh, and requested Li Po to read it to him. Then I asked Chu Teh to mail it, that he might have assurance that it had been sent.

He had a good laugh over this transparent artifice, but I could see that he was relieved.

"All right, Ts'an Tsan," he assured me, pushing his cap back with the gesture I knew indicated decision. "You may go. But where do you wish to go?"

"To Wu T'ai Shan (eastern Lake Superior region)," I replied steadily.

Chu Teh gave me a startled look. Wu T'ai Shan was entirely surrounded by the Japanese, and at that moment eight Japanese columns from the north, east and south were trying to smash their way into the area. These, however, were the very reasons that occasioned my request, for I wanted to see how these men of the Eighth Route Army fought. By going to Wu T'ai it would be necessary to pass through the enemy lines at least twice, thereby increasing the possibility of seeing action.

Chu Teh regarded me thoughtfully for a moment. Then a sympathetic smile spread over his honest face. He was a soldier and he could understand the desire of a soldier to see action.

"Hao (good)," he replied enigmatically. "You may go to Wu T'ai. And Li Po will go as your interpreter. I'll also send along your orderly and bodyguard."

I carried the joyful news to Agnes and Li Po.

"We'll celebrate with a pot of coffee," cried Agnes, and proceeded to dig into her precious supply.

It was Christmas Eve, and the patrol would depart on the day following Christmas. As we sipped our coffee we talked of the trip, and Agnes told of her experiences with the army.

"Do you know," she asked, "that this is probably the most continent army in the world? Have you noticed the comradely spirit which obtains between men and women in the army?"

I had noticed it, and I had wondered what the sexual relations of these men and women were.

"Continence is one of the virtues which is taught in the army. You never hear of attacks on women, and there is no prostitution in the areas which are administered by the army. Prostitution is regarded as exploitation of women, and it violates the tenets of their faith."

The conversation swung around to the significance of Christmas, and I suggested that we sing some carols.

"I don't know any carols," replied Agnes, "but I'll sing some negro spirituals."

"All right, you sing some spirituals and I'll play some carols on my harmonica," I compromised.

It was a memorable evening. A woman from Colorado and a man from Vermont celebrating Christmas Eve at the headquarters of a Communist army in the heart of China.

As the evening advanced Chu Teh and various members of his staff came in to join in the festivities. Chu Teh sang a solo, a plaintive ballad of his home province of Szechuan. And Tso Ch'uan did a sword dance.

It was Chu Teh who, with fitting perception, gave expression to a thought that must have been running through the minds of all when he remarked: "Here we have the Brotherhood of Man."

CHAPTER IV

"TSOU PA"—1,000 MILES WITH THE GUERRILLAS

I

THE day following Christmas dawned clear and cold. The sheepskin-lined coat would be none too warm on the mountain trails, I reflected, as I packed my haversack and rolled my sleeping bag. And yet, how much better prepared against the chill winter winds I was than were the men with whom I would march. Few had more than quilted cotton uniforms, and their bodies must be under-nourished after years of subsisting on millet and cabbage soup.

The patrol was forming outside the south wall when I emerged from the cozy room that had been my home for ten days. Medical supplies would be taken to Wu T'ai, and fourteen pack animals had been added to the patrol for this purpose. Two squads of fourteen men each comprised the escort, and all carried Thompson submachine guns. Half a dozen hsiao kweis (little devils) would also go with us, bound for duty in the north. In all we numbered forty-five, counting Li Po, myself and T'ien Tso-yao.

T'ien Tso-yao was only twenty-four, but he looked fully ten years older, so strenuous had been his service with the Red Army. He was a regimental commander in the 115th Division, and had been shot through the chest at the battle of P'inghsingkwan in September, his sixth wound in ten years (sufficient to win him the sobriquet of "six-wound T'ien"). Not yet fully recovered, he was eager to be at work again and was going to Wu T'ai to organize Partisans. His frail condition made it impossible for him to walk far, and so the army had provided him with the strongest mule it could find.

T'ien had a way with him. Patient, persuasive and courageous, he was a born leader. He was at his best when dealing with the lao pai hsing (the people), for his knowledge of their psychology was profound.

All was in readiness and Chu Teh came out for a word of farewell. Agnes Smedley bustled around sewing rents that appeared in packages of medical supplies, and cautioning the packers to take care that none of the precious contents was lost en route.

"Tsou Pa (let's go—or, we march)," commanded the young patrol leader. A "point" of half a dozen men started down the trail to the east. In a few minutes the rest of the patrol followed in single file. Behind trudged the pack animals, trailed by a small rear guard. The long trek had commenced.

I had not been informed about the route we were to follow. I knew only that we would go first to the headquarters of the 129th Division, nearly two hundred miles to the northeast. From there we would be sent across the Japanese-occupied Cheng Tai railroad into the Wu Tai mountain region. It was as though we were starting from Green Bay, Wisconsin, for eastern Lake Superior, and would follow narrow mountain trails which wound back and forth so much that the ground distance would be over double the air line distance.

At Hungt'ung we crossed the Fen river and struck into the mountains on a northeasterly course. Our pace was set at about two and a half miles an hour. On subsequent days this would be stepped up to ten li (three and one-third miles) an hour, a rate of march which seemed to be standard in the army. Hourly rest periods, such as are observed in Western armies, there were none. Instead we stopped for boiled drinking water every three or four hours. And there was no noon meal.

The equipment of these men was relatively light. In addition to his rifle or automatic each soldier carried an apron suspended just below his chest, containing three or four hand grenades of the potato masher type. On his back was a small, neat pack containing his blanket, extra socks (if he was lucky) and toilet articles. A rice bowl and an enamel cup hung from his belt,

Part of a regiment of Chinese guerrilla "Partisans," which operates behind the Japanese lines in the Wu T'ai district of Shansi province.

Members of a Village Self-Defense Corps transporting wounded from a guerrilla battle field to a hospital.

and chop sticks protruded from the top of one spiral puttee. Food, if carried, consisted of raw millet, which was encased in a narrow sack three feet long and slung over one shoulder. Including ammunition his accouterment probably weighed not more than forty pounds.

The hsiao kweis provided endless diversion as they joked among themselves or chased each other up the slopes that flanked the trail. We were still far from the enemy and there was no occasion to restrain them. One charming youngster of thirteen, just graduated from a radio school, plodded faithfully at my heels. Occasionally I would hear him muttering to himself: "Dit-da-dit, da-da-da, dit-dit-da-dit," as he endeavored to keep fresh in his mind the radio code.

It was still early in the afternoon when we stopped at the mountain town of Su P'u. The sixteen miles we had come were evidently considered sufficient for a first day's march. Tomorrow we would do twenty miles, and thereafter twenty-five and thirty.

The routine here was typical of what would take place at the end of each day's march. Calling on the village chief, the patrol leader asked if he could provide billets for our men. The army was obviously popular, for the troops were received with enthusiasm. Soon we were spreading our blankets, caring for our feet and preparing for the night's rest. Food was purchased and the cook prepared a sumptuous meal of millet, bean curd and cabbage soup.

Ching, a serious-minded youngster from Hunan, had joined our entourage as bodyguard. With the two other hsiao kwei and Li Po there were now five in our party. We shared a k'ang together, and as the days and weeks passed there grew up among us a rich and sympathetic fellowship.

In the evening Li Po and I worked on our diaries. Li Po would write a book when he returned. The boys busied themselves with studies, scrubbing clothes or examining each other's precious possessions, occasionally exchanging small items. T'ien came in and told stories of the long march from Kiangsi: how the Red Army had escaped the encircling ring of the Koumintang armies by a ruse, followed by a swift night march between the enemy positions; how the army had subsisted for ten days on grass roots while crossing the swamps of Ch'inghai.

Invariably we retired early, and by daybreak we were eating our breakfast of millet gruel. Before the sun rose the column was again on the trail.

The days that followed were much the same. The pace was grueling until muscles became set, but the mind was constantly stimulated by the changing panorama of hills and valleys. Here and there a shrine or a Buddhist temple contributed a distinctly Oriental touch. Of foliage there was little, except for the pine groves around the temples, for firewood was at a premium. And bird life was confined almost entirely to the humble magpie. But there was no monotony in the geological formations, and as the sun shifted from east to west the coloring of the hills changed from delicate purple to reds, greens and ambers.

The war had not yet come to this region and the people continued to live normal lives. They knew, though, that any day might see a Japanese column penetrating these mountain fastnesses, and they were apprehensive—and co-operative. At the infrequent rest periods townspeople brought steaming cauldrons of drinking water, and sometimes even offered the hard hsiao ping biscuit. It was winter and most of the people had little to do, for they had stored up food enough to carry them until spring. The more prosperous families had pigs and chickens, and they tended these and gathered firewood from along the river banks.

On the sixth day we came to the walled city of Ch'inchow, and stopped outside to await the pack train which had dropped behind. Quite accidentally we met an Eighth Route Army leader from the town, and learned that the commander of the 129th Division, Liu Peh-ch'eng, was here on his way south for a conference with Chu Teh. We decided to remain the night so that I might talk with him.

II

If the pack train had not been delayed we might have missed Liu Peh-ch'eng, the one-eyed commander, and we would also have failed to meet General Po Yi-po. General Po was the local representative of Governor Yen Hsi-shan, and he administered the affairs of ten counties, of which Ch'inchow was the headquarters.

Liu Peh-ch'eng had formerly been chief of staff of the Red Army. He was a serious-minded man of forty-four, whose right eye had been shot out during the civil war. A former Szechuan militarist, he was rated as one of the best tacticians and students of military history in the army.

"I have had little time for study during the past ten years," he told me rather wistfully, on the occasion of our first meeting. "Before I talk to you, though, I wish you would talk with General Po Yi-po. He represents the Governor of the province here, and we are trying to establish cordial relations with the Shansi officials. They are patriotic men, but they need to learn how to mobilize the people for resistance and how to fight guerrilla warfare. I'll come to see you this evening."

The atmosphere at General Po's headquarters was friendly, but it lacked the democratic quality which was present in units of the Eighth Route Army. Officers held themselves aloof, and soldiers bore an attitude of subservience. All had the class-conscious bearing of old China.

General Po was friendly, cordial, and something of a paternal autocrat. "How long can you stay?" he inquired. "Tomorrow we are assembling here all the troops and civil organizations which are located within fifteen miles and I would like you to see them."

I agreed to remain for a day.

He explained the steps which Governor Yen had taken to prepare the province for resistance. This was one of seven administrative districts into which the one hundred and five hsien of the province had been divided. Partisan groups had been organized, and the people were formed into societies. The titles of these societies were picturesque: Honesty—Salvation and Sacrifice—Dare to Die. I thought I saw the hand of the Eighth Route Army in a good deal of this. The form was much the same, but the leaders had not yet caught the spirit of self-sacrifice and devotion to the welfare of the people which made the Eight Route Army system work. These men of the provincial government were earnest, and they were sincere in their search for a formula with which to resist the invasion. Probably only time and bitter experience would bring an understanding that full and willing co-operation of the people is postulated on a self-denying and scrupulously honest leadership.

That evening Liu Peh-ch'eng came in for a talk.

"We have a complex situation in this province," he began. "Within the province there are three distinct political organizations, each with definite ideas as to how we should resist the invasion. In addition to the Eighth Route Army and the Provincial government, there are representatives here of the Kuomintang Party. We try to work with the other two groups without injuring their sensibilities. We hope, through example and persuasion, to convince them that the pattern of resistance which we have developed is best suited to meet the situation. We make mistakes, but we invite criticism—and we get results.

"Recently," he continued, "the Japanese sent five columns of troops to destroy my division. Our main force was in the hills near Ho Shun hsien, and the enemy columns approached us from the west, northwest and north. One of our companies ambushed and severely defeated one column of six hundred men. It then moved swiftly thirty miles across country and surprised a second column. The three remaining columns united and hemmed in our main force on the front and flanks. But that night we left a company to hold our positions on the hills and moved the bulk of the division to the rear and around one flank of the enemy. At daylight we attacked his flank, while Partisans assaulted his rear. This victory gave us fifty horses, a quantity of rifles and ammunition and several radio sets. In this operation we relied on the people to bring us information, and they did not fail us."

Comrade Liu wiped his glass eye and continued. "In Lin hsien, over in western Hopei, the women wear red jackets and green pants. Five of our Partisans dressed up in this type of raiment and sauntered towards the town. They were pursued by ten Japanese soldiers and fled up an adjacent valley, where our men lay in ambush. Those Japanese pursued no more women." Liu grinned complacently at the recollection.

"Sometimes we make effective use of rifles at distances up to five and six hundred yards," he said. "However, we prefer a close-in attack where we can use hand grenades. Just a month ago the Japanese sent a detachment of seven hundred men from T'ai Ku into our area. We kept them under observation until they reached a mountain pass. Here we had distributed a battalion of men on both sides of the road. We opened fire with rifles and machine guns. The Japanese replied with artillery, and we fought for an entire day. But the Japanese couldn't see us, for we were widely separated and well concealed. They retired with a loss of ninety men killed. We suffered not a single casualty." Liu's head was bowed in meditation as he concluded the narrative.

"Isn't there apt to be a conflict of authority between your leaders and the provincial officials?" I asked.

"We try to avoid any such conflict," he replied. "General Yen Hsi-shan is governor of the province, and we bow to his authority. However, we have his permission to employ our own methods for maintaining order in those hsien where our troops are operating against the Japanese. We endeavor to establish representative government in those hsien, and the Shansi officials co-operate with us. In some districts there is a mobilization committee, a united front organization which contains representatives of all political factions."

Liu was leaving for the south early the next morning, and I did not see him again.

"There's a missionary here to see you," Lo informed me the following morning.

I had not known that there was a foreigner in these parts. He proved to be the Reverend Edward Wampler, of Virginia, who represented the Church of the Brethren here. Later in the day I dined at his home and met Mrs. Wampler and their children, ages three and five. They proved to be earnest and practical Christians, and were highly respected by local Chinese for their unaffected way of life. Wampler was a practical farmer, and he supplemented his ecclesiastical work by aiding the local tillers of the soil to improve their methods. He showed me a flock of sheep of superior quality, raised from an imported registered ram, which was the pride of the community.

It was near noon when General Po came to take me to a wide plateau near the river where the troops had been assembled. Massed in front of an improvised platform were eight thousand human beings representing every stratum of local society. In the van stood three or four hundred children, and behind them ranged groups of women, peasants, merchants, various civic organizations and units of the village self-defense corps. The men carried weapons of various descriptions—ancient spears, scythes, and muzzle-loading muskets —Two regiments of Shansi troops and a company from the Eighth Route Army brought up the rear. This was China; tremendous manpower, child-like devotion, needing only the intelligent direction of earnest leaders to weld it into a strong, vibrant nation of incalculable power.

The meeting began with the reading of Doctor Sun Yat-sen's will, followed by three bows on the part of the multitude to the picture of Doctor Sun which was suspended above the platform. Cheer leaders led the shouting of slogans: Down with Japanese Imperialism—Unite to Defeat the Japanese Fascists —China Fights for the Peace of the World. Patriotic songs were sung, and General Po gave a highly emotional address in which he related specific instances of Japanese atrocities, with all the gory details, and called on those present to be ready to sacrifice themselves in defense of their soil.

When it was over the assembly was dismissed. Many remained to gossip, and the plateau took on the festive aspect of a county fair, with itinerant food vendors moving among the crowd.

III

When we left Ch'inchow our column was augmented by two hundred

Ho Lung, famous leader of the 120th Division of the Eighth Route Army.

Sung Sao-wen, Chairman of the Political Council of the Provisional Government of Shansi-Chahar and Hopei.

Nieh Yong-sen, the Eighth Route Army leader who organized Chinese resistance in the border region of Shansi-Chahar and Hopei.

Hsiu Shang-ch'ien, Vice-Commander of the 129th Division, Eighth Route Army, and organizer of Chinese resistance in Southern Hopei province.

and fifty men of the army who were returning to the 129th Division. The new detachment carried its own cooking gear, and I was intrigued by a huge metal pan which was rigged on a pack frame and carried on the back of a cook. Four feet in diameter and two feet deep, it towered above his head so that, viewed from the rear, it appeared to walk under its own power.

Hitherto we had not been bothered by ceremonies at the towns through which we passed, but General Po had evidently informed all and sundry that we were coming, and at every hamlet organizations of the people were drawn up to receive us. The climax came when we reached Wu Shang hsien. Here the Magistrate, a tall, imposing chap, met us at the city gate with a large entourage of county officials. There was much bowing and scraping, and Li Po and I were conducted through lines of cheering people (regimented, of course) to the yamen (office of the Magistrate). Here we sat for twenty minutes sipping tea and going through the ceremonious interchange of platitudes so familiar in old China. Finally the Magistrate conducted me to an elaborate residence where he intended that I spend the night. Chang and Lo examined the luxurious appointments with wonder mixed with amusement.

Without hurting the sensibilities of the Magistrate I tried to explain that I would prefer to remain with the patrol. I was making a bad job of it when Ching, the other bodyguard, rushed in. Without ado he brusquely informed the dignitary that I couldn't possibly stay here because it was too far from the patrol, and the patrol was responsible for me. Before the Magistrate could recover from his astonishment at this unorthodox explosion Ching grabbed me by the arm and piloted me into the street. As we walked along he winked impishly at me and whispered confidently: "I knew you didn't want to stay in that k'e ch'i (ceremonious) place."

It developed that T'ien, the old war-horse with the chest wound, had arranged for a room in the home of a baker. The Magistrate, having recovered his aplomb, followed us here. His reserve having been punctured, he proved to be a very democratic individual after all, and ordered an enormous dinner for us. This generous act served to raise him to the good graces of the hsiao kwei.

At sunup we were again on the trail, winding across frozen river beds and bleak mountain ridges. On the second day following we reached Liaochow, the headquarters of the 129th Division.

The headquarters was actually in a small village near the walled city. The army, I noticed, never placed its important nerve centers in cities. They were favorite targets for Japanese bombing planes.

Japanese overcoats were now much in evidence. This division was actively engaged with the enemy, both along the east-west Ch'eng-T'ai railroad, and along the Peip'ing-Hankow line which lay to the east. Supplies were captured almost daily.

In the absence of Liu Peh-ch'eng the division was commanded by Hsiu Shang-ch'ien, famed for his leadership of the Fourth Front Army during the civil war days. He was assisted by Chang Hou, the political director.

Hsiu and Chang made a fine team. Hsiu was short, thin and quiet, and his ascetic face had a way of expanding suddenly into a most engaging smile. He might easily have been called "The Fox." Chang was tall, robust and a bit boisterous in his address, reminding me somewhat of "Old Hickory." He was at his best when addressing a mass meeting, for then the persuasive power of his deep bass voice was impressive. Both were modest men whose first thoughts were for the people they led.

Soon after my arrival they looked over my wearing apparel.

"Is this the warmest coat you have?" asked Hsiu Shang-ch'ien.

"Yes," I replied, "but I also have sweaters and heavy underwear."

"Pu kou! (not enough)," he exclaimed. "It's bitterly cold in Wu T'ai. We have some lamb's wool which we captured from the Japanese. I'll have an extra lining put in your coat."

"And I'll have fur-lined socks and shoes made for you," added Chang Hou.

They were as good as their word.

When Li Po and I were settled in our quarters they came over for a talk.

Comrade Hsiu spread out a large scale map of the railway area. "We plan to send you across the lines here," he said, pointing to the vicinity of

Sho Yang. "The Japanese are active in this railway zone, but your patrol will be guided by members of the village self-defense corps over secret mountain trails."

He praised the work of these self-defense corps, saying that they aided the army in many ways.

"A corps is organized in each village," he explained. "It is composed of men who are unfit for active campaigning, and sometimes of boys as well. The corps gathers information of the enemy, prevents the Japanese from obtaining information of our movements, and relays the wounded from the battle field to the nearest hospital. Without their help we would be severely handicapped."

"Our mission," he continued, "is really two-fold: to thoroughly indoctrinate the people with the spirit of resistance, so that they will not lose heart even when their towns are occupied by the enemy; and to continually harass the enemy's lines of communication and ambush his patrols."

That evening a former Peip'ing college professor came to see me. Professor Yang Hsu-fang was until recently a member of the faculty of Peking Normal University. In his early fifties, he had for years been active in imbuing students with the spirit of nationalism and impressing them with the necessity for defending the national sovereignty. When the war came he put his convictions to work and led a group of students into eight hsien of southwestern Hopei which had been deserted by their former officials. Here he re-established law and order and organized a Partisan group which was keeping the Japanese worried. He had come across the mountains to Liaochow to study the methods of the Eighth Route Army. By no means a strong man, the rough guerrilla life must have called for no little fortitude on the part of this patriot.

A patrol from the 129th Division escorted us out of Liaochow. Henceforth those of us who were bound for Wu T'ai would be relayed by patrols from one headquarters to another. The twenty-four miles to the Brigade Headquarters of Tsen Ken were covered in record time.

Tsen Ken was different from the other leaders I had seen. He was thirty-two, and his beardless, bespectacled face suggested the student rather than the soldier. He had an abundance of nervous energy which found expression in ceaseless physical activity and a staccato manner of speech. Ten years before he had been one of Chiang Kai-shek's students in the Whampoo Military Academy, and at one time he is reported to have saved the life of the Generalissimo. The latter paid his debt in 1933, when Tsen was captured, by changing the death sentence to one of imprisonment.

Tsen had bad news for us. The Japanese at Shoyang were on the war path, and a battle was going on at this moment in that vicinity. Hsiu Shang-ch'ien had telephoned from Liaochow to send us fifty miles to the east where another route through the lines would be tried.

The eastward trek took us through Ho Shun hsien, where we had an amusing experience. The Magistrate was a young man who had done valiant work in mobilizing the people of the hsien, which had twice been invaded. He was eager to honor the foreign traveler and when we arrived at noon we discovered that a meal had been prepared for us. Ordinarily we ate nothing on the march, but this courtesy could not be ignored.

Evidently someone had informed the Magistrate that foreigners liked their food sweet, for when the dishes of rice, fried eggs, bean sprouts and fried chicken arrived each was covered with a layer of sugar nearly half an inch thick. Li Po and I suppressed our amusement with difficulty. We addressed ourselves to the dulcet dishes with determination and somewhat exaggerated manifestations of appreciation, for the feelings of our host must not be hurt. The latter appeared to be no less determined to enjoy the unfamiliar cuisine; this was a small sacrifice to make for a foreign guest. Only the hsiao kweis ate with true zest, for it was not often that their monotonous diet of millet was varied with such an elaborate spread.

In the afternoon we pushed on. The following day we reached Kao Lu, headquarters of an infantry regiment commanded by Chen Hsi-lien. Kao Lu was the provisional county seat of Si Yang hsien, the hsien city being occupied by the Japanese. This was further evidence of the determination of the Chinese to maintain control of the countryside where the Japanese occupied the cities.

One of Chen's companies had just returned from raiding a truck column on the highway which parallels the railway, and all sorts of captured equipment was on display. I admired a fur-lined suit (overall type with high bib, and with coat to match), and Chen insisted that I carry along one as a souvenir. I placed it in my baggage.

Captured diaries and operations plans were particularly enlightening, for they provided first-hand evidence of how the Japanese regarded the difficulties which were being encountered in this campaign. One of the diaries contained this note:

"Before we started today we were told that a small group of our army had been attacked at Chi Lung Chen. We moved carefully. At this place our regiment met the enemy for the first time. Because the people of the place are very dangerous we killed thirty young men and then left. We walked a short distance and then stopped."

On the following page appeared this final notation: "We are encircled by the enemy. Perhaps this is my end. I hope that we may have help from our army. God help us."

Evidently the soldiers of the Japanese army were not so happy about this campaign.

I had heard that Chen's regiment had on one occasion destroyed some twenty odd airplanes, and I asked him about it.

"It was like this," he told me. "The Japanese had an emergency landing field at Yamingpao. We kept it under observation and one evening our spies reported that twenty-four planes were there. I directed one battalion to attack the town to the north of Yamingpao, and another to attack the town to the south. The third battalion I led myself. We approached Yamingpao silently in the night. Two companies assaulted the garrison; the other two surrounded the landing field and destroyed twenty-two planes by setting fire to them with hand grenades. Two planes got away."

These stories I had been hearing began to make a picture. The invading army was crunching its way through the province like a huge elephant.

But the elephant was constantly bedeviled by hornets which swarmed around it day and night, stabbing, stabbing, stabbing. For food it was dependent on supplies from home, and sometimes the hornets descended on them in droves and carried them off. How long could the elephant survive under these conditions?

But the hornets had to live too, and here was another reason for the close co-operation between the army and the civil populace. The army protected the farmer, and the latter raised food which was divided equally among the populace, army and civilians alike.

Chen Hsi-lien informed me the next morning that he would accompany the battalion which would escort us through the lines. Chen was twenty-one, young even for a regimental commander in the Eighth Route Army. Ten years before he had joined the army as orderly for Hsu Hai-tung. Loyalty, a keen practical mind and great physical energy were responsible for his rapid advance. He had the appearance of a pugilist, and walked with a slight swagger, which was probably an unconscious manifestation of self-confidence.

Breakfast with the Magistrate delayed our start, though this ultimately proved to be providential. As we advanced north the terrain became more rugged and the mountains higher. We were approaching the edge of the zone in which the Japanese operated so frequently that the villages had mostly been evacuated. For this reason we stopped on the edge of the zone at Tsung Wu, in the middle of the afternoon. The following day we would make the dash across the lines.

It was another bright exhilarating day, and Li Po, T'ien, Chen and I lounged in the courtyard of our billet. A peasant came to see Chen. After talking to him the latter rose hastily and buckled on his Mauser. It appeared that a Japanese column was moving eastward down a valley which joined ours at Tung Yen T'o, a mile and a half north.

In a few minutes Chen returned and informed us that the situation was serious. He would have to take the patrol and fight. His headquarters (which contained radio equipment) would be established three miles back, up the mountain we had just crossed, at a place called Ch'ien Ai. Would we move back with it? We assented, for this was no time to embarrass him with our presence. But before we could leave the compound, artillery fire sounded close aboard. The Japanese were using their favorite method of reconnaissance—reconnaissance by fire.

We packed the mules hastily and started up the mountain. With us went scores of refugees from the village, a few household effects stuffed into blankets and thrown over their shoulders. Scores of others streamed across the floor of the valley towards the mountain on the other side.

Twenty minutes later, as we plodded upward, Li Po looked back towards the village. An ejaculation escaped his lips.

"Look," he cried. Coming around the base of the mountain and entering the town from the north was a troop of Japanese cavalry.

Early in the evening Chen joined us. By candle light he spread a map on the k'ang and gave us an estimate of the situation. An enemy detachment of five hundred men was at Tung Yen T'o. Another detachment was en route there from the north. The object of this force might be: (1) to block our passage to the north, (2) to search for food, or (3) to move on Kao Lu. Chen proposed to keep the enemy under observation and wait for an opportune time to attack. His mission was to get us across the railroad, so he would not attack unless necessary, but he would in any event keep between the enemy and his own base at Kao Lu. This was sound judgment.

"What would you have done if we had been north of Tung Yen T'o when this happened?" I asked.

Chen grimaced. "That," he replied, "would have been tough for us. We would then have been between the two forces. We can thank the Magistrate's breakfast for saving us from that calamity."

He explained that the reason we had not received earlier warning of the column's proximity was because it had started from its base at about the same time we had started from ours, and we had been marching on converging courses with a mountain between us. The people hadn't been able to get word to us earlier.

Li Po, T'ien and I remained at Ch'ien Ai during the next two days. We followed the operations through the messages which came back from Chen. The Japanese marched back and forth across the country, evidently trying to trap their pursuers. On the evening of the second day they attempted a ruse. Doubling back quickly over their trail under cover of darkness they laid an ambush near a converging valley. But this time the peasants were on the job. Chen was informed of the trap. Taking his patrol over the mountain he led it to the rear of the Japanese position. Just before daybreak he attacked. As soon as they could disengage themselves the Japanese withdrew towards their base at Si Yang, leaving behind fifteen of their dead. Chen's patrol had suffered one killed and two men wounded.

Chen had handled this engagement in masterly fashion. If all guerrilla leaders were as quick-witted and resourceful the Japanese would have to change their tactics if they hoped to survive this campaign, much less win it. Their weaknesses were all too obvious. They blundered around the country like blind men, for they lacked good information. Their columns were cumbersome, the men being weighed down with heavy impedimenta. Artillery slowed them still further. And their habit of abusing the people served to alienate those who might otherwise have been disposed to co-operate with them.

IV

The way was now clear for us to proceed—or we hoped it was. The patrol had spent three strenuous days, so we remained at Ch'ien Ai for a day of rest, and Chen sent the wounded back to Kao Lu.

Fifty students from Yenan joined our column, and among them was one girl. She was Chang Hsueh-hwa, the wife of Nieh Yong-sen, the military commander at Wu T'ai. She and the other students had recently graduated from the military and political training schools, and they were en route to Wu T'ai to organize Partisans and develop the people's organizations.

The students added to the gayety of the column. Their enthusiasm had not yet been mellowed by the hardship of active campaigning and the responsibility of making decisions which involved the lives of human beings. They were young, strong and filled with the willingness to sacrifice themselves for national salvation. Their packs were larger than those of the men of the army, for in addition to regulation gear they contained textbooks which would be useful in their work. Only Chang Hsueh-hwa rode a mule. The balance walked with the rest of us.

We struck into the mountains south of Niang Tze Kuan, following little-used trails. As we passed Tung Yen T'o, recently occupied by the Japanese, there was ample evidence of what such an occupation means. The town was in ruins. Every particle of woodwork had been stripped from doors and windows. Only the stark mud walls remained. A handful of old men, were burying the bodies of three of their number who had been shot out of hand by the undisciplined Japanese. One had failed to understand an order given to him by a tyrannical soldier; another had refused to k'ou t'ou (bounce his head on the ground) to an officer; and the third had been shot for no apparent reason except the whim of his assailant.

Our pace was not so rapid now—about two and a half miles an hour—for one company was covering our western flank by following a parallel mountain ridge. Another company was in the van, and the two remaining ones comprised the main body of the patrol.

No longer did the hsiao kweis cavort over the countryside. Every individual had his place in the column, and he held to it with dogged determination. We were in enemy territory now and unity was essential.

At three o'clock in the afternoon we paused in a deserted village to await the coming of darkness. The cooks prepared millet gruel, for we would be marching the night through. Five miles beyond lay the highway, and five miles beyond that was the railway. Chen Hsi-lien would remain herewith a small guard and the radio station. The battalion commander, K'ung Ching-teh, would conduct us through the lines.

K'ung wore one of the Japanese fur-lined suits, and walked with the undulating glide of a panther. He was a crack man on the trail, and he knew every man of his battalion by his first name.

Two hours later the command assembled and K'ung gave final instructions. No talking, no smoking and no coughing. Keep closed up and move as silently as possible. The advance guard would seize the town at the highway and hold it until we passed. The next company would then become the advance guard and would seize the rail crossing. That was all.

An air of tenseness pervaded the column as we wound down the slope, crossed a river bed and ascended the mountain on the other side. A gorgeous sunset suffused the western sky. As we reached the summit darkness closed about us, and off to the west a huge column of flame blazed on the side of a higher mountain. Was it a signal fire, or was it a peasant burning off his winter terraces? We speculated silently.

The descent was more perilous, for the trail was filled with smooth round stones which turned easily under foot. Behind me Ching, my bodyguard, fell and cursed softly as he picked himself up. Ahead faithful Li Po turned his head frequently to assure himself that I was near. And above the familiar indicators of the omnipresent dipper pointed to the north star which guided us.

The slope became more gentle, and the barking of dogs warned that a village was not far off. In the quiet of the night the barks sounded like trumpets giving the alarm. Probably the whole town would be astir.

But such was not the case. There was no sign of life about the lightless houses as we glided past. K'ung dropped back and took my hand. Together we dashed across a highway where the phantom figures of our soldiers were faintly visible on each side. Resuming a normal pace K'ung whispered in my ear "Ch'i Ch'e lu (the motor car road)," and moved swiftly into the darkness ahead.

The danger was only half over. In fact, the most perilous part of the journey lay ahead, for there was the possibility that the Japanese garrison at Niang Tze Kwan had learned of the highway crossing and would be waiting to nab us at the railway.

Swiftly we ascended another mountain. The tenseness throughout the column became more acute, driving us to greater effort. Stonewall Jackson's foot cavalry, I reflected, was a mere turtle compared to the speed of these men.

The five miles to the railway seemed like five hundred, but suddenly we were there. K'ung's reassuring figure appeared again. Again he took me by the hand and broke into a run. Pellmell we scuttled down a slope, across a small foot bridge, up an embarkment and through a culvert beneath the railroad. Arrived on the opposite side K'ung stopped short.

"Now I will return," he told me. "Company commander Teng will escort you to the north." He saluted punctiliously, wheeled about and glided back into the night.

K'ung's peremptory departure was a little disconcerting, for I had come to have great confidence in this silent, efficient leader. But apparently his orders were to see us across the railway and then return south with three of the companies.

This was no time for sentimentalizing, however, and the column was already plodding ahead. Niang Tze Kwan was only half a mile away, and we had captured four Chinese who were guarding the railway for the Japanese. Their absence would soon be known, and in a few hours a column would take up the pursuit. Our safety lay in reaching the higher mountain region to the north.

Crossing another low mountain, we dropped into a valley and followed it for what seemed hours. At last the trail became steeper. As we mounted higher the cold became more intense, chilling our perspiring bodies. My benumbed mind reflected vaguely on the number of mountains we had crossed this day. This would be the eighth. And I realized with amazement and a touch of chagrin that I was lagging. The blue-clad forms were scampering past me as though this were the first climb of the day. Grimly I set my teeth and concentrated on putting more power into my legs.

At the summit the men were sprawled on the frozen ground, most of them sound asleep. On this mountain top it was considered safe to catch a few moments' rest. My watch showed two o'clock.

I shall not soon forget the drama and the beauty of the scene here. It was bitterly cold, a sharp cold that pierced the marrow. Out of the eastern horizon a full moon was rising, its rich glow giving the adjacent hills a pale yellow hue and creating the illusion that we gazed into a phantom world. Overhead familiar constellations twinkled cheerily in a blanket of unbelievable blue. And all around was silence, save for the heavy breathing of the prostrate forms. But for these sleeping figures I might have been on a mountain top in Europe or America, so universal is the topography of night. But they were Chinese, and this was China, and those blue-clad forms were here because they sought to save this China from those who labored below to take it from them.

Commander Teng came over and sat beside me, looking intently into the eerie void from whence we had come.

"I wonder," he ruminated, "if they are following us yet?"

Getting up, he began awakening the sleeping ones, and the familiar command "Tsou Pa" was passed along.

The descent was steep and the footing precarious. Slipping and sliding down the mountain, we entered a valley which we followed to the north. The pace again became rapid and rhythmic. As the hours wore on the mind became numb to everything but the task of placing one foot ahead of the other. We resolved into automatons.

Dawn was breaking when we entered a friendly village. The people gathered firewood and made a huge fire in the open courtyard of a building. The only food in the town was wheat flour, and this was made into dough, cut in strips and boiled. I felt I had never tasted a more succulent dish.

While we ate, a peasant arrived from the south and informed the commander that a Japanese column was in pursuit. We had already covered forty-three miles since the preceding morning, but we must move higher into the mountains before we would be secure.

Again packs were slung on to the now weary backs, and we followed a stream bed which led into a massive range to the north. The valley narrowed to a gorge whose sides were almost perpendicular. Now the villages became clusters of mud huts terraced into the walls of the valley. Stunted pine trees began to appear, their short sturdy branches thrown out in gestures of defiance.

We had come eight miles when the gorge ended abruptly in a wall of rock over which a cascade of water charged into an ice-bound cavern. Crudely carved steps led up one side of the wall. Laboriously we climbed to the ridge of the mountain, where we had the sensation of being on top of the world.

It was the middle of the afternoon, and we had come fifteen miles since breakfast, when we encountered Partisan sentries outside a mountain village. Within the village we found ourselves again in the bosom of the army. Here was rest, warmth and food.

V

The march across the Ch'eng T'ai railroad and through the Japanese lines had revealed a number of interesting things about the Eighth Route Army. Fifty-eight miles had been covered in thirty-two hours, but the first stretch of forty-three miles had been accomplished in twenty hours—remarkable feat for an organization of six hundred men. Perhaps the most striking feature of this march was the absence of straggling. The explanation lay in the ethical indoctrination of the individual. Each man possessed the *desire* to do what was right; it was right to perform his duty; and it was his duty to reach the destination with the column.

The methodical manner in which the crossing of the enemy zone of operation had been accomplished was no less impressive. The towns which stood at the highway and railway junctures had been surrounded in such a manner as to prevent messages from being sent out, and to guard against sudden attack as well. The Chinese guards at the rail line had been captured without bloodshed. They would be sent back to headquarters, where an investigation would be held to determine whether their co-operation with the Japanese had been voluntary or compulsory. If it had been compulsory they would not be harmed. This enlightened policy ultimately served to bring the guerrillas the co-operation of a majority of the people who were constrained to live under Japanese jurisdiction.

Most important, however, was the revelation that the occupation by the Japanese of certain lines of communication was no barrier to the passage through those lines of Chinese armed forces. The conclusion was growing within me that so long as the people maintained the will-to-resist Japan could not control this country.

A good night's sleep restored depleted energy, and the next morning we were ready to move on. We parted from the men who had conducted us through the lines, and a patrol of Partisans escorted us towards Hun Tze Tei, a Partisan headquarters on the Fu T'o river.

These Partisans differed little from the regular army in uniform and arms, but they lacked the individual self-discipline so evident in old Red Army men. They were civilians who had taken up arms only a few weeks before, but their spirit was strong and they were willing to learn. The commander of this unit, and the political director, were Eighth Route Army veterans.

The most noticeable difference in this area north of the railroad was in the attitude of the civil populace. The people were more universally friendly and co-operative. It was as though their isolation had dissolved the shells of family complacency and induced a determination to aid each other. Faced with a common danger there was no place in their lives for prejudice and social barriers. The Eighth Route Army leaders, by providing a plan and a more equitable way of life, had given them new hope. Their response was spontaneous and unanimous.

As we moved along, the commander of the patrol explained the situation we were facing. It appeared that Hun Tze Tei was the objective of a Japanese force which was moving up the Fu T'o river from its base at P'ing San, fifty miles to the southeast. The commander was not certain where the Partisan headquarters had moved, but towards evening we found it in a village five miles south of Hun Tze Tei.

The commander of the Fifth Partisan Group was a hardy young veteran of the Eighth Route Army named Sen Kuohwa. He related the recent developments.

The Japanese column of a thousand men had been ambushed by his group and a regiment of Hsu Hai-tung's brigade twenty-five miles down the Fu T'o river. They had fought for three days in order to delay the column and afford the people of Hun Tze Tei time in which to evacuate women, children and food from the city. Now the Japanese had arrived there, but they would probably not remain long, for their food supply was depleted and their communication with P'ing San had been cut.

During the night word came that the Japanese were moving back towards their base, and in the morning we entered the town. It presented a pathetic sight. Part of the town had been burned, and six of the elderly men who had volunteered to remain as care-takers had been killed. I inspected the smoldering ruins and questioned some of the men who had been present during the occupation. The invaders, they said, were infuriated at finding no food or women. They had expressed their indignation by burning and shooting.

Our next destination was the brigade headquarters of Hsu Hai-tung, which lay ten miles directly north. The Fu T'o river, a swift-flowing stream, lay between, and the bridge had been destroyed.

The patrol leader was reluctant to ford the river, but the alternative was a twenty mile detour to the west. We decided that the saving in distance was worth the risk of crossing. Although the temperature was zero, most of the men stripped to their bare skins and waded through the waist high waters, holding their clothes and equipment above their heads. I felt that my high leather boots furnished more protection, but when I reached the other side my clothes were frozen solid. Li Po and the patrol leader were horrified and rushed me into the home of a peasant, where I thawed out and shifted to the fur lined socks and shoes which had been provided by Hsiu Shang-ch'ien at Liaochow. The balance of the march was made without incident.

Hsu Hai-tung was another peasant who had given abundant evidence of his qualities of leadership. In appearance he was tall and large of frame, while his face bore the expression of kindliness which I had found in Chu Teh. He was a leader of the Nathan Bedford Forrest type, believing in getting there "fastest with the mostest men."

That evening we talked, over our peanuts and tea, and he related a few of his war experiences. I had heard that every person in his home hsien in Hunan who bore his family name had been put to death during the civil war. "Yes," replied Hsu Hai-tung, "but that is all past. Now all Chinese are brothers, and Chiang Kai-shek is our leader." This sentiment I found to be universal in the Eighth Route Army. Bygones were bygones, and now all Chinese were brothers.

It was with a feeling of sadness that we left T'ien Tso-yao here. He was to assume command of his old regiment, for the man who had replaced him when he was wounded had been killed in the battle of Hun Tze Tei.

Again we headed north, and for three days we averaged thirty miles a day. Our destination was Fu P'ing, in western Hopei province, now the headquarters of the guerrilla forces in the north.

Late in the afternoon of the third day we entered the city. It was a gala occasion. Nieh Yong-sen, the commander, met us on the outskirts and escorted us along a line of troops and organizations of the people over a mile in length. No foreigner had penetrated this region since the war began and the people were eager to show what they had accomplished.

A group of merchants in long black gowns saluted as we passed, their faces beaming with good will. Close beside was a group of peasants in quilted trousers and short black jackets, open at the throat. They regarded with unabashed curiosity this foreign devil with the red face and clumsy shoes. A women's society carried small paper pennants which bore the characters "welcome American friend." Their hair was bobbed, a symbol of their emancipation. But most appealing was the children's society. They ranged in age from five to fifteen, and they obviously gloried in the fact that they were accorded the dignity of a place in line with their elders.

That night I met the officials of the Border Government at dinner, and I had an opportunity to examine these men who were responsible for maintaining Chinese sovereignty in this region far in the rear of the Japanese advance.

Nieh was the brains and driving force of the organization, though he would not admit it. He was short, thin and unprepossessing, but his eyes shown with intelligence, and the lines of his mouth indicated strong determination. He had studied in France for three years, and he wore his military cap with a slight tilt such as is affected by many French officers.

The Governor of this region was Sung Sao-wen, a former Shansi provincial official who had once been Magistrate of Wu T'ai hsien. He was chubby, jovial and be-spectacled.

I learned that this area, which was completely surrounded by the Japanese, contained about ten million people, and was called the Provisional Government of Shansi, Chahar and Hopei. It contained about forty thousand square miles of territory, comparable in size to the state of Ohio. After dinner Nieh took me to his office where the walls were covered with large-scale maps on which colored pins neatly located the positions of opposing troops.

Nieh's task, he said, was three-fold: to prevent the enemy from occupying the area; to harass the enemy's lines of communication; and to extend his own control gradually to those adjacent areas in which Chinese authority had not yet been re-established. From the military standpoint he held an important strategic position, for his base occupied a hub, protected by mountains, from which his forces could lash out against the enemy in any direction. The Japanese, on the other hand, must work in from the perimeter. When they attempted to surround him he struck first one detachment and then another, defeating each separately.

People's organizations had been developed in all the hsien, and the people were already selecting their own village officials. Ten days previously the representatives of the forty-five hsien embraced by the region had met at Fu P'ing. A committee of nine members, of whom Nieh was the only

Communist, had been selected to govern the area, and Sung Sao-wen had been appointed chairman. The plans worked out at this meeting were ambitious. They included the establishment of a bank and the development of an economic program which aimed at economic self-sufficiency.

The area was self-supporting except for munitions, which had to be brought in through the lines. Taxes, which had been reduced, were sufficient to provide revenue for support of the government and the army. There was a military academy with four hundred students, most of whom had come from the universities of Peip'ing and Tientsin.

Jurisdiction had been established over only a few hsien which lay to the east of the Peip'ing-Hankow railroad, but others were in the process of being taken over. Eventually the government planned to establish its authority in all districts which were not actually occupied by the Japanese, inculcating in the people the will-to-resist, and teaching them how to resist. Representative government would be established everywhere.

These plans spelled trouble for the invaders if they materialized. I wondered to what extent they would be placed in practice. Six months later I paid Nieh another visit and was able to see that his plans were not merely air-castles.

I did not wish to retrace my steps on the return trip, so it was arranged that I should move west across the Wu T'ai mountain area, pass through the lines along the T'ung P'u railway, and visit the divisional headquarters of Ho Lung as I moved south along the west side of T'aiyuanfu. After a day of rest, Li Po, the three hsiao kweis and I departed with a mounted patrol for the west.

Returning for a moment to our geographical analogy, Fup'ing would occupy a position on the map of North America corresponding to that of a point a hundred miles north of Sault St. Marie, Michigan, and T'aiyuanfu would be where Marquette, Michigan, is located. We would virtually be striking west across the northern part of Lake Superior, with a view to moving south between Marquette and Duluth, Minnesota, and then returning to Green Bay, Wisconsin, where Chu Teh's headquarters was located.

After we had climbed the heights of Great Wall Mountain our progress was rapid, for we followed the valleys of the Wu T'ai plateau. Majestic mountains towered above the narrow canyons. At strategic points sentries from the village self-defense corps examined our passports and waved us on. Occasionally organizations of the people came trooping down from some lofty village and hastily lined the sides of the trail to greet us as we passed. At night leaders of such groups assembled in our sleeping quarters and told of the nature of their work. Everywhere the people were organizing, marching and singing the new patriotic songs.

I was especially interested in the percentage of people of various categories who had enrolled in the salvation societies. Usually the highest percentage was in the children's groups, where the proportion ran from seventy-five to eighty percent. The women's organizations were lowest, with an average of thirty percent. They were unaccustomed to having interests outside their homes, and in some cases their men-folk were reluctant to see them change their habits. But the press of circumstances had made minds more receptive to new ideas, and progress, though slow, was steady.

One day we visited the hospital of the army, established in a Buddhist temple. Here I found sixty wounded from the battle of Hun Tze Tei. They had been relayed over the mountain trails in record time by members of the village self-defense corps.

On the fourth day after leaving Fu P'ing we reached Wu T'ai hsien, having come a hundred miles. This walled city presented a picturesque sight as we approached. The walls, a hundred and twenty feet in height, were terraced. A soft blanket of snow lay over the land. The terraces of the crenelated walls were black with people who had come out to welcome us. Stopping only long enough to exchange greetings with the Magistrate and other officials, we rode on to Tung Yen, where a foot patrol was waiting to take us through the enemy lines.

The T'ung P'u railroad was more lightly held by the Japanese than the

Ch'eng T'ai had been. We crossed near Kwo hsien, dropping into the Fu T'o valley at night and winding snake-fashion over the quarter mile surface of the frozen river. We would have made a fine target on the river, but our presence was undetected. Beyond lay the railroad, and beyond that a mountain pass where we found an outpost of the army. The railroad, we discovered, had been stripped of its rails for a stretch of thirty miles to the north of here.

We were now in the bailiwick of Ho Lung, well known for his aggressive campaigns in Hunan during the civil war, and now exceedingly active against the Japanese in northwest Shansi. His headquarters lay one hundred miles to the southwest. The route lay through bitterly cold and wind-driven valleys, and required five days of travel.

Ho Lung was stout, roly-poly and something of a swash-buckler. In a way he was rougher in manner than other high commanders of the army I had met. But beneath this outward bravado there was a deep sympathy for the under-dog. I could picture him as a sort of Chinese Robin Hood who robbed the rich to give to the poor. On the street he loved to tease children, and often he would pick up a protesting child, carry it under his arm for half a block, then send it off with a copper or a piece of candy to gladden its heart.

Here was the same systematic organization of the people I had witnessed in Wu T'ai. Ho Lung's division had entered the region four months before with fifteen thousand men. This number had now been trebled through the enlistment of Partisans.

I was eager to return to the south now, and after a day with Ho Lung we started on the four days' march to Li Shih, where a truck would be awaiting us.

It was the fifteenth of February when we reached Li Shih. Here we had startling news. The Japanese had commenced an intensive invasion of Shansi, and were moving in this direction. It was doubtful, said the truck driver, if we would be able to get through Fenchow, for one enemy column was headed for that city.

I particularly wanted to stop at Fenchow long enough to talk with one of the foreign missionaries and ascertain their condition. Doctor Walter Judd was there, or had been when I commenced this trip, and I hoped to see him. The truck driver promised to accommodate me.

Tank traps were being constructed along the highway as we proceeded. Outside the gray walls of Fenchow no sign of life was visible as we approached. At the northwest gate a sentry from a Shansi army lounged listlessly. The Japanese, he said, were three miles east of the city. At this alarming bit of news the driver stepped on the accelerator and sped through the gate. I glimpsed an American flag and shouted for him to stop—to no avail. Swinging dizzily through the empty streets we passed out of the city and charged down the road to the south. An hour later we drew up before a temporary supply depot of the Shansi army, having left the city twenty miles behind.

While we were eating dinner word came that the Japanese were not far from here either. Trucks began to fill with supplies, and presently a long lightless caravan motored south through the night. At three o'clock in the morning we stopped at Wu Cheng hsien and sought shelter. The town was filled with soldiers, but after some haggling we managed to secure the use of a k'ang in the home of a merchant. On this we slept in two hour relays.

As rapidly as possible now we pressed on towards Linfeng, where I had first met the army back in December. But progress was slow, for the road was filled with columns of marching troops headed north to meet the invasion. They comprised divisions of General Yen Hsi-shan's armies, and the men lacked the spirit and discipline of those with whom I had been marching. Their faces were listless and their feet dragged as they trudged along the frozen road. They knew not why they fought except that they had been ordered to do so. Officers, sitting haughtily in their saddles, rode up and clown the column urging them on. Here was lacking that unanimity of spirit which energized the Eighth Route Army.

At Linfeng Yang Li-san informed us that Chu Teh would leave the next day to take his headquarters into the field. We shifted to a dilapidated bus, the one in which I had come north nearly three months before, and drove to Hungt'ung. The headquarters we found in a different village from where we had left it.

Chu Teh looked worn, but his welcome had lost none of its cordiality. The situation in Shansi, he said, was serious. The Japanese had sent five divisions into the province. One was coming across country from the southern Hopei border, evidently bent on capturing Linfeng. He would move east tomorrow to direct operations. Seven Shansi and Kuomintang divisions had been placed under his command, in addition to his own army. This, it seemed to me, was marked recognition of his ability.

We talked until the wee small hours, with his wife, K'an K'e-ch'in, sitting by and taking notes. She was a peasant woman who had made the long march, and she had become a trained political organizer. Broad of face and buxom of body, she was an able helpmate for her distinguished husband. She had an infectious smile which never lost its sparkle, and she never interfered in the affairs of the army, being content to devote herself to organizing women in the villages—and to darning her husband's socks.

At daylight Chu Teh clanked into my room attired for the trail. I went out with him to see the army off. Half a hundred pack animals were loaded with supplies. As many bearers of the army carried metal boxes suspended from shoulder poles. These would contain the army records, operations plans, captured documents and the estimates of situations. Both men and animals were decorated with bits of foliage to make them less conspicuous from the air.

Chu Teh embraced me and joined his marching men. For an hour Li Po and I watched the long serpentine column until it disappeared into the mountain haze beneath the rising sun.

VI

This brief insight into life behind the scenes with the Eighth Route

Army revealed new potentialities in China's war of resistance. Here, it seemed to me, was the answer to the challenge of Japan's modern military machine. This machine could hardly prevail against a populace inspired and trained to continue resistance and prepared to endure the hardships which such resistance might entail. It could not destroy an army geared to outmarch and outsmart its opponent in a protracted guerrilla war. Its effort to conquer Shansi was about as effective as an attempt to plow the ocean. The important question was one of supply.

The supply problem had yet to be solved. Some small arsenals had been established in the mountain fastnesses, but these were inadequate to keep an army going indefinitely. Food for the armies and the people could be provided if agriculture was intelligently directed, and if harmonious relations continued to prevail between the army and the people. But as time passed there would arise a need for manufactured articles which would have to be met. Such goods were still dribbling into the country, and even found their way into the interior. But a stiffening blockade would diminish this flow. And so the pressing problem was to re-establish some form of industry within the country. It would have to be de-centralized and broken up into small units in order to reduce vulnerability from the air. Preferably the units should be set up in proximity to the source of supply in order to simplify the problem of transportation of raw materials. It should also be made attractive to the people in order to stimulate their co-operation.

There was a broader aspect of China's problems that had to be considered. Shansi was only one small part of the nation, and if this nation was to survive it seemed imperative that the pattern of resistance which had proved to be so effective there be extended to all parts of the Republic. Here were obvious difficulties, for the antagonism of many Kuomintang leaders for the Communists was so bitter that they would be reluctant to adopt any plan which had been devised by the latter. The second major problem, then, was to overcome this antagonism. Probably only one man could do it, and as I turned my face towards Hankow I speculated as to the willingness of Chiang Kai-shek to undertake the task of indoctrinating his subordinates with the spirit of practical self-sacrifice which animated the leaders of the Eighth Route Army. Would he be willing to mobilize the people for resistance and afford them the civil rights and social equality which alone could command their unqualified devotion?

CHAPTER V

TAIERCHWANG—CHINA WINS A VICTORY

I

CHU Teh had given me permission to take two of the hsiao kweis, Lo and Chang, to Sian with me. Ching had been offered a post in the intelligence section of the army, and he preferred to remain. None of these boys had ever been in a large city, nor had they ridden on a railroad train. In fact, the trip down from Li Shih was their first experience in a motor vehicle.

Li Po would stop at Linfeng to do some writing. I also wished to stop in Linfeng long enough to have a talk with Governor Yen Hsi-shan, and so we journeyed there together by train, after watching the departure of Chu Teh's headquarters.

Theoretically Yen Hsi-shan exercised supreme authority in Shansi. As commander of the Second War Zone he was responsible to the Generalissimo for the conduct of military operations in Shansi and Suiyuan provinces. Actually, as we have seen, the operations in those areas behind the Japanese lines were conducted in accordance with the ideas of the Eighth Route Army leaders, though with General Yen's tacit consent. The latter was primarily interested in regaining control of his province, from which, in the past, he had amassed a comfortable fortune. He was astute enough to recognize the advantages of the pattern of resistance developed by the Eighth Route Army, and he accepted it because the alternative was the complete loss of his province.

I had seen at first hand the conditions which obtained in the province. Now I was interested in seeing the titular head himself.

I was conducted to General Yen's headquarters by his English speaking secretary, Mr. Balson Chang, an earnest and enthusiastic young man who had graduated from Yenching University at Peip'ing, and who regarded his chief as a sort of demi-God. The headquarters was located in an inconspicuous village several miles south of Linfeng.

Entering the office of the Governor I found a somewhat paunchy individual of sixty-odd years who was engaged with studied poise in examining the operations maps which covered the walls. His long gray mustache drooped at the ends, after the fashion affected by the old mandarins. He greeted me cordially, albeit a little ponderously, and I got the impression that he was an old man who was very tired.

We discussed the military situation in the north, and he told me of the progress of the new Japanese drive. Although Linfeng actually fell to the Japanese four days later, at this time General Yen did not appear to be greatly perturbed.

I asked him for the designations of the divisions which comprised his army, mentioning those I had encountered on my way south. He started to name them, failed to recall either the numbers or the names of the commanders of some, and called on a staff officer to refresh his memory. When I asked for a statement of his basic military policy he drew himself up and cleared his throat as though he were preparing to deliver a profound bit of wisdom.

"China," he began pontifically, "must break the Japanese political plan. We must counter this plan by developing the national revolutionary struggle. " He slumped back in his chair with an air of supreme complacency.

It was a little pathetic. But the truth was that Yen Hsi-shan was more of a merchant than a general. For twenty-six years he had governed Shansi, and he had placed great emphasis on the development of industry and merchandising. In his younger years he had been active in instituting social and political reforms, but as time passed there had grown up around him a bureaucracy which, in an increasing degree, usurped the prerogatives of government and used them for personal aggrandizement. Now the Governor was an old man and while his instincts were benevolent he was dependent more than ever on his subordinates to direct the affairs of the province. When I left him he manifested his good will by placing his private railway car at my disposal for the trip south to Fenglingtu. As things developed, he had no further use for it anyway.

Li Po and I parted at Linfeng. We would meet later in Hankow, but this we did not know now. It was with a feeling of deep tenderness and profound regret that I left this brave and self-effacing companion. His was a rare friendship, for he was consistent in his loyalty and devoted at times even when my own nerves were frayed and my tongue not too well controlled.

The rail trip Lo, Chang and I made in the height of luxury. We had the Governor's car to ourselves, and I was continuously amused by the reactions of the two boys to this type of travel. They examined the appointments of the car with meticulous curiosity, emitting exclamations of astonishment at such unfamiliar arrangements as swivel chairs, porcelain wash basins and sleeping compartments. Within a few hours, however, their self-possession had returned, and by the time we reached Fenglingtu I heard Lo discoursing learnedly to a Shansi soldier on the subject of trains in general and the merits of first class travel in particular.

We crossed to the south bank of the Yellow River, accompanied by hundreds of refugees who were fleeing the Japanese advance, and entrained for Sian.

After nearly three months of primitive life the Guest House at Sian, with its baths and hot running water, seemed like the last word in modernism. I repossessed the baggage I had left when I departed for Shansi, and prepared to return to Hankow, where I would write the official report of my observations. But first I wanted to show the hsiao kweis the sights of the city.

Immediately I ran into difficulties. These boys had accepted me as an equal during the weeks we had traveled together and I wanted to express my appreciation in some way. I knew that they possessed little money, for the pay of the men of the Eighth Route Army runs from one dollar a month for the fighter to six dollars for the Commander-in-Chief, Chu Teh.

I started my round of entertainment by taking them to dinner at a modest restaurant. Always interested in prices, they asked the waiter what the meal cost. The nominal price of a dollar and a half (about thirty cents in U. S. currency at the time) shocked them, and they refused to eat. It required all of my eloquence to induce them to share food which I had ordered and which, I assured them, would otherwise be thrown away.

Then we wandered about the streets window shopping while I enjoyed vicariously their amazement and enthusiasm over the variety and quantity of articles on display. I made a mental note of those which intrigued them most, and later slipped back and purchased them. For the most part they were simple articles such as jack knives, harmonicas, mirrors, fountain pens and watches—things that would be useful in the army.

When later I offered them to the boys they flatly refused to accept them, though their eyes regarded them longingly. It wouldn't be "right" for them to accept gifts from me; there was no reason why I should spend money on them. They had everything they needed! Finally in desperation I said: "Look here, it's a sound communistic principle for those who have to share with those who haven't, I can easily afford these articles, and if you don't take them I'll simply throw them in a junk heap." My logic struck home and they accepted the things tenderly, wrapped them carefully in their cases, and scuttled for their quarters. I hoped I wasn't undermining the morale of the army.

When my train left that night Chang and Lo were on the station platform proudly displaying their wrist watches and jack knives.

II

Wuhan is the name which is customarily given to the metropolitan area which includes the three cities of Hankow and Hanyang, located on the north bank of the Yangtze, and themselves separated by the Han river, and Wuchang, which lies opposite on the south bank of the Yangtze.

Madame Chiang Kai-shek (née Song Meiling), First Lady of China, caught in a reflective attitude during the Battle of Hankow.

Madame Sun Yat-sen (née Soong Ch'ing-ling), widow of the Father of the Chinese Republic, and one of the three famous Soong sisters.

When I returned to Wuhan in early March I found that it had become the capital of a nation at war. Here were the offices of the civil departments of the government, the military headquarters of the Generalissimo and the Embassies of foreign governments which were accredited to China.

Hankow was the seat of the foreign concessions, though at this time only the French actually operated a concession, the Japanese area having been taken over by the Chinese, and the former British and Russian concessions having become special administrative districts. In Hankow were located the embassies, the foreign business houses and many of the offices of the Chinese government.

The arsenal was the most important feature of Hanyang, though there were factories and poor residential districts as well. At Wuchang was the Generalissimo's headquarters. Here also were several foreign missions, and a number of universities. Wuchang was the terminus of a railway which extends north from Canton, and over this line now came the bulk of China's war imports.

The center of military operations had shifted from the Shanghai-Nanking sector to the area around Hsuchowfu, where the rail line from Tientsin to P'ukow crosses the east-west Lunghai line. By air Hsuchowfu lay about three hundred and fifty miles northeast of Hankow, but the route by rail was much longer, for it was necessary to go north to Chengchow, nearly three hundred miles, and then east along the Lunghai for another two hundred miles.

The Japanese were driving towards Hsuchowfu both from the north and from the south. Their air force had extended its activities far into the interior in an effort to destroy the more important Chinese supply bases and lines of communication, and also to terrorize the populace and break their will-to-resist. Hankow at this time was coming in for special attention from the Japanese aviators.

Ambassador Johnson was living with Consul-General Paul Josselyn, in his commodious flat, as were Douglas Jenkins and Captain James McHugh, and I was invited to join this jovial group. Three exceptionally pleasant weeks followed. The days were spent in writing a report of my observations in the north, and in the evenings there were gatherings with friends, both foreign and Chinese.

I thought I had known the Ambassador well during the years at Peip'ing, but here under the stress of war conditions he was manifesting a degree of fortitude and cheerful optimism which inspired all who came in contact with him. A prime asset was his ability to relax completely at intervals during the day. He was particularly fond of games, and at this time Patience Poker was a favorite. Each day after lunch and dinner a few of us would battle at this innocuous game with such zest that the war was temporarily forgotten.

Agnes Smedley had come to Hankow to engage in work for the Chinese Red Cross Medical Relief Commission, and I found her established in the home of the Right Reverend Logan Roots, American Episcopal Bishop of Hankow. Agnes' indefatigable energy and forthright manner of speech had won her the respect and admiration of most of the foreign colony, for they recognized in her a refreshing sincerity and genuine devotion to her ideals. Through her I met the Bishop, and came into a rich and lasting fellowship.

Bishop Roots was no ordinary churchman. At this time he was on the eve of retirement after forty-odd years of work in China which had brought him the confidence of the rank and file of the nation. Included in his large circle of intimate friends were most of the government leaders, including the Generalissimo and Madame Chiang Kai-shek. Tolerant and liberal in his views, one could find in his drawing room leaders of the Communist Party, as well as those of the Kuomintang. Here was a man who both practised as well as preached the doctrines of Christ, and his influence on the thought patterns of China's leaders was measureless.

One day Doctor Hollington Tong, the very able Vice-Minister of Public Relations, came around to conduct me to an interview with Generalissimo and Madame Chiang Kaishek. Holly, as he was affectionately known to the newspaper fraternity, had graduated from an American university, and had subsequently edited and published newspapers in China. He was a trusted friend of the Generalissimo, whose biography he completed in 1937.

We crossed the Yangtze to Wuchang and drove to the simply furnished pavilion which served the distinguished couple as a residence. I had not seen either since the occasion of the state burial of Doctor Sun Yat-sen at Nanking, in 1929, and I wondered how time and the responsibilities of office had affected them.

Presently short, decisive footsteps sounded in the outer room, and Madame Chiang entered followed by the erect form of the Generalissimo.

Madame Chiang fairly radiated charm. It was not the frivolous charm of youth, though she was not lacking in vivacity. Rather it was a mature graciousness born of an inward peace and a consciousness of being an instrument of destiny, with the power to serve her people.

Both greeted me cheerily and Madame Chiang seated herself before the table on which I had arranged my maps. The Generalissimo continued to stand until his wife directed him to be seated. Turning to me she explained: "The Generalissimo is still troubled by the back injury he sustained at Sian, and it is unwise for him to stand long."

I regarded this man who for the past decade had controlled the destinies of China. He had aged greatly since I last had seen him, and his short cropped hair was graying rapidly, but he had gained in poise and self-confidence. Also he was more mellow and mature. His brilliant black eyes met mine with steady, almost relentless, gaze. Here was intelligence, loyalty and stubborn determination.

For an hour I told of my experiences in the north and answered their incisive questions. I expressed my confidence in the loyalty to the Generalissimo of the Eighth Route Army leaders, and described the steps being taken by them to develop representative government in the areas behind the Japanese lines. When I mentioned my feeling that the will-to-resist of the people in the Wu T'ai mountain area was the strongest I had seen anywhere, and that their co-operation was better, the Generalissimo wanted to know why.

"I believe," I replied, "that it is due to the fact that they are completely surrounded by the Japanese, and that the common danger they face inspires them to subordinate certain individual liberties in favor of co-operation. They are further inspired by the self-sacrificing character of their leaders."

His face gave no indication of his reaction to this idea. In fact, the Generalissimo's face could be called inscrutable without exaggeration. His Olympian self-possession is one of the reasons for his successful leadership—this and his profound self-confidence. He is politically astute, and he has built a strong personal integrity through the habit of keeping the few promises he makes. His inscrutability operates to give the impression to each political group that he secretly sympathizes with the doctrines of that group.

At the end of an hour they rose to go. I asked him to place his autograph in my note book and he graciously acquiesced. The pencil he was using contained red lead in one end and blue in the other. He poised to write, saw that the red point was down, quickly flipped the pencil over and wrote with the blue point. It was a split-second gesture, but it implied much.

Back in Hankow, Hollington Tong took me for luncheon to the home of Doctor H. H. Kung, President of the Executive Yuan and Minister of Finance. Here we found Randall Gould, forthright editor of Shanghai's only American-owned newspaper. Randall Gould's insistence on printing the truth had brought the bombing of the newspaper premises recently by Japanese-inspired terrorists.

Doctor Kung was another friend of long standing. In appearance he was a bit on the corpulent side, affected a short cropped mustache, and wore spectacles. After receiving his education in American universities he returned to China to head the Oberlin missionary college at T'aiku, in Shansi. He married Ai-ling, eldest of the famous Soong sisters, amassed a fortune through business investments and entered politics. Since the establishment of the National Government at Nanking, in 1927, he had served in the cabinet as Minister of Industry and Commerce, Minister of Finance, and now held a post which made him tantamount to Prime Minister of the Republic. He is probably proudest, however, of his ancestry, being a direct descendant of the Master Kung who is popularly known to foreigners as Confucius.

Also at Doctor Kung's table on this day were the so-called Christian General, Feng Yu-hsiang, a strapping man of benign manner and studied speech,

General Ho Ying-ching, the Minister of War, and Mr. Chen Kung-po, formerly high in the Kuomintang councils, but now at odds with the Generalissimo. Within the year he would join Mr. Wang Ching-wei in attempting to form a puppet government under Japanese tutelage.

General Feng Yu-hsiang, who now held the post of Vice-Chairman of the Military Affairs Commission (of which the Generalissimo is Chairman), was the most picturesque member of this group. He was over six feet in height and broad of beam. He prided himself on being a man of the people and in former years when he was at the head of the Kuominchun army he wore the most disreputable clothes in the army, hiked with his troops or rode on the front seat of a truck beside the driver. In 1930 he essayed a trial of strength with the Generalissimo, in conjunction with General Yen Hsi-shan, and lost. But his name was still one to conjure with in many parts of the country, and his patriotism was beyond question in this anti-Japanese struggle.

General Ho Ying-ching was something of an enigma. He was short, bespectacled, and smilingly placid of countenance. In the early years of the Nanking government he had been one of Chiang Kai-shek's most trusted lieutenants, as was evidenced by his frequent despatch to deal with critical situations where loyalty was a prime requisite. However, at about the time the Generalissimo was detained at Sian, in December of 1936, some unrevealed development altered this intimate association. While outwardly there was no indication of a lack of confidence in him it seemed significant that he had received no important command post in the field.

As I chatted with these men who were directing the affairs of the nation I could not resist contrasting the physical comfort in which they lived with the strenuous self-discipline of the Eighth Route Army. There was no question of the earnest patriotism of the two groups of leaders, but they represented antipodal schools of thought. Not only the outcome of the war with Japan, but the development of a strong, united nation in the post-war period, would depend on the ability of these two groups to work out a formula acceptable to both. If I had correctly sensed the temper of the people it would of necessity have to be a formula which would result in a government which was of the people, by the people and for the people, for the democratic instinct was strong in the nation.

Distinguished visitors came at infrequent intervals to the Ambassador's table, usually flying up from Hongkong to have a quick look at China's war capital. Best known of these, probably, was John Gunther. With his charming wife he came to lunch one day, and we were afforded an unparalleled opportunity of getting first-hand information of affairs in Europe. The conversation was not all one-sided, and Gunther, in his buoyant, vibrant manner, fired questions about the progress of the war. The questions were penetrating and showed an amazing comprehension of the Oriental scene, but after every fourth or fifth question Mrs. Gunther would put one which pierced to the heart of the subject. Here, we concluded, was a reportorial team of the first water.

One of the top-flight Communist leaders was in Hankow as Vice-Chairman of the Political Training Department of the Military Affairs Commission. Chow En-lai was the scion of a Mandarin family, and a man of culture and refinement. But he was no less self-disciplined than the men I had seen in the north. Slender, of medium height, and gentle of manner, he had a way of listening to a conversation with an air of complete detachment which was most deceiving. His was one of the most brilliant minds in China, and his judgment carried weight in the councils of the National Government. In the early days of the Kuomintang he had been Director of Political Training at the Whampoo Military Academy, and in 1927 it was he who organized the workers' army which delivered Shanghai to Chiang Kai-shek.

One evening I was sitting at dinner with Agnes Smedley, Chow En-lai and one or two others. Agnes was holding forth in strong language on the failure of foreign journalists to report the true facts to their papers. Chow gazed off into space, apparently paying no attention to the tirade. But presently he sat up, cupped his chin in his hands, with elbows resting on the table in characteristic manner, and remarked quietly: "If the journalists always published accurate accounts of current events there would be no need for the historians."

III

Towards the latter part of March I was ready to go again. Having observed the character of guerrilla operations I hoped now to see something of the positional warfare on the Hsuchowfu front. General J. L. Huang, generous friend of Nanking days, assisted in securing the necessary credentials, and one day I took train for Chengchow (Lansing, Michigan), at the junction of the Peip'ing-Hankow and the Lunghai railways. Here I paused for a day or two in order to sense the probable focal point of operations and determine if the officials were agreeable to my presence there.

Doctor Sanford Ayers directed the Baptist Mission hospital at Chengchow, and his home had become an oasis for itinerant journalists and attaches. Although I arrived late in the evening and was a stranger, I found Doctor Ayers still up and waiting to see who might come in on the late train.

The doctor had his hands full, for his usual quota of civilian patients had been increased measurably by the steady trickle of wounded who drifted in from the east. He was never too busy to listen to the woes of a Chinese client and frequently I have been at table with him when someone in distress appeared. Without waiting to finish his meal he would quietly arise and conduct his visitor to the clinic.

One evening while we were at dinner word came that a train from Hsuchowfu had just arrived with a thousand wounded soldiers. The Chinese military surgeons wondered if Doctor Ayers would assist in examining the dressings and segregating the cases which required immediate attention.

Doctor Ayers gathered his group together and we went to the train. In the group were Doctors McClure, a Canadian, Hankey, an Englishman, and Tremewan, a New Zealander.

The wounded were lying in box cars, coal cars and passenger coaches. Only three days had elapsed since they left the front, and although the wounds had received first-aid treatment, gangrene had set in in many cases. About fifty such cases were removed to the hospital and the night was spent in emergency operations.

Most significant was the fact that the wounds were the result of gunshot, indicating that the men had been up against the machine-gun defensive framework of the Japanese positions. This meant that the Chinese were attacking, for at Shanghai the majority of the wounds had been from shell and bomb fragments.

General Ch'eng Ch'ien, who commands the First War Zone, with headquarters at Chengchow, received me warmly and assured me that General Li Tsung-jen would be glad to have me visit the Hsuchowfu front. He was a tall man, slow of movement, fifty-seven years of age, and wore a wide brushlike mustache. Until recently he had been Chief of Staff for Chiang Kai-shek. The following day he sent me east by train, with Mr. Pao Shih-tien as interpreter.

On the same train went Archibald Steele, of the *Chicago Daily News*, Walter Bosshard, a Swiss who represented the *Holstein Press*, and the "History Today" motion-picture group, which was piloted by old friends of the War Area Service Corps: General Theodore Tu, Jack Young and Chuk, the Generalissimo's photographer.

The "History Today" group had recently made a picture of the Spanish War, called *Spanish Earth*. Now they hoped to record for the West China's struggle for independence. The director, Joris Ivens, and the cameraman, John Ferno, were citizens of the Netherlands. They were assisted by Robert Capa, a young Hungarian who also made photographs for *Life* magazine. Capa, too, had made camera studies of the Spanish war, and he had an extraordinary sense of drama. All were profoundly interested in reflecting life in its unadulterated aspects, and were fearless in their search for truth.

Troop trains were pouring into Hsuchowfu, but despite the heavy traffic we made the two hundred mile trip in record time. If Chengchow is regarded as corresponding in location to Lansing, Michigan, then Hsuchowfu would be in the vicinity of Erie, Pennsylvania. Its importance lay in the fact that here the railroad from Tientsin to Nanking crossed the east-west Lunghai line.

We found a cordial welcome at the Presbyterian Mission hospital, pre-

General Ch'eng Ch'ien, former Chief of Staff of the Chinese Army, and now commander of the First War Zone, with headquarters in Honan.

General Li Tsung-jen, distinguished Kwangsi province leader, commander of the Fifth War Zone, and director of the operations at Taierchwang and Hsuchowfu.

sided over by Doctor McFadden, a hearty Scot, and Mrs. Greer, a doctor in her own right, with over forty years of medical work in China.

The normal population of this city was about 700,000, but many had evacuated to the west. However, the city still had the appearance of a thriving metropolis. Uniforms were prevalent in the street, for Hsuchowfu was now the hub of a defensive system which extended in a semi-circle from the north around to the east and thence to the south. Optimism was strong, much stronger than in Chengchow or Hankow. It is a curious fact that in war the closer one comes to the front the greater the confidence of troops and people, and the less one sees of fear and pessimism.

At the headquarters of the Fifth War Zone I found General Li Tsung-jen. Short, thickset and in his middle fifties, General Li had an air of business about him. In his simple manner of living he more nearly approached the standards of the Eighth Route Army than any other Central Government leader I had met.

The Japanese, he said, had been compelled to give up an attempt to envelop the west flank of Hsuchowfu, and now they were driving for Taierchwang, a town on a branch line of the Tientsin-P'ukow railway which lay to the northeast about forty miles. Another column was moving towards Taierchwang across country from Tsingtao (Kingston, Ontario), the principal seaport of Shantung province. Thus far he had been able to prevent these columns from joining. On the south the Japanese advance from P'ukow had been held up at P'engp'u, nearly a hundred miles away.

General Li approved my request to join one of the divisions at the front. As a matter of fact, he said, he was going to the field headquarters of General Sun Lien-chung, commander of the Second Group of Armies, on the Taierchwang front, that evening, and he would be glad to have me join him on his special train. I accepted with alacrity.

When I arrived at the station that evening I found that the "History Today" group and Irving Epstein, of the *United Press*, were also going. And when the special train drew alongside it contained not only General Li but General Pai Chunghsi, Deputy Chief of Staff for Chiang Kai-shek, as well. It was dusk when we got under way for the east.

Generals Li and Pai were the leaders of the Kwangsi group, most powerful group in the country next to the Kuomintang and the Communist parties. Their presence here was further evidence of China's unity, for until the autumn of 1936 they had been violently antagonistic to the Nanking government.

Both of these men were rated as exceptionally able military leaders, and some felt that General Pai had the best military mind in the country. Both took a prominent part in the northern expedition of 1926-28, but they revolted against Chiang in 1929 and retired to Kwangsi province, in the south, where they instituted social and economic reforms and built a crack army. Along with the Communists they called for a strong stand against Japanese encroachments after the 1931 invasion of Manchuria. In 1936 the Generalissimo succeeded in negotiating a peace with them which brought their support again to the side of the Central Government. In some quarters their administration in Kwangsi was called a rightist government, and in others it was termed national socialist (though not of the Nazi variety). Actually it appeared to be a paternal dictatorship, with representative government being developed in the towns and counties. In any case Kwangsi, in recent years, seemed to have enjoyed the most efficient administration of any province in China.

In appearance and by inclination General Pai was something of a military ascetic, and his rigid self-discipline and devotion to the study of tactics and strategy have placed him in the top stratum of China's military leaders. He is a Mohammedan, and his influence in retaining for China the loyalty of the Mohammedans of Chinghai, Kansu and Ninghsia has been invaluable.

About forty miles east of Hsuchowfu the train turned north on to the branch road which follows the Grand Canal to Taierchwang. With all lights extinguished we moved slowly north for another thirty-five miles until we reached what appeared to be a military railhead. Here were several spurs for the unloading of supplies and the loading of wounded. And here General Sun Lien-chung came aboard for a midnight conference with his superiors.

Our baggage was unloaded and distributed among soldier bearers who filed off in a long serpentine column into the night. We must have looked something like a Hollywood cinema group going on location, what with tripods, cameras and other photographic paraphernalia. As we trudged over the ill-defined footpath an occasional gun thundered off to the north, emphasizing our proximity to the theater of battle. At four o'clock in the morning we reached our destination, a tiny village on the reverse slope of a hill. Rawhide cots were awaiting us, and in short order we were rolled up in our blankets for a few hours of sleep.

IV

We were awakened at seven by the low rumble of artillery fire, and Teddy Tu announced that General Sun Lien-chung had invited us to breakfast with him. After rather hasty ablutions, we joined the General in the sun-flooded courtyard of the home which served as his headquarters. He had been in conference most of the night and his face showed the signs of strain. His welcome was hearty, and we distributed ourselves around a table to which orderlies presently brought dishes of noodles, fish and rice.

General Sun was a northern Chinese, and his huge frame stretched to a height of six feet. For years he had been a trusted subordinate of Feng Yu-hsiang in the old Kuominchun army. Extensive educational advantages had not been available to him, but he had studied, observed and practised the military art for thirty years, and had become a sound practical leader. He was one of the few military men in China who had no political axe to grind, and devoted himself strictly to military tasks. This was probably responsible for his singular success. From General Feng he had learned the value of invoking the co-operation of the people, and his well disciplined army was indoctrinated with this policy. Not the least of his assets was his ability to let his staff work for him, reserving to himself the prerogative of making decisions, a faculty which few Chinese had learned at this time.

Also present was the Chief of Staff, General Chin T'ienjung, a brilliant officer in his early thirties who had been trained in the Central Military Academy under the supervision of German officers.

After breakfast General Sun took me into his office and stood before his operations map.

"The 10th Japanese Division," he began, "was sent along this branch railroad from the north to occupy Tsaochwang and Yihsien." He indicated two towns which lay respectively thirty and twenty miles north of Taierchwang. "It was to effect a junction with the 105th Division, which was en route across country from Tsingtao and Kaomi." Here he drew his finger across Shantung province in a southwesterly direction from the seacoast towards Lin Yi (Buffalo), sixty miles northeast of Taierchwang. "But we countered by sending General Chang Tze-chung's army to Lin Yi and by placing General T'ang En-po's army between Lin Yi and Taierchwang, so as to prevent the two enemy divisions from joining."

We seated ourselves on a bench before the map, and he lighted a cigar, after handing me one. Smiling reminiscently, he continued:

"I arrived in this area with my army on the 20th of March, and the 31st Division met the Japanese 10th Division at Ni Ko on the 23d, relieving Szechuan troops. My plan was to draw the Japanese south to Taierchwang, which stands on the north bank of the Grand Canal. Here I felt we could make a strong stand while other divisions of my army closed in on the flanks of the enemy, thus bringing him into a salient. I depended largely on the rashness and overconfidence of the Japanese leaders, who are contemptuous of our military strength.

"Thus far," he concluded, "the plan has worked beautifully. We hold a line along the Grand Canal, and we hold the western two-thirds of the walled city of Taierchwang. The Japanese are in a salient twenty-five miles deep and fifteen miles across. We are now endeavoring to cut their line of communications to the north, and to destroy the Taierchwang force."

I had come over here expecting to see a desperate battle for the defense of Hsuchowfu. Now it appeared there was a chance I might see a Chinese victory. The issue depended on the ability of the Japanese to re-enforce their 10th Division, and on the enterprising leadership of General Sun. The latter, I felt, had the edge.

During the next three days we visited various parts of the front. Medium artillery of 155 millimeter size was firing at ranges of from ten to fifteen thousand yards. Battery and battalion commanders were young officers who had been trained in the military schools at Nanking under German supervision. They were thoroughly familiar with the latest methods of computing firing data and for observing and controlling the distribution of fire. The effect of this fire I was to see later.

The observation post of one battery was on a hill half a mile to the west, and in advance of the battery. From here I could see the battle positions in the vicinity of Taierchwang and also the target of these guns, a Japanese artillery position behind a rim of trees two miles beyond the city. The area to the north was a vast plateau out of which cone-shaped hills rose sharply. Small walled villages, with low watch towers rising from diagonally opposite corners, were spaced from three to five miles apart. In the fields farmers patiently planted wheat, millet and sesame, apparently oblivious of the shells which whined over head and which occasionally exploded near by. From the distant battle lines came the faint putt-putt of machine guns and the sharp explosions of trench mortar shells. It was a lazy sort of battle, for the Japanese were on the defensive, and the Chinese preferred to conduct their assaults at night.

Suddenly high explosive shrapnel began exploding at the base of our hill. Apparently the Japanese were trying to get the range of this observation post. The battery commander directed that the observers shift their telephones and instruments to a hill east of the guns, and we returned to the gun position. Fifty salvos were fired before the explosions ceased, and all burst short of the hill. Probably, I concluded, the eyesight of the observers was poor, for no artilleryman with good eyes would fail to bracket a target with his third salvo.

A squadron of Chinese planes had come over from the south to bomb the Japanese positions north of the Grand Canal. Now one returned, its engine sputtering, and glided to a landing in a field behind us. Instantly soldiers ran out from the adjacent village with stalks of kao liang (a type of sorghum which looks much like corn), and in a few minutes the plane resembled a huge stack of kao liang.

It proved to be a Russian pursuit bi-plane, using a Curtis-Wright motor, and was piloted by a young Chinese from Kwangsi. Its armament consisted of two light machine guns Synchronized to fire through the propeller.

The following day we went forward to where the seventy-five millimeter guns were pounding the Japanese positions from a range of five thousand yards. As we watched the fire of the camouflaged guns infantry of the twenty-seventh division trailed by in single file, on their way to re-enforce the west flank of the line which was being tightened about the enemy.

General Chin led us by a circuitous route over to the east flank, where we found windlasses from village wells which had been set up to look like artillery.

"Here," he said, "is another example of the inaccuracy of Japanese artillery fire. Three days ago we erected these dummy guns and then used one real gun to fire rapidly from various points along the line. The Japanese expended a great amount of ammunition in an attempt to destroy this position, but they didn't even hit one of the dummy guns."

That night when we were back at headquarters chatting around a small wood fire in the courtyard, General Chin expanded further on the relative merits of Chinese and Japanese tactics.

"One of the most flagrant errors of the Japanese," he said, "is over-confidence. They are in a bad way here because they thought we would retire before a show of force. They depend on artillery fire and aerial bombing to blast a path for their infantry. But we counter by causing our troops to dig shelters which give reasonable protection from shells and bombs. When the enemy infantry approaches, our men come out and meet them with heavy machine-gun fire. The Japanese infantry fights by the drill book. When the drill-book instructions don't work, they are lost."

I recalled the hundreds of small pocket drill books which I had seen in captured Japanese effects in Shansi.

General Chin continued: "Our attacks are conducted at night when the Japanese cannot use their aviation, and when we are too close in for them to use their artillery. We direct these assaults so as to bring our troops into hand-to-hand conflict with the enemy infantry, for our men are superior in big sword fighting."

That night the tempo of the battle rose to a crescendo. Before daylight General Chin came to our sleeping quarters waving a message excitedly in his hand.

"We have driven the Japanese out of Taierchwang," he cried.

We arose hastily and gathered around a large scale map which General Chin brought from the office.

"Last night," he began, recovering his composure, "General Chih, who commands the 31st Division, reported that the Japanese were using tear gas. We decided that this indicated their situation was desperate. General Sun ordered him to assault. At four o'clock this morning about four hundred of the enemy broke out of the northeast gate of the city and joined those outside in a general retreat towards Yi hsien. The remaining two hundred barricaded themselves in a building in the southeast corner. We tried to get them to surrender, but they would not. So we set fire to the building and smoked them out. All were slain."

The date was the seventh of April, and China had won her first major victory.

General Sun Lien-chung had retired for much needed sleep, but General Chin assured us that we might enter the captured city early in the morning. This would be a real "scoop" for the "History Today" group, for they would have exclusive pictures of the great event.

We ate breakfast amid a babble of excited speculation. Would this break the Japanese drive to the south? Had China finally gained the upper hand? Would the Generalissimo exploit his advantage? Even here at the scene of the victory these questions could not be answered. China had won a victory, but the Japanese would probably move promptly to vindicate themselves.

V

It was nearing nine o'clock in the morning and a brilliant sunlight suffused the plain around Taierchwang, bringing into sharp relief the greens and yellows of early spring, as we approached the city. Overhead three Japanese observation planes droned back and forth as they inspected the scene of last night's disaster. Along the railroad an armored train inched its way ahead, preceded by a pilot engine and a squad of soldiers who examined the roadbed for land mines, and flanked by squads of infantrymen who proceeded on foot in single file. Columns of stretcher bearers plodded across the fields bearing wounded towards the dressing station at the railhead.

At the canal soldiers lounged around the entrances of innumerable dugouts. Others pushed artillery carriages across the pontoon bridge that had been improvised of canal boats and barges. On the north bank were more dugouts and the main firing positions of the Chinese. A few hundred yards to the east lay the battered walls of the city itself.

Inside the walls was a scene of utter destruction: buildings blown to bits, streets littered with debris, dugouts everywhere, and trees bullet-scarred and shorn of their branches. What a hell this must have been during the fighting!

General Chih Feng-chen had already moved the headquarters of the 31st Division into the city, and here we found the General talking with General T'ien Chen-nau, commander of the 30th Corps.

I was surprised at the youth of General Chih, expecting to find an older man in command of the division which had borne the brunt of the fighting here. Instead I found a short, broad-shouldered man of thirty-four whose crisp black hair was brushed back in a wide pompadour. His trousers were of tan gaberdine, fastened loosely around the ankle with strap and buckle, after the fashion of the old Zouave trousers. These were topped by a short blousy windbreak of the same hue, and of Western cut.

His personality was dynamic and he related in short picturesque phrases the events of the past few days. In the main his narrative agreed with the salient facts we had already learned at General Sun's headquarters.

"Over towards the east side of the city," he explained, "the officer in charge telephoned me that the Japanese had launched a gas attack. I asked him what it was like. He said it made the eyes smart and burned the nostrils. I

A group of refugees in the Taierchwang (Shantung) area, seeking shelter from a Japanese aerial attack.

The town of Taierchwang after the Chinese victory. Note the utter desolation caused by the fighting.

Chinese woman and her child attempting to salvage some the family heirlooms from the ruins of her burned home in o Teh, Northwest Shansi province.

A pontoon bridge across the Grand Canal near Taierchwang, constructed by the Chinese of canal boats. In the background may be observed some of the Chinese dugouts which dotted the northern bank.

said, 'Use your masks and don't give way—it's only tear gas.' Then I ordered a reserve regiment to move in and assault. We used hand grenades and big swords. The fighting was hot, but the Japanese gave ground. At four o'clock this morning the only opposition was from a building in the southeast corner. We called on them to surrender, but they continued to fire. So we burned them out. This is a part of what we captured." He indicated stacks of rifles, grenades, machine guns, records, diaries, drill manuals and three long metal tubes which had contained tear gas.

General T'ien Chen-nau had been quiet during this narrative. He was an older officer, one of the old-school Chinese, but a man of kindly disposition. Now he suggested that we look over the area.

We went first to the eastern third of the city, which had been held for a week by the Japanese. Climbing over sandbag barricades and stepping gingerly through barbed wire entanglements we came into a city of the dead. The Japanese had not had time to bury all of their killed, though black patches of ashes here and there indicated a last minute attempt to incinerate some of the bodies. At one place an elderly Chinese peasant lay sprawled in the street, the feet of a pair of geese still clutched in his lifeless hand. Farther on was the body of a woman, an unborn child protruding from her ruptured abdomen. It was all too ghastly for words.

Moving to the field outside the north wall we found four tanks disabled, the bloated bodies of their crews lying outside. The tanks were of medium type, each carrying a fifty-four millimeter gun and two six-point-five millimeter machine guns.

General Chih described the manner in which they had been disabled.

"The enemy," he said, "attempted to attack the north wall with twenty tanks. We had anti-tank guns on the wall, but we had also sent soldiers out individually to secrete themselves in the folds of the ground. Each man carried eight hand grenades, divided into bundles of four each. When a tank came abreast of him he threw the bundle of grenades into the treads. Of the twenty tanks thirteen mere disabled in this manner or by the anti-tank guns. The others withdrew. Nine of the tanks were dragged away by tractors under cover of darkness, but these four remained."

We had heard of a Japanese artillery position at Shaochwang, two miles to the north, which had been destroyed by Chinese artillery fire, and where nearly three hundred horses had been killed, and in the afternoon General Chih sent a patrol of fifty men to conduct us there.

The outward trip was without incident. Far to the north the dull booming of artillery told that the enemy was not near. Shaochwang proved to be a small group of farm houses. In front of the houses at regular intervals were the wheel marks of artillery carriages. The ground around the guns was pock-marked with shell holes. A dozen ammunition trucks and trailers lay at one side of the buildings in a disabled condition. The walls of the buildings were piles of rubble. Within the walls were the bodies of twenty-five or thirty horses; while others were scattered about the area. Evidently the Chinese 155's had got the exact range of this position.

Twilight was gathering as we started back. It had been a full day. For Ivens, Ferno, Capa and Epstein it had been a profitable day, for they had obtained news pictures which none could pre-empt. And for the Chinese it had been a day of victory. All were in good spirits. Towards the head of the column someone struck up a song. Suddenly it was cut short. A series of shots followed, and the patrol scuttled for a ditch on the left of the road.

Peering ahead from my position in the middle of the column I saw a grotesque form floundering in a shell hole off to the right of the road a matter of forty yards. I moved up to the ditch opposite the hole.

One of the patrol, it seemed, had seen a blanket in the shell hole and had attempted to fish it out with the muzzle of his rifle. A fusillade of shots came from beneath the blanket. A Japanese soldier, wounded in the foot, had taken shelter under his olive drab blanket in this hole.

The whole business was a bit pathetic, for the man would not surrender, and from time to time he raised his arm beneath the blanket and fired a pistol blindly in the general direction of the patrol. The patrol opened fire, but he presented a difficult target except at the infrequent intervals when he raised his arm to fire. Eventually a soldier crept off to the flank and threw a grenade.

It dropped nearer to us than to the Japanese, and he was soundly berated by his provoked comrades. But the next one hit the edge of the hole and ended the uneven engagement.

The fight may have seemed unfair to a spectator, but the brave Japanese would not give up, and being concealed under the blanket one could not say which way his gun was pointed. It was one of those tragedies that goes with war, which is a sordid business at best.

Back at Taierchwang there was considerable chagrin on the part of the army commanders that the area had not been properly mopped up before we ventured forth, but enemy stragglers are to be expected on any recently won battle field, and observers who go to the front cannot reasonably expect to have their path strewn with roses.

Generals T'ien and Chih accompanied us back to headquarters, which had been moved nearer the town. Here General Sun Lien-chung was waiting dinner for us.

It was another memorable evening. For the first time within the memory of any man present China had won a victory against a foreign enemy who possessed modern military equipment, and these were the men who had led her forces on the field of battle. They could be pardoned if they seemed exultant. Six months ago, even a month ago, resistance had seemed futile, and they had fought simply because it was not in their nature to relinquish their soil without a struggle. But hope of prevailing against the military might of Japan had been small. Now the opponent had been vanquished in a pitched battle, and though he might come back to win tomorrow, they knew he was not invincible. Thenceforth the memory of Taierchwang would be for the Chinese people a symbol of hope and a spur to greater effort.

General Sun sent out for some huang chiu, the mild yellow rice wine, and we drank to a new, strong and united China. Teddy Tu sang two new songs he had just written, "Self Sacrifice'' and the "Flag Song." The others caught the air, and the walls of the courtyard resounded with their rollicking voices.

Presently General Chih asked: "Have you ever heard how our soldiers evaluate the effectiveness of weapons?"

I had heard the troops pooh-poohing the dangers of aerial bombing, but I wanted to hear his explanation.

"Well," he rejoined, "they say that the Japanese bombs are not as effective as their artillery fire; that the artillery fire is not as effective as the machine-gun fire; but, they insist, our hand grenades are more effective than the Japanese machine-gun fire, and our big swords are the most effective of all."

We laughed at this simplified analysis, but the soldiers' viewpoint was understandable, for in hand-to-hand combat they had gained a victory.

I asked General Sun how the Japanese had happened to escape.

"We occupied the villages around Taierchwang," he replied, "but the area between the villages was not properly covered."

I suspected that he had heeded an old Chinese proverb which warns that an enemy should never be completely surrounded, for if there is no way of escape he will fight more fiercely, knowing that he is doomed.

There was another observation which troubled me. The principal defensive positions of the Chinese had been established along the north bank of the Grand Canal. This was contrary to the orthodox custom of placing a strong natural obstacle, when it is available, in front of the defenders. I mentioned the matter to General Sun. A twinkle came into the General's eyes.

"Centuries ago," he replied, "there lived a famous Chinese general named Wu Tze. He is credited with having remarked that it had been his observation that soldiers always fought best when there was an obstacle at their rear." We all chuckled at this witty rejoinder, for the answer was that the Chinese had not been pushed hard enough to compel them to make a strong defensive stand behind the canal. From the north side it was easier to launch the attacks which finally routed their opponents.

VI

A few clays later I left this pleasant company and journeyed back to Hankow. The Japanese were bound to launch a strong offensive to wipe out the disgrace of this defeat, but thy would require time in which to bring up re-enforcements. The Chinese seemed to be reluctant to push their advantage, possibly because they were somewhat stunned by their success, or perhaps because they feared they might be led into a trap. In any event there would be no unusual action for several days.

At Hankow I talked with General von Falkenhausen, the chief of the German military mission, about the battle. I had had several talks with him on my previous visit to the city, and as a result I had great confidence in his professional judgment. The doubts I had entertained about the loyalty to China of this military mission from the nation which had strong and sympathetic relations with Japan had been dissipated, for I recognized in General von Falkenhausen a man of high personal integrity. I felt then, and I am still of the opinion, that he rendered faithful and valuable service to the Chinese cause.

The General was tearing his hair because the Chinese were not following up their advantage.

"I tell the Generalissimo," said he, vehemently, "to advance, to attack, to exploit his success. But nothing is done. Soon the Japanese will have eight, ten divisions before Hsuchowfu. Then it will be too late. Now they can destroy this small Japanese force, for the morale is low. The blow would shake the confidence of the people at home." He threw up his hands in despair.

Well, this was China, and it was China's war. China would have to fight it in her own way. Who could say whether what to us of the West seemed to be mistakes were in fact grave errors which imperiled her cause. A victory such as Taierchwang was due as much to Japanese arrogance and incompetence as to Chinese valor and ingenuity. Japan would be more wary in the future, and China's army was not yet strong enough to prevail against a determined Japanese offensive. China's strength lay in time and the vast reaches of her terrain. By skillfully using these factors China could prolong the war and reduce the test of strength to the basis of economic endurance. And so, while a victory was of great psychological value, Generalissimo Chiang probably reasoned that it was not to be interpreted as a sign of China's general military superiority. The broad policy must be one of defense which would continue to exhaust his opponent, and cause that opponent to dissipate his strength by occupying a wide front, while preserving the integrity of the Chinese forces.

Perhaps the most significant factor in the Taierchwang victory was the fact that the troops employed there worked in harmony with the civil population. General Sun Lien-chung had instituted the system of ethical indoctrination in his army. His men fought for an ideal—the salvation of China. And they realized that the civil populace were their allies, and treated them with respect and consideration. The people responded by continuing to work in the battle area, tilling the fields and co-operating with the troops.

The lion's share of the glory went to Sun Lien-chung, as the commander on the field, and to Li Tsung-jen, who commanded the War Zone, but equally important to the final outcome were the operations of the armies which lay to the east. General Chang Tze-chung's army, operating north of Lin Yi, stopped the Japanese 105th Division, and General T'ang En-po's army, which lay between Lin Yi and Taierchwang, supported General Sun, on his left, and General Chang, on his right.

T'ang En-po was another military leader who steered clear of politics. It was he who conducted the gallant defense of Nankou Pass, northwest of Peip'ing, at the beginning of the conflict, and here at Taierchwang he again proved his ability by inflicting heavy losses on the enemy and capturing a number of prisoners.

CHAPTER VI
CHINA'S FOUNTAIN-HEAD OF LIBERALISM

I

THE war was now in the last quarter of its first year. I had witnessed operations on two positional warfare fronts, and on the guerrilla front as well. Of the two types, the latter appeared to be best suited to the accomplishment of China's objectives of denying Japan the fruits of victory, and of prolonging the war until China could become strong enough to evict the invaders. But the success of this type of resistance depended on a strong people's movement, especially in those areas which had been penetrated by the Japanese. I had inspected a small portion of this area while with the Eighth Route Army. Now I considered the possibility of making a survey of the entire area behind the Japanese lines, from Suiyuan, in Inner Mongolia, to the seacoast in Shantung. This would show not only the potential strength of the People's Movement, but would afford an opportunity to observe the degree to which the united front between the Kuomintang and Communist parties was actually working, for military units of both parties were represented in the north.

The trip I contemplated making would be the equivalent of starting from Dubuque, Iowa (Sian, Shensi), moving north to Duluth, Minnesota (Yulin, Shensi, on the Suiyuan border), then continuing a hundred and fifty miles northeast into Canada, swinging east and southeast to the north shore of Lake Huron, and returning to Lansing, Michigan (Chengchow), by passing between Detroit and Port Huron. The ground distance would be about fifteen hundred miles.

As usual, I told no one of my plans. Secrecy is assured only when plans are not communicated. However, I deferred making a definite decision until I reached Chengchow, for it might be advisable to return to the Hsuchowfu front before essaying the northern trip. The Japanese were massing troops for a renewal of the southern drive.

Peter Fleming had come out from England to gather material for a series of articles for the *London Times*. He wanted to have a look at the Hsuchowfu front, so we decided to travel together, at least as far as Chengchow.

In his early thirties, Fleming had already made a name for himself as the author of travel books on Brazil, China and Central Asia. Quiet and unassuming, he was a delightful traveling companion. The usual fourteen-hour train trip from Hankow lengthened into two days, for air raids were frequent. At each alarm the locomotive was uncoupled and run ahead a few hundred yards, while the passengers spread out over the fields, or sought shelter in ravines, culverts or folds of the ground. Just as the train arrived in Chengchow a particularly vicious air attack was launched on the city. Throwing our baggage into rickshas we dashed for the Baptist Mission hospital compound, with the rickshas close on our heels.

A dozen journalists were in the city seeking transportation to Hsuchowfu. Some had been here a week. But the Chinese were pushing re-enforcements to the east, and had no time to bother with civilian passengers.

From General Ch'eng Ch'ien we learned that the Japanese concentration was being made at Tzeyang, a hundred miles north of Hsuchowfu, from which point they could strike either to the east or to the west of the latter city.

I was beginning to think that perhaps I ought to go to Hsuchowfu first when Colonel Joseph Stilwell, our military attaché, arrived and announced that he was going there. My own course was now clear. There would be no occasion for two American observers on the Hsuchowfu front. Peter Fleming could accompany Colonel Stilwell, and I would go west to see what could be done about getting to Inner Mongolia. That night I entrained for Sian, three hundred miles to the west, where I had started and ended the winter trip with the Eighth Route Army.

I had heard that there was a truck road of sorts from Sian to the Communist political headquarters at Yenan, two hundred and fifty miles north of Sian, and thence to Yulin on the Shensi-Suiyuan border, two hundred miles farther north. My plan was to go first to Yenan, where I would spend a few days talking with Mao Tse-tung and other Communist leaders, and then move up to Yulin, where I hoped to find a patrol which would escort me to the headquarters of General Ma Chan-san, in Inner Mongolia. From that point I would trust to chance and the generosity of guerrilla leaders to enable me to work my way across north China to Shantung province. The trip would be about fifteen hundred miles in length, and if I was lucky I could do it in five months.

After reaching Sian I called on the Governor, General Chiang T'ing-wen, again. The military units in Yulin and Mongolia came directly under the Central Government, and the Governor was able to act for the Generalissimo. He received me cordially.

"You are seeing a good deal of our war, Ts'an Tsan," he said in greeting.

"Yes, General," I replied. "And now I hope to see more."

I outlined my plan briefly, and then added: "I was much impressed by the value of the co-operation of the people with the army in the occupied regions. This is a development that is vital to your resistance, it seems to me, and I want to see how extensive it is. Moreover, the world has little knowledge of the extent to which the people are maintaining Chinese jurisdiction in the occupied districts. The Japanese say that their control is supreme. From what I have seen, I challenge this statement. If I personally inspect these regions in their entirety I will be in a position to testify to conditions as I find them."

"But, Ts'an Tsan," he remonstrated, "such a trip will be extremely dangerous. Why do you undertake such dangers?"

For a moment I was at a loss for a reply. I had not stopped before to examine the urge which prompted these expeditions, being conscious only of trying to place my finger on the key elements in this conflict. But now I realized that behind the desire to fulfill an official duty there was a deeper urge.

"General," I replied, and I spoke from the heart, "I come from a country whose people regard liberty and equality as inalienable rights. We have suffered much in an effort to preserve these rights in my country. In the Chinese people I have observed this same love of liberty and equality, and I am convinced from what I have seen that they are ready to sacrifice comfort, homes and their lives that it may be preserved for their children. We cannot, as a nation, take sides in this conflict, but as an individual I can inspect the character of your efforts to resist the invasion, even in the most isolated spots, and give my report to the world. The risk is one which any of my countrymen would gladly take in the name of liberty."

I had not intended to be either dramatic or sentimental, but liberty and equality were so much a fundamental part of my concept of human rights that I realized now my soul had unconsciously been revolted by the ruthless manner in which I had seen them trampled under foot by the Japanese invaders. And conversely, I had seen in the Chinese efforts the same spirit which had animated our own ancestors at Lexington, Trenton and Valley Forge.

General Chiang was strangely quiet, and recovering from my reverie I discovered to my amazement that tears were coursing down his bronze cheeks. Wiping them away he said huskily: "Ts'an Tsan, I had no idea that any American understood so well the cause for which we fight. You will have my full cooperation."

This was the man who was reported to deal so harshly with the Communists, and who, I had been told, ruled with a rod of iron. But he was human, and obviously his love for his country was no less strong than that of men who governed by less arbitrary methods. He was the product of a different environment and training, and his pattern of thought could not be changed over night. I have never since been able to regard Chiang T'ing-wen as the hard-boiled bigot he is frequently painted.

At the Eighth Route Army office I found Lin Tso-han (sometimes known as Lin Pai-chu), the dignified and grayhaired chairman of the Special Administrative District of north Shensi, which is the home base of the Chinese Communists.

Lin was the grand old man of the Chinese Communist Party, his membership dating from 1922. His gray hair, which flowed back from a high forehead, and his equally gray mustache, gave him a distinguished appearance, while an ill-fitting pair of spectacles, which he frequently allowed to hang from one ear, added an air of benevolence. He was the son of a schoolmaster, and had been educated in the classics. At one time high in the Kuomintang councils, he denounced Chiang Kai-shek when the latter set up a right-wing government at Nanking in 1927, and fled to Russia, where he studied for four years. On his return he joined the Chinese Soviet in Kiangsi as Minister of Finance. Now he headed the Special District as well as the Eighth Route Army office in Sian.

My plan was received with enthusiasm by Comrade Lin, and he gave me letters of introduction to Mao Tse-tung and other leaders at Yenan.

When I was here previously I had been the instrument for bringing together Lin and Professor Musse, a Swiss who headed the League of Nations Anti-Epidemic unit in Sian. The latter had brought a hospital unit with him and was eager to set it up in the Eighth Route Army area, having heard that the army took care of its wounded, but sorely needed medical supplies and equipment. Now I asked for news of the unit.

"We sent it to Yenan," replied Comrade Lin, "but the League of Nations wants to exercise too much supervision over it."

I determined to examine into the matter when I reached Yenan.

Lin said that a truck with medical supplies would leave for Yenan the following day, and there would be room for me on it.

That night General Chiang T'ing-wen gave a dinner for me, which was attended by most of his staff. In Chinese fashion I was seated opposite my host. The General made a short, moving speech, and then with great formality he passed around to me six letters of introduction, one by one. There were letters to Generals Tun P'ao-san and Kao Suan-chen at Yulin, and to Generals Ma Chan-san, Fu Tso-yi, Ho Chu-kuo and Men P'in-yueh, in Inner Mongolia. He also offered to send me north by truck, but I informed him that the Eighth Route Army had already arranged to do so.

With Chiang's blessing I returned to the Guest House to prepare my traveling gear for the long trek.

II

"You'll get through in two days if there's no rain," opined Doctor Eric Landauer, of the League of Nations Anti-Epidemic Commission, as he checked the last of the medical supplies into the truck. "If it rains God knows when you'll arrive."

The truck was of American make and the canvas top carried two large red crosses painted on each side. My traveling companions were a Canadian nurse, Miss Jean Ewen, of Vancouver, three Chinese students (a boy and two girls), who hoped to enter one of the training schools at Yenan, and a Shanghai Boy Scout, who was in charge of the truck. The Scout was an attractive youngster of nineteen named Kua Chi-teh, and he wore the official Scout uniform with all the trimmings, including scout knife and whistle. He was full of energy and initiative, and he had a cheerful smile and a solution for every difficulty.

All except Kua clambered into the body of the truck, and we made ourselves as comfortable as possible on top of the medical supplies and baggage. Kua rode with the driver.

Jean Ewen had spent five years nursing in a Catholic mission in Shantung, and spoke Chinese with great facility. She had returned to China a few months before with Doctor Norman Bethune, as a volunteer for medical work with the Eighth Route Army. Sent to Shansi, she arrived at Linfeng three days after I had left, in February, and one day before the Japanese arrived. Forced to flee with an army detachment towards the Yellow River, to the west, she had had a grueling experience, for the column had been bombed and machine gunned by planes daily, and on one occasion a bomb had exploded so close that she was partially covered by earth. But the experience had not dampened her ardor, and now she was returning to Yenan with needed supplies. During the three days of the truck trip she proved her mettle by being always cheerful and never complaining of the interminable dust or the lack of comfortable

Mao Tse-tung, distinguished leader of the Chinese Communist Party, in the courtyard of his abode in North Shensi province.

accommodations.

We crossed the Wei river on a railroad bridge and headed for the loess hills of north Shensi. The loess soil pulverizes easily, and the wheels churned it out of the sunken road into a billowing cloud which settled on us like a shower of yellow powder. But we were moving north, and nothing else mattered.

Towards evening we rolled into Tungkwan hsien and found a room in the home of a tinker. Only one room was available, but it had two k'angs separated by a narrow passageway. Jean and the two girls rolled up in their blankets on one, while Kua, the boy student and I occupied the other. One cannot be squeamish about conventions when traveling in China.

We were up at five-thirty, and after a hearty breakfast of bean curd and millet we moved on over the dust-filled road. Now we began to climb, and soon were able to survey the severely barren yellow cliffs which extended to the right and left of the road as far as the eye could reach. A characteristic of loess is that it shears vertically. Time and the elements had so eroded the peaks that they looked like fantastic beings of a pre-historic age. Only occasional terraces of millet, nursed by obscure farmers, relieved a scene of desolation.

Steadily moving up over a road that constant travel had cut deep into the crumbling soil, we occasionally skirted a precipitous cliff or dived swiftly into a valley, to ford a rocky stream bed. Once we came to a river, wide and deep, and crossed on a ferry which was sculled by an ancient boatman with a long scraggly beard, who still wore the queue, formerly symbolic of loyalty to the emperor, wound around the top of his head. That night we stopped in the mountain village of Lao Tsun.

The town was filled with troops of the provincial government, and we could find no place to stay. As a last resort we went to the commandant, and were received coldly by an officious young zealot who regarded with ill-concealed contempt these people who were en route to the Communist headquarters.

Ignoring the rest of us, he addressed himself to the three students. Why were they going to Yenan? To enter a school? But the Kuomintang had schools, and in them the students were well fed and provided with comfortable accommodations. Didn't they know that at Yenan the students subsisted only on millet ? And they lived in caves ? His smile was ingratiating.

But the students were adamant. Their replies were courteous, but succinct. Their minds were made up, and neither sarcasm nor bull-dozing could change them. After thirty minutes of this inquisition the Commandant gave up and informed us that we might sleep in the school that night.

With curious students crowding around, we spread our blankets, Jean and the girls on the benches, and the rest of us on the teacher's platform.

The next morning we reached the border of the Special Administrative District, and stopped for baggage inspection, as though we were entering another country. Later I asked Mao Tse-tung the reason for the inspection and was informed that it became necessary after two spies were found in the District.

Towards the close of the day we entered Yenan. The ancient town stands at the junction of three valleys, and caves in the sides of the loess walls of the valleys provide homes for thousands of students who come here seeking a new way of life. The caves extend for miles, and from a distance resemble the cliff homes of swallows or bats. They not only solve the housing problem, but protect the occupants from air attack as well.

The civil population lives in the town, and as we drove through the business district I was impressed by the absence of filth, so common to inland villages of China. The flagstone streets were clean, and the houses, with their doors thrown wide, appeared to be equally fresh and attractive. The number and variety of shops were remarkable, for they included tailors, barbers, restaurants, apothecaries, and shops offering an assortment of small merchandise.

In front of the post office we were hailed by Doctor Wentzler, of the League of Nations Anti-Epidemic Commission, who led us to his office and relieved us of the medical supplies. The students were taken in charge by a representative of the school board. Kua would remain with the truck, and Jean and I went off to a group of caves.

Jean had her own cave, and I was parked for the night in the cave recently vacated by Doctors Norman Bethune and Richard Brown, the latter of the Canadian Church Mission. Both had departed for Wu T'ai Shan to work in the hospital I had visited last winter.

My cave was high on a cliff to the west of the town, and was reached by a footpath which led to a loess ledge that extended in front of a group of twenty caves. It was about twenty feet across by thirty feet in depth, and the crescent shaped roof was twelve feet high at the center. At the back of the cave a k'ang had been provided by the simple expedient of leaving an earthen platform the width of the cave, and about eight feet in depth. The k'ang had no fire box, of course. Shelves had been carved from the sides of the walls, and the front of the cave was closed by a wall of earth to the height of the door, which was centrally placed. A lattice-work window, covered with paper, rested atop the wall and provided a certain amount of light.

I was only to remain here one night, however, for on the following morning an official of the local government conducted me to the official Guest House in the village. A cooperative restaurant next door provided a good assortment of food. Comrade Wang, fiftyish, serious minded and companionable, was assigned as interpreter. He had recently returned from a long prison sentence at Nanking occasioned by his political convictions.

The camaraderie here was much the same as in the Eighth Route Army. There was the universal kindliness, the absence of restraint, and an honesty and frankness which were attractive and refreshing. Everyone looked you squarely in the eye, with an absence of either arrogance or timidity. The life was rough, but all shared equally, and they were happy and contented.

Insofar as I was concerned, however, there was a measure of suspicion which I had not sensed in the army. One day, for example, three men of the Central Committee of the Party came to my room. They were ill at ease, but finally one broached the subject which had brought them. Had I not taken a bird's-eye picture of the town from a ledge the morning before? I assured them that I had not; that I never took pictures without Comrade Wang's approval. Turning to him I said:

"The last pictures I took were of the exercises on the recreation field yesterday. Do you remember?"

He nodded his head in assent.

Continuing, I said: "I don't want any shadow of a doubt to exist in your minds, so I wish you would take this film and have it developed."

Assuring me that there had probably been a mistake, they took the camera and departed. The following day camera and negative were returned, but I noticed that two exposures had been removed, though this fact had not been mentioned. I recalled that the missing exposures were of a sword dance and a demonstration of bayonet practice.

The matter worried me, for it entailed an element of deceit which was in contradiction to the high ethical standards I had come to associate with these men. I mentioned the matter to Comrade Wang, and in another day the exposures were returned with the explanation that the young men had been overzealous in attempting to guard what they regarded as training secrets.

The largest proportion of the students who came to Yenan entered K'an Ta, the military academy. At this time the student body numbered six thousand. The curriculum was much the same as the one I had seen in the school in Shansi, which was modeled on this one. The length of the course was four months, and the graduates went out to lead units of the army, of the Partisans, or to organize the people in the invaded districts.

Three miles out one valley was the North Shensi Academy (known as Shen Pei), the political training school where men and women were trained for political leadership. The fifteen hundred students lived in caves high above a natural amphitheater, wherein they congregated to hear open-air lectures.

I visited the classes of both schools, and addressed the students. They were interested in knowing of the progress of the war in other theaters. And they particularly wanted to know the attitude of the United States towards this struggle. Why hadn't America done something about her obligations under the Nine Power Treaty?

I stressed the fact that the signatories of this treaty were obligated only to respect the territorial and administrative integrity of China. And then I said:

"Look here, supposing the situation were reversed and America were a weak nation comparable to China. And let us assume that Mexico was an aggressive nation like Japan. If Mexico should invade the United States just how interested would you people here in the heart of China be about coming to our assistance?"

They saw the point. "But," they remonstrated, "America is powerful. And your spokesmen have stated repeatedly that you stand for justice, and for morality in international relations. We don't expect the United States to fight for us, but we don't feel that the aid you are giving our oppressor is in harmony with the principles you preach."

There was no adequate answer to this point except to remind them that in a democracy national decisions of great moment cannot be determined until the will of the majority has been made manifest, and such a manifestation takes time.

These boys and girls, most of them in their late 'teens or early twenties, were mentally keen and physically active. They had come here because of their confidence in the honesty of these leaders, and because of a deep faith in the ability of these leaders to mold China into a strong nation, where there would be equality of opportunity for all. Most of them had walked the two hundred and fifty miles from Sian. Every moment of their waking lives here was filled with activity: studies, dramatics, singing, lectures on politics, economics, hygiene and ethics, and with mountain climbing and other exercises designed to strengthen their physiques. Food was the monotonous diet of millet—two meals a day—but it kept body and soul together. When money was available they went to one of the restaurants in the village and splurged on a plate of Pa Pao Fan, the delectable sweetened rice mixed with fruit and nuts, for their bodies were starved for sweets.

III

One evening Comrade Wang took me to see Mao Tse-tung, the famous leader of the Chinese Communists. Mao slept in the day time and worked at night.

A single candle lighted the room in which he worked, and when I entered I came face to face with a tall man whose leonine head dominated a well built body. Crowning the massive head was a mane of jet black hair, parted in the center and thrown back carelessly. Kindly eyes regarded me thoughtfully from a face that suggested the dreamer.

A gentle smile suffused his countenance as he gave me a warm firm handclasp. "Welcome," he said in a soft, low-pitched voice. "I have heard of your wanderings with our army, and I am glad to welcome you here."

The pale candle light, the severely plain appointments of the room, whose only furnishings were a k'ang, a wooden table and a few shelves of books, and perhaps above all the abstract air of Mao himself, gave the atmosphere a quality of otherworldliness. We seated ourselves at opposite sides of the table, and Mao called softly to the guard outside the window to bring tea and peanuts.

Here was the man whose mind had provided the foundation for China's modern liberal thought and whose flare for organization had established the bases on which rested the structure of the present Communist Party in China. With Chu Teh he had led his people over the six thousand miles of hazardous terrain to the comparative security of these loess hills. And it was his extraordinary perception which was responsible for the pattern of resistance which was operating so effectively in Shansi and Hopei to neutralize Japan's superiority in modern weapons of war.

We talked late into the night, and our conversation covered the war, the political situation in Europe and America, the development of political thought down through the ages, the influence of religion on society and the ingredients of a successful world organization. He was an idealist, but there was a sound practical side to him as well.

"So long as our people have the will to endure hardship," he said, "and the will to continue resistance, China cannot be beaten. That will can only be built and sustained if the people have confidence in their leaders and are provided with hope for a better way of life. We try to provide these essentials by training leaders to live simply, administer justly and strive earnestly to aid the people to solve their problems. We believe that the better way of life lies in developing democracy and teaching the people how to govern themselves. Economic life, we feel, should be on a co-operative basis. Communism is not an immediate goal, for it can be attained only after decades of development. It must be preceded by a strong democracy, followed by a conditioning period of socialism."

He filled an old pipe with some of the long, stringy, yellow Chinese tobacco, and I made a mental note to send him a new pipe and some American tobacco.

"China," he continued, "is like a gallon jug which Japan is trying to fill with a half pint of liquid. When her troops move into one section, we move to another, and when they pursue us we move back again. Japan hasn't sufficient troops to occupy all of China, and so long as the people are determined to continue resistance she cannot control by political means."

He added that Japan has no main direction in her campaign in China. "A drive is made here, and ancther there. Instead of throwing a large force in at the beginning, re-enforcements have been brought in piece-meal. But her greatest mistake has been in the attitude of the army towards the Chinese people. By burning, raping and slaughtering they have enraged the populace and cemented the will to resist."

"What are the plans," I asked, "of the Chinese Communist Party for the post-war period?"

Mao's eyes gazed off into space as though they sought to penetrate the haze that cloaked the future. Slowly he replied: "We hope to perpetuate the present entente with the Kuomintang, looking to the establishment of a real democracy with a two-party government. We believe that the state should own the banks, mines and communications. The producers' and consumers' co-operatives should be developed, and we favor the encouragement of private enterprise. Finally, we feel that cordial relations should be established and maintained between China and those nations which are willing to meet us on a basis of equality."

There was certainly nothing very radical about these points. The banks, mines and communications were already owned by the Chinese government, in whole or in part. And there are many in the United States who feel that the co-operative idea is the answer to the growing friction between capital and labor. As for equality in international relations, this idea had gained ground rapidly in official American circles prior to the present conflict.

I recalled the controversy I had heard about the League of Nations hospital unit, and asked for his comment.

He smiled slowly. "We welcome such units, and we welcome those foreigners who come to help us. But the trouble with so many foreigners is that they soon want to dictate. They must remember that this is China, and that while their advice is eagerly received, we are the ones to decide if and how it will be used. With regard to the hospital, the foreign doctors wanted to give the patients in it better treatment than we can afford the patients in our own hospitals. It would mean that there would be inequality of treatment, and this is a question which must be studied carefully. The problem will be solved, but in our own way after due consideration."

Occasionally Mao would get up and pace the room as he talked, puffing on pipe or cigarette. His movements were graceful, even to the gesture of his hand when removing the pipe from his mouth.

Turning to the situation in Europe I ventured the opinion that Britain would fight if Germany invaded Czecho-Slovakia.

"No," replied Mao emphatically. "Britain will not fight for Czecho-Slovakia. If Germany should thrust to the southwest, Britain would fight, but she is not ready to fight for Czecho-Slovakia."

The following October, at Munich, Mao's prophecy was proved correct.

He returned to the struggle with Japan. "There are various types of besiegements," he ruminated. "Japan has us besieged at Wu T'ai, where we are surrounded. And both Japan and China use the device of the salient, such as Sun Lien-chung used at Taierchwang. But we have another type. Take the Japanese garrison at T'aiyuanfu, for example." Here he pushed a tea cup over

The student body of the North Shensi Academy, training school for political leaders at Yenan, Shensi, listening to a lecture. Note the loess cliff in the background.

The patrol from General Ma's Cavalry Army, which accompanied the author from Mongolia to Shansi, preparing to cross the Yellow River opposite Ho Kiu.

to represent this position, and around it he placed four other articles to represent Chinese positions. "Northeast of T'aiyuanfu is our force under Nieh Yong-sen, in Wu T'ai; to the northwest is Ho Lung; Lin Piao is to the southwest, and Chu Teh is to the southeast." He grinned mischievously. "The Japanese cannot move in Shansi without being pounced on by one of our patrols."

Then he added: "As Shansi is the strategic key to north China, so is the Wu T'ai region the key to Shansi. Japan cannot control the province so long as we possess Wu T'ai."

Whimsically, and with twinkle in his eye, he concluded: "Another type of besiegement would be for the United States and Russia to join with China in besieging Japan. That would be an international besiegement."

It was early in the morning when I left Mao. I was to see him again before departing for the north, for he had promised to go into the matter of my proposed trip, but the vision of him which would remain with me was this picture of a humble, kindly, lonely genius, striving here in the darkness of the night to find a peaceful and an equitable way of life for his people.

IV

I had come to know two foreign communists who lived here in Yenan. One was a German, known as Li Teh. The other was an American doctor, said to be of Armenian descent, who was called Ma Hai-teh.

Li Teh was about forty, of medium height and clean shaven. He wore thick glasses, and was inclined to be irritable at times. His past was shrouded in mystery, but he obviously had had a military background, and it was said that he had fled his native land because of the unpopularity of his communist leanings. In 1933 he was smuggled into the Soviet area of Kiangsi, and became a military adviser for the Red Army, making the long march with it. Here he instructed in the military academy.

Jean Ewen introduced me to him, and he promptly and bluntly accused me of being a spy. I assured him that I was not, and pointed to the fact that the army in Shansi had suffered no harm as a result of my presence.

Eventually we became good friends, for his extensive knowledge of military subjects gave us a common meeting ground. He maintained a large and well selected library. A popular book on Field Artillery, by Major General Harry G. Bishop, of our army, had been carefully, and not too favorably, annotated.

"Artillery in the American army must be in pretty tough shape if this book is any indication of the methods it uses," he remarked darkly.

I assured him that the book did not represent the tactics and technique of artillery as we now practised them.

He lived a solitary life, reading voraciously, and for exercise charging out over the valley floor on a small Mongolian pony.

In the cave next to Li Teh lived Doctor Ma Hai-teh, who advised on medical affairs. His past, too, was unrevealed. I made no attempt to pry into the private affairs of either man.

Ma was short, of dark complexion, and sort of an eternal optimist. His cheerful, hearty way, and the fact that he had learned to speak Chinese with amazing facility, made him extremely popular in the army.

Over in Shansi men had asked me eagerly: "Do you know Ma Hai-teh? He speaks Chinese almost as well as we do."

I met Ma late one afternoon down in the village, and invited him to have dinner with me. He agreed and we started for a restaurant famous for its Pa Pao Fan (the sweetened rice concoction). As we walked along Ma was hailed almost at every step by students and shop keepers, men and women alike. To each he would reply: "Come on down and have dinner with us."

I was amused by the generosity with which he dispensed my hospitality, for I realized that he knew I was not pressed for money.

By the time we reached the restaurant I felt like the Pied Piper of Hamlin, for in our wake were a dozen or more of young men and women, laughing, joking and thoroughly in the spirit of the occasion.

It was great fun, and wholly informal. Individuals ordered what they wanted and then got up and left, or sat around and told stories of past experiences, without any sense of obligation or restraint.

One day Comrade Wang asked if I would like to see Lo Fu. Indeed I would, I had heard of the efficient secretary of the Party, who seldom saw foreigners.

We walked out to the cave, three miles north of town, where Lo Fu lived alone. In a room that was flooded with the morning sunlight, and surrounded by shelves of books in the German, Russian, English and Chinese languages, I found a short, pleasant-faced man who I judged to be in his late thirties. A pair of spectacles emphasized the studious caste of his face.

He welcomed me with a manner that was both charming and unassuming. Talking easily on a wide variety of subjects he finally got around to the relations between the Communist and Kuomintang parties, and expressed confidence that a formula would be worked out which would permit the two parties to continue working together after the war. Aggression, he felt, must be curbed before there could be hope of world peace. In this connection he emphasized that China was fighting the battle of the democracies in Eastern Asia.

Towards the end of the conversation he addressed me in English, and I discovered that he understood the language, though he spoke it haltingly. It developed that he had spent a year and a half in the United States about the year 1920, and had attended a Western university.

Lo Fu's one eccentricity was an aversion to being photographed. I had secured pictures of the other leaders, but he was firm on this point. I got no picture.

Back at the Guest House I found five youths waiting for me. They bore a note from Mao Tse-tung, and they wished to accompany me on my trip. I was somewhat nonplussed at the thought of assuming responsibility for five boys—for that was what it would amount to, as they had had no experience on the trail—and I suggested that two, or perhaps three, might come along. But, no, they were a cultural group, and they worked together. Either all went, or none.

They were fine-looking chaps, ranging in age from twenty-one to twenty-seven. Auyang was a dramatist, Liu was a novelist, King a journalist, Lin San a poet, and the youngest, Wang Yang, was a photographer. Some of them had been trained at the Lu Shun Art School, a cultural school here which was named for the celebrated liberal writer, who died in 1936. I liked their spirit, their youthful enthusiasm and their earnest desire to aid their country. Their object was to collect material along the way which they would later utilize, each in his own medium, to stimulate the people to greater effort.

The more I thought of the proposition, the more I felt that they should be encouraged. Moreover, it would be great fun having this group of intelligent youngsters along, and there was much they could teach me about the progressive movements in China.

"Good," I said, "we will go together."

They were ecstatic. Speculating excitedly on the probable route we would take after reaching Mongolia, we went out to a restaurant to celebrate our entente with plates of Pa Pao Fan.

Auyang spoke English with fair fluency, having studied it in school at Shanghai.

"Comrade Liu," he said, "is our leader. But we are following you on this trip, and we hope you will correct our faults."

This attitude was reminiscent of the Eighth Route Army. Auyang said he thought that Mao Tse-tung would provide a truck to take us to Yulin. This would save us a hundred and fifty miles of walking, and speed our journey.

V

I saw Mao Tse-tung again next day, and he confirmed the authorization for the truck. The road was now being repaired, having been washed out by the rains, but it should be ready in two days.

That afternoon Hsiao Ching-kwan came to see me. Hsiao was the commander of the rear echelon of the Eighth Route Army, a post that carried responsibility for the defense of the Yellow River defense line.

A huge man with a hearty, boisterous manner, he had a way of thrusting his body forward as he walked, as though his long, vigorous legs were not carrying him as rapidly as he would like them to. He had spent a number of years at the Red Army Academy, at Moscow, and was considered to be an able tactician.

The river, he said, was itself a formidable obstacle to any army which wished to invade Shensi from Shansi, and the west bank was strongly held by several brigades of the army. Thus far no Japanese unit had succeeded in crossing, but even if they should succeed, the rugged loess hills of Shensi favored effective guerrilla operations, which only an overwhelming invading force would be able to withstand. Comrade Hsiao's manner was full of confidence.

As the time for departure approached I checked my equipment again with a view to eliminating everything that was not absolutely essential. The sleeping bag I had taken on the Shansi trip had offered difficulties, especially when pack animals passed through narrow defiles. So I had cut my bedding down to two blankets (it would still be cold in Mongolia). These were wrapped in oil cloth to protect them from moisture. Changes of clothing and extra shoes went in a ruck sack, along with my few books. A third sack carried my wash basin, tea kettle and rice bowl. On my person I planned to carry a haversack containing photographic equipment (exposed and unexposed film), notes, diary and maps. These items I wanted to make certain would not fall into the hands of the Japanese, for such an eventuality would seriously embarrass my hosts. The possibility of my own capture was remote so long as I trusted myself to Chinese hands. Finally, a special waist belt would carry a cup, camera case, compass and jack knife. Chop sticks reposed in a shirt pocket.

In contrast to the fur-lined garments of the winter trip, I now wore khaki shirt and shorts, while my headgear was a pith sun helmet. The tall lace boots with composition soles were still my favorite foot gear, for they were comfortable and the composition soles gripped rocks better than leather, and their endurance was equally good. For an occasional change I carried broad-toed shoes and wrap puttees.

During the winter trip I had carried only four pieces of reading material: Emerson's *Essays*, a companion of many years, two booklets of the British Three Penny Library: *An Introduction to Geography* and *The Basis of Law*, and a copy of the *Reader's Digest* for the month of September, 1937. At Hankow I had added three volumes to this collection.

In Shansi I had been so impressed by the similarity between the doctrines I saw being practised by the Eighth Route Army and the people and the doctrines of Christ that when I prepared for the present trip I selected a pocket volume of the New Testament with a view to reading the four gospels systematically and comparing Christ's doctrines with what I saw being applied around me. To this volume I added *The Education of Henry Adams* and *One Hundred and One Famous Poems*.

It was the fifteenth of May when we assembled at the Guest House and loaded our sparse equipment into the waiting truck. A large crowd of students had turned out to see the five boys off. Jean Ewen was going to a hospital at Chingkien, half way to Yulin, and she would accompany us that far. A squad of soldiers as escort completed the party.

The eager, earnest students seemed to symbolize the spirit of this place—that spirit of liberalism which was doing so much to inject new life into the heritage of an ancient civilization. Soon they would go out steeped in those ethical principles so vital to the building of a sound and equitable social order, dedicated to lives of service to their countrymen. Perhaps the most important lesson they would carry would be the example of self-sacrifice.

"Tsou Pa," cried the truck driver. The familiar phrase sent us scrambling into the truck. The motor roared, the students shouted a final slogan: "Down with Japanese Imperialism!" We were off.

CHAPTER VII
THE CHINESE FRONT IN MONGOLIA

I

MONGOLIA-BOUND at last! The prospect of entering that fabulous region by a side door, instead of by the usually traveled rail route from Peip'ing, was exciting. Moreover, mystery had surrounded the activities of Chinese troops on this extreme northwest flank since the Japanese had completed the occupation of the Suiyuan railway line by capturing the terminus at Paot'o, the preceding October. Best known and most picturesque of the leaders of Chinese resistance in that land of vast deserts was General Ma Chan-san, the doughty Manchurian who first broke into international headlines in 1931-32 when he opposed the Japanese invasion of Manchuria, and made a strong stand along the Nonni river. Now he was reported to have a cavalry army which was giving them a good deal of trouble in Suiyuan.

As our truck lurched over the road north of Yenan the five boys discussed General Ma. His wile, and his courage in challenging the Japanese in those years before the war, when the policy in China was to appease, had made almost a legendary figure of him. They were no less eager to see him than I.

Already I had begun to discern the individual characteristics of the boys. The personalities of all were charming, though each was distinctly individual. Strange to say, the leader was not the eldest. Liu was a native of Hopei and had been educated in Peip'ing. He was tall, slender and graceful, and he carried himself with a quiet dignity that was natural and unaffected. It was probably his remarkable self-discipline which caused him to be selected as leader, for during the five months we were together I never saw him lose his self-control. When called upon to make a decision he calmly examined all sides of the question, and then made up his mind. Any action which involved the group as a whole was considered by them jointly. At the end of each day's journey Liu would lead them aside, at some convenient time, and they would hold a meeting in which each discussed his observations and criticised himself. They were seeking to perfect their conduct and their self-possession, and to add to their knowledge and broaden their understanding of life. The leader of such a group had to be a man of spiritual serenity and exceptional patience.

Auyang was the most versatile of the group. He was twenty-three, and a native of Hunan, though he had been raised in Shanghai. From his actor-father he had inherited a talent for dramatics and a singing and speaking voice that was both deep and rich. He knew the Chinese stage from "A" to "Z," and had had experience in both acting and playwriting. Without preparation he could sing selections from the old Chinese classics, in the falsetto so much admired by the ancients, or any of the new popular war songs. Probably because he spoke English, Auyang and I became greatly attached to each other.

The poet, Lin San, had been born in Kwangtung, though he had lived most of his life in Siam. He was the eldest of the group, being twenty-seven. He spoke little Mandarin, which was the dialect of the others, and for this reason he came in for a good deal of good-natured joshing. They would laughingly say that I was more Chinese than he because my Mandarin was better. Lin San would look at me with a wry smile and nod his head in agreement. He was a sad, dreamy-eyed individual, as poets should be, I presume, and was frequently buried in his own thoughts. Later, when we would pass a particularly attractive spot while marching, one of the others would say, "Lin San, there's a romantic setting; you should write a poem about it." To which gentle jibe Lin San would retort, "Such a setting might have appealed to the old school of poets, but the moderns go to the front for their inspiration."

Ching, the journalist, was lanky, angular, and reminded me of Down-East Yankees by his rustic humor and sound common sense. Although only twenty-five, he had fought with the Volunteers of Manchuria after his native province was invaded by Japan, in 1931. His life had been a hard one, and it had toughened his body and tempered his spirit. But his heart was as tender as a woman's, and he spent much time talking with the peasants, especially those who were old and whose care-lined faces and gnarled, calloused hands told of hardship and devotion. It was Ching who always had a practical solution for a pressing problem. And it was Ching who labored with me at night when I was trying to add more characters to my Chinese vocabulary.

But it was Wang Yang whose irrepressible good humor kept us light hearted, even when meals were scant and far between. Wang Yang was the youngest, twenty-one, and a native of Chekiang. He had spent most of his short life in Shanghai, and until recent months he had been a carefree motion picture photographer, with not a thought in his head about political matters. But he had fallen in love with a girl who was a revolutionary. It was no fly-by-night affair, but a deep and absorbing passion which, almost overnight, had raised him to maturity, as he proved by renouncing his former gay and heedless ways and following his beloved to Yenan, where he entered the political training school. He was less self-disciplined than any of the others, and this trip was part of a conditioning process for him. It was impossible not to like him, and difficult even to chide him for any of his impulsive indiscretions, so appealing was his frank, quick smile, and so earnest his desire to do the right thing. His one English word was "beautiful," which he pronounced expressively "beeeutiful." Whether it was a charming landscape or a razor-back hog that I pointed out, he would flash his infectious smile and cry: "Beeeutiful."

With such a group as companions life was never dull.

The country through which we passed after leaving Yenan was much the same as that I had seen when approaching the town: desolate loess hills, with precipitous descents, and equally difficult climbs out of stony stream beds. There was no canvas top on the truck to break the infiltration of dust, and soon we all looked like yellow gnomes.

We stopped at the small dust-covered village of Li Chai Chin the first night, and the boys displayed their culinary ability by preparing the dinner of eggs and noodles. At six o'clock the next morning we were again on the road, and towards evening we approached the walled city of Chingkien. Here the country began to show evidences of rock, and picturesque temples appeared, on the summits of cone-shaped hills.

Jean Ewen left us at Chingkien to work in the local Eighth Route Army hospital. Although she would be the only foreigner in this area, the prospect did not seem to disturb her, and she departed with a cheery smile and a reassuring wave of the hand. Partings are like that when there is work to be done and the workers have the sense of mission.

Twenty-five miles north of Chingkien we climbed to the top of a mountain range and had a magnificent view of the surrounding hills, looking much like the crests of waves on a storm-tossed sea. Pear trees began to appear near the villages, the pear peculiar to China—hard as a brick-bat, and deliciously sweet. Trees, rocks and fields gave the country a less forbidding appearance, and after another twenty-five miles we came to Suiteh, a walled city with many temples, built on the side of a hill overlooking the junction of two river valleys whose lush green banks brought exclamations of pleasure from the boys.

There was an Eighth Route Army garrison at Suiteh, which is only thirty miles west of the Yellow river. Stopping only long enough for the meal which the commander insisted on providing, we crossed to the east side of the Wu T'ing river on a fine new nineteen arch bridge, and continued north through the green and fertile Wu T'ing valley to Michih, headquarters of another army unit.

Michih was near the southern edge of the desert country, and after a night's rest we embarked on the fifty mile trip to Yulin over a road which led across dunes of shifting sand. It was a tedious process, for the truck bogged on every incline, and on one occasion two hours of digging were required to retrieve it from a hole into which it had slid. At sundown we reached Yulin (corresponding to Duluth), a desert metropolis built around an oasis, five miles south of the point where the Wu T'ing river flows south through the Great Wall of China.

II

The letters from Governor Chiang T'ing-wen brought a cordial reception from General Tun P'ao-san, commander of the New First Army and 21st Corps, as well as from the commander of the 86th Division, General Kao Suan-chen. Trimly dressed officers, wearing the red and gold tabs of their rank on the edges of their military tunic collars, escorted us to elaborate quarters in an old Chinese home, where we had three rooms and a courtyard to ourselves. Such treatment at the hands of Central Government officers was a new experience to the boys, but their equanimity was not disturbed.

Auyang and I went to call on General Tun the following morning, for we were now among people who observed conventions and the social amenities. The General was in his fifties, tall and thin, and his head as well as his face was shaved. He received us graciously, and I explained the presence of the five boys with me, adding that the cordiality of their reception here afforded added proof that the united front between the Communists and the Kuomintang was more than a mere phrase.

"We have never had a foreign military officer up here," replied the General, "and we appreciate your interest."

Then he proceeded to give me a thumb-nail sketch of the military situation, bringing a military map to the table.

"The Japanese not only occupy the railway into Suiyuan, but they also occupy strategic points in the area between the railway and the inner loop of the Great Wall, in Shansi, which lies to the south from fifty to one hundred and thirty miles. The Yellow river, you notice, enters Suiyuan from the west, and makes a broad sweep to the south a few miles east of Paot'o" (160 miles north of Yulin). Here he indicated the point where the river bends south and becomes the boundary between Shensi and Shansi provinces.

"What Chinese troops are opposing the Japanese in Mongolia?" I asked.

"Our force is called the North Route Army," he replied. "General Fu Tso-yi, the Governor of Suiyuan, is the commander, and I am vice-commander, in addition to commanding the New First Army and the 21st Corps. My own army guards the Shensi-Suiyuan border. All of the other troops except General Ma Chan-san's cavalry army, are east of the Yellow river and north of the Wall. General Ma operates in the Ordos desert country to the west of the river."

I asked what he considered to be the mission of the army, and he replied that it was charged with preventing further penetration of the Japanese to the west, guarding the Shensi entrance to China proper, and harassing the garrisons along the railway.

He promised to provide a patrol to escort us to General Ma's headquarters, which was a hundred and seventy miles to the northeast.

Back at our quarters I found an invitation from General Kao Suan-chen to attend a field meet which was to be held by his division on the following day.

The hour was early when we went out to the athletic field which occupied a plain near an attractive tree-shaded pond, over towards the east wall. The deep green of the foliage contrasted sharply with the billows of yellow sand which lay beyond the wall. As we approached the entrance Auyang drew my attention to the American flag which flew beside the Chinese, over the gate. I carried a small one in my haversack, but this was the first time I had seen one flying since I left Hankow.

General Kao met us at the gate. He was short and wore a closely cropped mustache. Greeting us amiably, he led the way across the field past lines of soldiers drawn up in athletic uniforms which consisted of singlets and shorts. At the far side we entered an improvised pavilion made of bamboo and woven straw, and took seats around a table from which we could observe the events. Evidently the 86th Division believed in doing things in style.

But despite all this ceremony General Kao struck me as being a man of simple habits. He was the old-fashioned, practical type of soldier, and had spent most of his life in the northwest, the last twenty years right here in Yulin with the 86th Division. His attitude towards his men was paternalistic, and though he was illiterate he knew human nature, and possessed the knack of inducing men to work together in harmony.

The track and field events got under way forthwith. For the most part they were of the type which are popular in the United States. The events were competitive, with companies and battalions pitted against each other. The stellar affair was a game requiring skill and agility, called "Leaping the Horse. " The dummy "horse" consisted of a leather covered log, seven feet in length, four feet high at the head, and two feet high at the rear. The trick was to run towards the "horse" from the rear, dive through the air so as to land on the horse's head with the hands, and then swing the feet forward through the hands and land standing up in a sand pit. The exercise was performed by companies, with the men following each other at close intervals. Any who failed to land on his feet and maintain his balance received a demerit. It was great fun for both participants and spectators.

"We hold these meets every month," General Kao told me. "Patrol duty along the border is strenuous, and when the troops return here for regular rest periods we try to keep their minds and bodies active by providing athletics, dramatics and schools."

That night we had a chance to see one of their amateur theatrical performances. It was held in an open-air theater, with soldiers playing the parts of actors in an old classic drama, using the costumes and paraphernalia of an ancient dynasty. This was the type of thing which deeply interested Auyang, and the next day I saw him in conference with the leaders of the dramatic group, offering criticism and receiving new ideas from them.

The life here presented another aspect of the contemporary Chinese scene. Neither the army nor the people were concerned particularly with political ideas. But the very remoteness of the place had caused the development of a spirit of camaraderie between officers and men, and between the army and the people, fostered, no doubt, by the paternalistic attitude of the leaders. Essentially these people were concerned with developing their own self-sufficiency, though the army could be depended on to carry out its appointed tasks with devotion so long as it was well paid and cared for.

The Wu T'ing river passes through the Great Wall a few miles north of the city, and General Tun insisted that we see this historic spot. The Chief of Staff, General Hsu, took us out on the following day. South of the Wall sandstone cliffs overlook the river, and below them eucalyptus and weeping willow trees add to the beauty of the setting. Hsiung Shan Ssu, a Ming dynasty temple, is carved out of the sandstone cliff on the east bank, and the cliffs on the opposite bank bear the epigrams of famous sages of history, carved in huge characters, distinguishable three miles away.

The next point of historical interest was the Chun Po T'ai, a pyramid-like structure which stands in majestic solitude close by the Great Wall, and two miles east of the river. It differs from the pyramids in that its sides are terraced, while on the top terrace stands a temple, with roof corners turned up to ward off the devils. Here the generals of the Ming dynasty assembled to receive their final orders for the campaigns against the Mongols. The view from the temple is superb. Off to the north the desert extends as far as the eye can reach, in undulating billows of yellow sand, and to the east and west a line of crumbling watch towers is all that remains of the Great Wall which the Emperor Shih Huang Ti built nearly 2200 years ago.

On the return trip we visited the narrow gorge through which the waters of the Wu T'ing river cascade, after passing beneath the ancient P'u T'o bridge. Buried under the bridge, we were told, are the bodies of emperors of the Five Minor Dynasties (A. D. 907-960).

Time had brought few changes to this remote outpost of the Chinese nation during the past thousand years. But the future would be different. At some early date, no doubt, the waters in this gorge will be harnessed to provide power and irrigation for the undeveloped areas of northern Shensi.

Back at Yulin we visited a unique industrial school, a modern structure terraced into the side of the hill which dominates the east side of the city. Here three hundred boys and girls were being taught how to spin and weave wool, and how to make leather products. The school is operated by the provincial government, and makes excellent blankets, sweaters, gloves, rugs and various types of leather goods.

It was time to be thinking about moving along to General Ma's headquarters, and our hosts promised a patrol for the next day.

I went for a stroll alone in the streets that evening and encountered a Spanish priest who had been in the northwest for forty-five years. He spoke no English; so I resurrected my Nicaraguan Spanish, and as we walked along together he related some of the local gossip.

"See that building ahead of us?" He indicated a curious structure, three stories high, which straddled the street. "That is a memorial to a former commander of the 86th Division, who committed suicide," he chuckled at the incongruity of raising a memorial to a suicide.

A one-legged man was brushing the street in front of a saddle shop with a handful of brush twigs. The venerable father thrust a thumb in his direction, "Know how that man lost his leg? He escaped twice from prison and they cut it off so he couldn't run any more."

We passed a camel caravan, and my companion gave it a wide berth. "Never get near the heels of a camel," he warned. "Often camels are mean, and they have a vicious kick."

Father Francisco, as he told me to call him, had little interest in the outside world. Years of isolation had caused him to adapt himself to his environment. He lived alone with a few servants in the church compound, surrounded by a high wall, and his interests were centered here, where he had spent most of his life. Of China and Mongolia he had a vast store of knowledge, and I would like to have spent more time with him.

III

General Tun had been lavish in his hospitality, and now he not only provided us with a mounted patrol, but sent each of us a blanket, sweater and leather despatch case, products of the industrial school.

We selected our own animals from a group that had been provided, and Wang Yang entertained the crowd which had gathered to see us off by selecting a high-strung animal that took the bit in his teeth when Wang had only one foot in the stirrup. Wang landed in a heap at the feet of the Chief of Staff. But he came up smiling, as usual, and a second try proved more successful. With shouts of farewell, we got organized and headed northeast, following the general line of the Great Wall.

Our first objective was Shenmu, a trading center on the Mongolian border eighty-eight miles away. Progress the first day was slow for whether on foot or horseback we sank into the sand at every step. That night we stayed in a cave village, carved out of the side of a loess gulch.

We reached the dividing line between the desert and the loess country on the following day. In one valley the line of demarcation was so sharp that the north side was sand and the south was clear loess. At a village in this valley we stopped for a breakfast of millet gruel. While we were eating we heard a disturbance in the courtyard, and looking out we observed a column of children parading into the yard dressed in the white sack cloth used for mourning. The column was headed by a man who rang a large bell violently as he led his charges into one room of the house and then another. The purpose, Auyang said, was to drive out the devil of a man who had died in an adjacent house.

On the third day we reached Shenmu, a county seat located in a fertile valley, with picturesque temples crowning the adjacent hills. It had been an important rug-making center before the war, but now fewer caravans of wool came from Mongolia, and the occupation of the rail lines in Shansi had cut off the markets. A cavalry patrol from General Ma's army was waiting to conduct us north over the remaining eighty miles to his headquarters.

As we proceeded north the character of the soil changed from loess to rock and hard pan. We jogged along easily, following valleys for the most part, and on the morning of the third day we reached the nondescript village occupied by the headquarters of the T'ing Tsin Army (always at the front).

The soldiers of our patrol, and those we met, were Manchurians, or men from the northern provinces of China, and rode their horses as though they were part of them. Each man wore a badge on the sleeve of the left arm, above the elbow, which bore the letters "T A" above a diagonal line, and the letters "K D," below it, with a numeral. They indicated that the wearer was a member of a cavalry division of the T'ing Tsin Army.

We encountered many Mongolian and Manchurian soldiers, as we entered the village, who were wearing the olive drab uniform of the Japanese puppet armies. They did not appear to be prisoners, and I asked the patrol leader for an explanation. He grinned and replied: "They've deserted the Japanese and come over to us."

Proceeding to a large compound which belonged to a county official, we were met by General Ma's Chief of Staff, General Wang T'ing-san, a studious appearing man of fifty, whose actions were slow and deliberate. General Ma, he explained, was indisposed, and would see us on the following day. He had, however, sent over his personal orderly to assure that we were made comfortable.

The orderly was a funny little man, in his middle fifties, I judged, who had personally attended the General for a score of years. He had a staccato manner of speaking, and his hands were always busy gesticulating, buttoning and unbuttoning his tunic, or toying with a short ox-tail riding crop. Apparently he used narcotics in some form, probably opium, for he was subject to alternate periods of depression and elation. In the latter condition he delighted to stand in the middle of the courtyard, draw himself up to his full height of five feet two inches, and with Napoleonic dignity direct the lesser orderlies to perform certain chores which had not been done to his taste. Then he would come to my room and gossip aimlessly about life in the army, or regale me with stories of the prowess of his general.

From him I learned that the General was sixty-two, and that he smoked a little opium each day—not enough to hurt him, you understand—just sufficient to assure him a few moments of relaxation. He arose at dawn, but he slept in the afternoon, except when the army was on the march. The army had just returned from a march which had taken it clear around the Japanese garrisons that occupy the railroad. They had crossed the railroad west of Kweihua, cutting it as they went, then proceeded fifty miles north, turned west, and ridden out to Wuyuan, a hundred miles west of Paot'o, where they had replenished their food supply. They had returned here by a route that took them south of Paot'o.

In the evening the boys and I wandered through the narrow cobblestone streets, and I was able to sense the spirit of this army. The men walked with the slight swagger typical of cavalrymen, and there was apparently no attempt to keep their uniforms either neat or uniform. But they were good-humored, and their morale was excellent. Those who were not natives of Manchuria came from Suiyuan, Chahar or Jehol—a great many from Jehol. They were eager to fight their way back to their homes, an ambition which, I learned later, was shared by their General. It was this hope which sustained them, for they had received no indoctrination which associated the war in their minds with a crusade for the integrity of their race and nation, or with the development of a better way of life. They were fighting to regain their homes, and their devotion was to the leaders they knew personally, and who had proved their skill and courage in battle. The brutality of the Japanese army had done much to stimulate their will to fight.

IV

The Chief of Staff came over early the next morning and cleared up a good deal of the confusion that was in my mind about the relation of the Mongols to the war.

It seemed that out of the two million people in Suiyuan, only 150,000 were Mongols. The balance were Chinese (Hans, he called them) who had come in after the railway was built, and who lived in the railway zone and south of it.

The Mongols were organized into Leagues (Mengs), and each League contained a number of tribes, called Banners, each numbering from 1,000 to 7,000. The Mongols, he said, were nomads whose chief occupation was raising cattle, sheep, goats and horses. There were two major Leagues in Suiyuan, the Wu Lan Ch'a Pu Meng, in the north, with Yuen Wang as Prince, and the I Ke

General Ma Chan-san, the elusive Manchurian leader whose death was officially reported to the Japanese Emperor by the army leaders in 1932. He now commands a Cavalry Army on the Mongolian front.

Chia Meng, in the area south of the Yellow river, with Sa Wang as Prince.

The Japanese had seized on certain differences which had arisen between the Princes and the Chinese government, based largely on the fact that Chinese immigrants had deprived the Mongols of rich grazing lands, to drive a wedge between the Princes and China. Many Princes were susceptible to bribery, and had gone over to the Japanese. The most important of these was Teh Wang, who was now head of the puppet government in Chahar, with headquarters at Kalgan.

The hope of the Chinese, the Chief of Staff thought, lay in the young Mongols, who desired to break away from the feudalistic control of the Princes, and who were keenly aware of the dangers of a Japanese over-lordship. General Ma had been working with these younger Mongols, and many who had joined the Japanese puppet army had since come over to the T'ing Tsin army. The total number was estimated to be four thousand.

This was a startling piece of news. If General Ma could continue to absorb the enemy's puppet troops it would be a greater contribution to the Chinese cause than victories on the battle field.

In the afternoon the Chief of Staff took us over to General Ma's quarters, in the wing of a Lama temple. As we entered the courtyard a short, wiry figure in the uniform of a general (oblong gold tabs on each side of the collar, at the front, with two gold stars superimposed on each) danced lightly down the steps of the building across the way, and without ceremony came out to meet us with impetuous courtesy. Here was the man whose death had been reported officially to the Japanese Emperor by a harried army commander six years before. For a corpse he was extraordinarily agile.

The story of General Ma's resistance to the Japanese invasion of Manchuria in 1931 has become a legend which is known throughout the nation. Charged with defending the northernmost province of Manchuria, he refused to capitulate to the invaders. They tried to bribe him, and eventually he allowed himself to be persuaded to accept the post of Minister of War in the Manchoukuo government. One day, after he had secured a large sum of money and a considerable quantity of arms and ammunition from the Japanese, he quietly went off on an inspection trip. Returning to his army in north Manchuria he declared himself in revolt against the puppet government and its overlords, and continued to resist until he was driven over the border into Soviet Russia. In one battle his horse and saddle were captured, and the Japanese thinking (and hoping) that he was dead, officially reported his demise to the Emperor.

General Ma led us into a room which served as an office, and we seated ourselves around a table, the General sitting forward on the edge of his chair with an attitude of eager intensity. His was a dynamic personality, and he consciously dominated any group he was with. He talked with machine-gun rapidity, displaying a keen sense of humor. These spasmodic surges of humor caused the parchment-like skin of his face to break into a maze of fine wrinkles, and spread the wide, short-clipped mustache into a long line of gray and black speckles. His black, bead-like eyes burned with intensity, yet there was in them both shrewdness and kindliness.

Without waiting for questions he burst into a narration of what he had done since emerging from retirement at the beginning of the war. There was no false modesty about him, and yet his frank egotism was not obnoxious because it emanated from a child-like quality of unquestioned self-confidence. I could see why his men adored him, for he was completely honest and devoid of fear.

"When the Japanese attacked Lukouchiao," he said, "I was living in retirement in Tientsin. I had returned there after retiring into Russia from north Manchuria. Immediately I offered my services to Generalissimo Chiang Kai-shek, and was asked by him to go to Tatung (north Shansi) and assume command of one of the cavalry brigades in General Ho Chu-kuo's division. I went to Nanking for a conference first, for I hoped to persuade the Generalissimo to allow me to lead a cavalry army into Jehol. But that was not feasible. I arrived in Tatung on the 23d of August and took command of the brigade. General Tsao Chun-sho was also there with part of his Shansi-Suiyuan cavalry army. But we were poorly organized and unprepared to make a strong resistance.

"We fought delaying actions as the Japanese advanced to the west along the railway. They had three Manchurian divisions opposed to us. General Li Ta-chow, who commands the People's Army of Suiyuan, and a Mongol leader named Pai Hu-feng, came to our assistance, but after a three-day battle Kweihua fell, and we retired to Paot'o, at the end of the railroad.

"General Tsao Chun-sho had now been recalled to Shansi by Yen Hsi-shan. The Japanese brought up a motorized force of 2,000 men, and Paot'o fell on the 20th of October.

"I then retired to Wuyuan, one hundred miles further west, and began to reorganize my army."

This narrative was delivered in explosive sentences, embroidered with personal opinions of the various Chinese leaders, some of them most uncomplimentary.

"General, how about these troops I see in your army who are wearing Japanese uniforms?" I asked.

He chuckled and replied: "Manchurians and Mongols are my friends. They don't want to serve the Japanese, but many had no alternative. And others had no political knowledge. But they know that they can trust me, and they know that I will fight to the bitter end to get their homes back for them. I send out my emissaries to talk to those who are serving in the Japanese puppet armies, and these emissaries convince them that if they unite with China we can drive the Japanese out.

"The first group to come over was brought by Ching Te-chuan. He now commands one of my divisions. At present about four thousand men of my army were formerly with the Japanese. They came over with their arms and ammunition. Just today a Mongol named Han Yu-chun brought his company of 400 to us. You will see him at dinner. And a month ago a Manchurian named Mo Sing-ya led his entire regiment to my army. He also commands a division now."

General Ma then told how he had helped relieve the pressure of the February-March drive of the Japanese in Shansi by recapturing Tokato (on the Yellow river in Suiyuan) and threatening Salachi. He had been hampered by a shortage of ammunition, but when a supply arrived early in April he had set forth on a series of raids which had taken him to the north of the railroad. Salachi was captured and the railroad cut. Moving north, he occupied Wu Chuan, and then turned west and rode out to Wuyuan, the grain growing region west of Paot'o.

I had heard that the Japanese had offered a reward for General Ma's head. Was the story true?

The General chortled. Yes, they had posted a reward of $500,000. The Imperial General Staff was embarrassed by the liveliness of the ghost of the man they had solemnly reported as dead. They couldn't officially recognize the existence of this thorny warrior, but they had promised the reward to any who would bring in his head.

Auyang had accompanied me to the interview, and now the other four boys arrived for dinner. The General was interested in their work and asked Liu and Auyang to organize a cultural group in his army, and to give some advice on political training. They agreed to do this, and a conference was held later in the evening.

The Mongol leader, Han Yu-chun, arrived as we were going in to dinner. I liked this young Mongol. He held his fine head with an air of quiet and inoffensive dignity. His wide-spaced eyes were frank and intelligent, and his mouth was both firm and sensitive.

The food that was placed before us was mysterious in form and seemingly endless in variety. There were, General Ma informed us, ninety-six different parts of the sheep which were edible. He had, however, directed that the cook serve only the choice portions. The grilled kidneys and cubes of lean meat were delicious, but I drew the line at stewed sheeps' eyes.

It was the fly season and two soldiers wafted long horsehair plumes over the table to keep the huge insects from resting too long on the food. The rhythmic movement of the plumes reminded me of the punkahs used to fan Indian and African potentates.

After dinner, as we stood around the courtyard digesting the sumptuous meal and belching our pleasure in proper Chinese fashion, a middle-aged man of peasant type, wearing a slovenly uniform with the markings of a general, entered the yard, and was greeted explosively by General Ma.

"Meet one of our heroes," he cried to me. "This is La T'ai Liu."

Liu looked uncomfortable and ill at ease. As the General related his story he shifted uneasily from one foot to the other, a deprecating grin playing about his homely, honest face.

His full name, the General said, was Liu Chin-san, but so extraordinary had been his achievements that the people of his home town of La T'ai had awarded him the name of the town as a token of their regard.

It seems that when the Japanese entered La T'ai they killed Liu's son and raped his daughter. Liu was deeply moved, and instead of accepting this insult to his family he decided to do something about it. As the days passed he watched warily for an opportunity to strike at the ruthless oppressors. One night he discovered four soldiers asleep in his home, with no one on guard. With a knife he used for butchering sheep he killed them. Already he had a plan. Calling on some relatives to help him, he formed a small Partisan group, armed the men with the rifles he had captured, and led them against a small Japanese garrison. As the group captured more rifles he recruited men from among the neighbors. His band grew to the size of a platoon, a company, a battalion. General Ma heard of his work and asked him to join the T'ing Tsin army. Now he commanded a brigade in the army.

As I went to my quarters that evening I contemplated these two new elements, each of great potential significance to the cause of Chinese resistance, which had just come to my attention. There were thousands of Chinese peasants who were equally as resourceful as Liu, and who had suffered comparable injury to their sensibilities. What a potential explosive they were, especially in those areas controlled by the Japanese. And this practice of the Japanese puppet troops of deserting to the Chinese. By what means could the Japanese combat this tendency? I was to have more knowledge of this matter the next day.

Fortuitously, Mo Sing-ya, the young Manchurian leader who had brought his regiment over to the T'ing Tsin army, came to town the day after my conference with General Ma, and the latter sent him over to see me.

He was an attractive fellow, twenty-eight years old, and bursting with geniality. He talked easily, and with enthusiasm.

He had graduated from the Liaoning Military Academy, in Manchuria, eight years before, and at the time the Japanese invaded his native land, in September, 1931, he was in Peip'ing with the Young Marshal, Chang Hsueh-liang. He returned to Manchuria and fought with Partisan forces for two years, but became convinced that their cause was hopeless until outside support in the form of money and supplies was received. So he changed his plan.

He enlisted in the puppet army of Manchuria with the idea, he assured me, of deserting to the Chinese forces at an opportune time. He was sent to an officers' training school, and because of his previous military experience he soon became an instructor. For two years he was kept under close observation by the Japanese officers, but finally they were convinced of his loyalty, and he was promoted rapidly to the post of regimental commander. In December, 1937, his regiment was sent to the Suiyuan front.

On the 26th of April he learned that one of General Ma's units was approaching. He had already discussed with his officers and men the matter of going over to the Chinese, and they had agreed unanimously. There were ten Japanese "advisers" with the regiment, but a force of one thousand was due to arrive in a few days. The time had come to strike.

Waiting until the day the Japanese re-enforcements were due, they killed the "advisers" and ambushed the approaching column. Then they fled to the hills, and two days later contacted General Ma's army.

It was a stirring story of courage, ingenuity and patriotism. As he finished it the Mongol, Han Yu-chun arrived. I wondered if he knew Teh Wang, the Mongol who was the chief puppet at Kalgan.

Yes, Han knew Teh, and he had talked with him earlier in the year.

"Is there any chance that Teh may come to the Chinese side?" I asked.

Han didn't think so. "Teh is a very unhappy man," he said. "He agreed to co-operate with the Japanese because he felt that the Mongols had not been treated fairly by the Chinese government, and he hoped to gain certain advantages for his people. But the Japanese have not kept their promises, and furthermore, Teh is kept under close surveillance. He told me that there were only three Chinese who could save him: Chang Hsueh-liang (the Young Marshal who held Generalissimo Chiang under detention at Sian), Ho Ying-chin (the present Minister of War), and Ma Chan-san."

I had heard Chang Hsueh-liang referred to with affection by his former Manchurian comrades, and with respect by Mongols and Chinese. Evidently his name carried great weight with these people of the north. It might be possible for the Generalissimo to use him to advantage here, instead of punishing him for the Sian kidnaping by keeping him in detention.

V

General Fu Tso-yi, I had learned, was at Ch'ing Shui Ho, east of the Yellow river, and was preparing for a counter-offensive. I was eager to see him before he became engrossed in active military operations, and General Ma said he would send us with a patrol to General Fu's headquarters.

On the way up from the south I had rather suspected that Chiang Kai-shek would use this North Route army for a counter-offensive against the Japanese right flank while his adversary was busy trying to break through at Hsuchowfu. I had secretly hoped that by coming to Mongolia at this time I might be on hand to observe such an operation. Strategically the movement would be sound, for the Japanese had drained their garrisons in other parts of China in order to assure that the failure at Taierchwang would not be repeated at Hsuchowfu. Thus, by attacking the garrisons along the Suiyuan railway there would be a good chance for success, and in any event it would probably alarm the Japanese and draw troops from the eastern front. Perhaps this prospective move of General Fu's was the forerunner of such a counter-offensive.

We decided to leave on the morning following the day when I had talked with Mo Sing-ya. We prepared our equipment for the trail, sewed on buttons and washed clothes.

At one of their private conferences the five boys had decided they would like to do something for the wounded here, and they asked what I thought about it. Grand idea, I said, and we collaborated in preparing a package which contained cigarettes, candy, peanuts and nuts. There wasn't much of a variety to choose from in this town.

The gesticulating major-domo of the orderlies led us to the hospital, which was a private residence which had been taken over for the purpose. The wounded lay on k'angs in the dark, cheerless rooms, fanning themselves to keep the flies away. Most of them had been wounded during the last foray of the army north of the railroad.

Their wounds were neatly bandaged, and their accommodations were not as bad as some I had seen in other parts of China. But as we strolled along from room to room the chief surgeon suddenly burst in upon us, and in a highly excited manner wanted to know what we thought we were doing. Explanations failed to assuage his ire. We should have requested permission from him, be informed us angrily, before coming to the hospital.

The episode was a striking example of the part that "face" plays with the old-fashioned Chinese. If we had notified him of our intention to visit the hospital he would have spent a day preparing the place for inspection. By coming unannounced we had seen the hospital under normal conditions. He felt that he had lost "face."

I paid a farewell call on General Ma that evening, but the next morning when we were preparing to leave the General entered in riding attire, with his staff trailing at his heels. He would escort us on the first five miles of our journey, he said.

We made a colorful picture as we left the town. With General Ma were two of his divisional commanders, as well as his staff and coterie of orderlies. Some wore the uniform of the Japanese puppet army, with the peaked forage cap. The General sat his strapping bay stallion as though the two were molded of one piece. He might be dynamic in his conversation and informal in his hospitality, but on horseback he was the commander, erect, stern and rather formidable.

General Mo Sing-ya, young Manchurian who brought his Japanese sponsored regiment over to the Chinese side in 1938, and who now commands a division in General Ma Chan-san's army.

"La T'ai" Liu, the fifty-two year old Chinese peasant of La T'ai, Suiyuan province, Inner Mongolia, who recruited a brigade of volunteers with which to oppose the Japanese.

Where the trail turned out of the valley he bade us farewell, a gallant figure, a burning patriot and an implacable enemy.

We rode on towards Ho Kiu, the city which stands at the extreme northwest corner of Shansi, where the Great Wall crosses the Yellow river. General Fu's rear echelon was there, and would provide an escort to Ch'ing Shui Ho.

The distance to the Yellow river was about forty-five miles, but most of the route lay through valleys, and we moved rapidly. As we approached the river the terrain became more rugged, and a good deal of shale rock appeared in the hills. Climbing a long slope we entered a village near the top and passed through a moon gate (circular in shape) which pierced the ridge. The view which burst upon us was breath-taking, both in its majestic beauty and because it was so unexpected.

Two miles distant the broad waters of the Yellow river swept down from the north between banks of deep green foliage. Below us a multitude of cone-shaped, stratified hills spread out to the north and south, the reds, browns and tans of their strata brilliant in the late afternoon sunlight. We paused at the top for a few minutes to drink in this master painting.

Zig-zagging down the ridge we rode out through the picturesque hillocks to the river's edge, where a junk waited for us. Horses went over the side with us, and boatmen sculled us across, aided by the current. On the opposite bank we remounted and rode towards the walled city of Ho Kiu (which would correspond in location to Port Arthur, Ontario, northeast of the Minnesota border).

VI

Bad news awaited us at Ho Kiu. We suspected it when the Chief of Staff of the 35th Army, General Miao Yu-t'ien, met us in the city. The Japanese had initiated an offensive of their own, and the army was moving south from Ch'ing Shui Ho. The set-back was only temporary, he told us, but it would be a day or two before General Fu could see us, and in the meantime it was wise to remain here. The Chief of Staff was very evasive, and he vetoed all suggestions that we go to the front.

The next surprise was the news that a Norwegian missionary was living in the city. It had been arranged for me to stay with him, while the boys were to occupy an adjacent house. I demurred at the idea of being separated from them even by this distance, until I saw Peter Torjesen, the missionary. He had not seen another foreigner for nearly a year, and he was starved for knowledge of the outside world. The boys understood.

This sojourn at Ho Kiu proved to be one of the doldrums into which we occasionally slipped in the course of the trip. It was difficult to obtain facts about the military situation. The Chief of Staff was courteous, and he did all the conventional things a host should, but he did not provide reliable information. He was of the old school, given to evasion, procrastination and deceit—all with a bland smile and a gracious manner.

The city had been held by the Japanese for a short time in March, and the Magistrate, also a product of the old order, fed us much propaganda about the atrocities they had committed (they had committed enough without need for exaggeration), and about the courage and efficiency of the county officials.

By the third day I had become uneasy about all this uncertainty. Something had to be done, and I went over to confer with the boys. They, too, were glum, but they had news for me. Auyang had discovered a Ming Hsien unit here. The name meant nothing to me, and they explained that it was a patriotic young people's organization. The objectives were: (1) to foster honesty in public office, (2) to improve the welfare of the people, and, (3) to promote better co-operation among the people for resistance to the invasion. The organization numbered about eighty thousand members in the country, and they were sworn to dedicate their lives to its objectives. They worked quietly, and sought to insinuate themselves into village, county, provincial and national organizations in which inefficiency and corruption were evident. Only members knew the identity of other members, and Auyang had found six here in the city.

The leader of the local group came over for a talk, and from him we learned the truth about the local situation. He was a quiet, frank youngster, and wholly unprepossessing.

General Fu Tso-yi's army was fighting at P'ien Kwan, only twenty-five miles to the northeast, and the battle was evidently going against the Chinese. The Chief of Staff was here to prepare for the retirement of the army, either across the river, or to the south.

We then learned of what had happened here in March, when the Japanese came in. The city had been defended by General Ho Chu-kuo's army, which retired across the river ahead of the invaders. The troops were undisciplined and poorly cared for, and before leaving they looted the town and abused the people. Much of the damage which had been reported to me as having been done by the Japanese, was actually the work of the Chinese troops. Even the Magistrate had run away to Shensi. But, the youth said with a wry smile, he would not do so again for the Ming Hsien had pointed out to him the error of his ways, and they were keeping him under observation. In case the Japanese entered, the Magistrate's office would be set up in the hills outside the city where he could continue to look after the affairs of the people in the rural districts.

Later, in other parts of China, I frequently encountered members of the Ming Hsien. They represented all shades of political thought, but invariably I found them to be honest and dependable.

On the fourth day of our stay the atmosphere of the city became tense with apprehension, and Torjesen prepared to take women and children into his compound. The boys and I decided that a decision must be made. We had hoped to be able to move east through southern Suiyuan, but obviously the guerrillas were not sufficiently well organized for this, so the alternative was to move southeast to K'o Lan, where we could make contact with Ho Lung's division of the Eighth Route Army. I went to the Chief of Staff.

He was not so bland now, and he admitted that a battle was in progress at P'ien Kwan. I requested him to telephone General Fu and say that I desired permission to join him at the front today, but if that was not considered feasible would the General authorize a patrol to escort my party to K'o Lan, starting tomorrow, a distance of a hundred miles. The call was made, and General Fu authorized the patrol. Evidently he was anxious to have us out of the way.

At daylight the next day we were packing the mules when units of the 35th Division streamed into the city. The Japanese had captured P'ien Kwan and were moving on Ho Kiu. The populace became panic stricken, and as we moved out of the city to the south many joined our column, carrying a few of their belongings.

The sequel to this story of Ho Kiu I did not learn for several days. The Japanese did not capture the city on this occasion. A brigade from the Eighth Route Army came up from the south and struck their line of communication, forcing them to double back to P'ien Kwan, where they dug in.

The most pleasant part of the stay here was the opportunity to know Peter Torjesen. He was a man of faith and courage. I learned from people in the city that when the Japanese came in March, Torjesen brought as many women and children into the mission compound as it would hold. He guarded the entrance personally. On several occasions Japanese officers attempted to secure women from the compound, and to each he steadfastly denied permission. When some became insistent and threatened to bring soldiers and take the women by force, he calmly replied: "You'll take them over my dead body." The attempt was never made.

CHAPTER VIII

TEST TUBE FOR NEW CHINA

I

MY experience in Mongolia made it clear why the Chinese effort there had not been more effective. Theoretically China had a group of armies in that region, under the high sounding title of North Route Army. Actually there was little co-operation between the four groups. Ma Chan-san, although a gallant soldier and doing effective work in bringing levies of the puppet armies over to China, was decidedly an individualist. He felt that his prestige entitled him to receive orders directly from the Generalissimo, though he co-operated with General Fu Tso-yi after a fashion. General Ho Chu-kuo was the special representative of Governor Chiang T'ing-wen, of Shensi. Thus, Fu Tso-yi was assured of direct control only over his own 35th Army and that of General Men P'in-yueh. Even the latter was inclined to operate somewhat on his own initiative.

What was needed in Mongolia was a supreme commander who possessed a sound military background, and whose prestige was such that he would command the respect and cooperation of all subordinate commanders, and of the Mongol, Manchurian and Chinese people as well. The alternative was a commander with a big name, and a chief of staff with a comprehensive knowledge of tactics and strategy.

After leaving Ho Kiu our patrol moved south along the east bank of the

Yellow river. We would go first to Pao Teh, fifty miles south, and then turn east and cross the mountains to K'o Lan, another fifty miles.

The patrol was a fair sample of the character of the 35th Army. The men were a good sort, but they had no money and were evidently expected to forage for food in the country. As a result the people kept their food hidden. Under pressure they would produce a little millet, but they were sullen and far from being co-operative.

At the village where we stopped for the night I asked a peasant if he could get a chicken for our group. I had heard that there were some in the vicinity. No, he said, this was a very poor country. There were no chickens. I suspected that it was a question of money, and placed a few coins in his hand. His face brightened momentarily, then resumed its doleful expression. But he sidled off, mumbling that he would see what could be done. In half an hour he returned and pulled a chicken from beneath his shirt.

We reached Pao Teh at noon the next day. There are really two cities here. The old walled city stands high on a bluff on the south side of a valley which comes from the east, while the new city lies in the valley itself, close beside the Yellow river. On the Shensi bank, a mile away, sprawls another city—Fu Kuo. The importance of this site is due to a caravan route, which comes down from Mongolia, and extends eastward to T'aiyuanfu, the capital of Shansi.

Pao Teh had been twice occupied by the Japanese, and on the last occasion they had burned the old city, on the bluff, and part of the new city. But of this I was to learn more from the Norwegian missionary, George Rinvold, whom I found here.

Rinvold was outstanding, both as a man and as a missionary. He was living here with his wife and four children, three charming girls of eight, six and four years, and a baby boy. Like Torjesen at Ho Kiu, they had not seen a foreigner in nearly a year.

I declined an invitation to stay with them, explaining that I did not wish to leave the five boys. "But," exclaimed Rinvold, "we expect the boys to come, too. We have ample room for all of you." I sensed his sincerity, and was pleased, for I had encountered missionaries who were reluctant to admit Chi-

Students of a Mongolian and Tibetan school in Wu T'ai Shan, Shansi province. These children study each day the Chinese, Mongolian and Tibetan languages.

Part of the student body of the Military Academy which is located behind the Japanese lines, in the Wu T'ai mountains. Most of these men were university students from colleges in the Peip'ing-Tientsin area. They are singing a patriotic song.

nese into their homes, evidently feeling that their mission was to evangelize rather than fraternize. Of course we would come, I said.

We spent a delightful evening in this hospitable home. It was a little piece of Norway set down in this remote, dust-blown region of northwest China, but the Chinese of the city came and went as though it were the home of one of their own people. Rinvold's influence in the community was profound.

In addition to his church he had organized an industrial training school, equipped with eleven hand looms, which were engaged at this time in making bandages. They needed some No. 16 cotton thread, Rinvold said, and as soon as I got to a town where there was a military radio I sent off a message to our Ambassador, in Hankow, to see what the Red Cross could do about it.

As wounded began to arrive in the city Rinvold organized a hospital which could care for them while they were waiting for transportation to the south. It was still operating when I came through.

He told me about the Japanese occupation of Pao Teh. When they came the first time, early in March, they left a garrison of nineteen men in the walled city. A few weeks later a Chinese detachment crossed the river and exterminated the garrison. A second Japanese column from the east recaptured the city, and in retaliation for the loss of the garrison the commander decided to burn it. Rinvold pleaded with him not to take such drastic action, but he was adamant. Then Rinvold asked him to spare the block in which the mission was located. The commander finally agreed to do so if Rinvold would sign a statement which said in effect that the commander of this detachment of the Imperial Japanese Army had graciously acceded to the request of the missionary to spare his property. But Rinvold wanted to be sure that the promise would be fulfilled before placing his signature on the document, and he stalled for time. While he was still with the commander one of his Chinese evangelists entered and informed him that the building next to the church was already on fire. The commander, he told me, was much embarrassed.

Rinvold accompanied us for the first five miles of our journey the next morning. Then, with a pat on the shoulder and a quiet "God bless you," he turned back alone to return to his family and duty. A gallant Christian, with a wife no less plucky. On the evening before she had made a remark which impressed me deeply. "This is our duty, and we are glad to be here," she said, "but—" as though she were thinking aloud, "I *would* like to talk to a foreign woman once in a while."

II

We virtually sang our way into K'o Lan. The boys were now inured to life on the trail, and were in fine fettle. Auyang would strike up a song, and the others would fall in line. Soon all would be singing, suiting the rhythm to the cadence of their step. It was exhilarating.

After our depressing experience along the Yellow river, the atmosphere we found at K'o Lan was like a spring tonic. It was alive with optimism, happiness and good will.

K'o Lan was a mobilization center for northwest Shansi, and there functioned here a general mobilization committee whose members included representatives of the Kuomintang and Communist parties and officials of the Shansi government. It was probably the best example of co-operation of men and women of varying political opinions that I saw in China. All possessed the true spirit of self-sacrifice, and all were richly imbued with the desire to save China from foreign domination. These leaders had learned the value of self-abnegation and of co-operative effort, and they had experienced the inner satisfaction that derived from the knowledge that no one within their orbit of influence enjoyed advantages which were not available to all. Consequently, they inspired confidence, and the ethical doctrines they practised were adopted whole-heartedly by the people.

The most forceful figure in this scene was the chairman of the general mobilization committee, General Su Fan-t'ing, a member of the Kuomintang Party. He was a man of high integrity, earnest, thoughtful, energetic and self-effacing. He was heartily supported by the governor of this administrative district, which comprised several counties, Yang Chi-hsien, a man of paternalistic proclivities.

This experience at K'o Lan served to re-emphasize the importance of integrity in leadership, and the relative unimportance of ideologies. Above all it emphasized the value of individual self-discipline in developing an equitable and happy social relationship.

The high point of our stay here was a mass meeting which was held in a pouring rain. I had agreed to speak, and when we reached the field we found between twenty-five hundred and three thousand people standing around informally, singing "Now's the Time for Sacrifice."

Realizing by now that the Chinese judge a talk largely by its length, I spoke for an hour. Occasionally a youth would break in peremptorily to shout a slogan, as if to revive the audience. At the end a twelve-year-old boy was invited to lead in the singing of another song. With consummate self-confidence he stepped out, announced the title, raised his hands, counted "one, two," and they were off.

The rain continued to fall, but despite this inconvenience the crowd remained for another hour and a half to see a patriotic drama which was enacted on an improvised stage. People with such indifference to personal comfort can absorb a lot of punishment.

III

Lin San, the poet, had been having trouble with his feet, and now he decided to accept an invitation to remain here and work with the general mobilization committee.

The boys and I had decided that our best chance to get across Shansi and into Hopei was to go through the Wu T'ai region, which I had visited in the winter. Apparently the Eighth Route Army was the only guerrilla force which had organized the areas behind the Japanese lines. In order to carry out this plan it was first necessary to go to Ho Lung's headquarters, which was at Lan Hsien, thirty-five miles away. We covered the distance in a day.

On my previous visit my chief impression of Ho Lung had been that of a swashbuckler. Now I came to know him better, and I found that beneath the outward appearance of bravado there was tenderness and an earnest sense of responsibility.

His division had been fighting continuously since I had seen him, cutting the enemy's communications between Tat'ung and T'aiyuanfu, raiding garrisons hither and yon, and harassing those columns which attempted to penetrate the hinterland. One of his brigades had moved a hundred and seventy miles northeast, into the heart of the Japanese-occupied region, and was now fighting in Chahar province, in Inner Mongolia.

Ho Lung showed the strain of this strenuous program. He had lost weight, and his manner was less buoyant, but he had not lost his optimism or his confidence in the soundness of his tactics or ethical doctrines.

With customary efficiency and despatch Ho Lung arranged for a patrol to escort us through the Japanese lines along the T'ung P'u railway, and into the Wu T'ai region. In a few days we were en route northeast, over the trail I had traversed in February. We would go to a small town in the hills near the railroad, a distance of ninety miles, where a pack train was being assembled, and make the crossing on the night of June twenty-second.

We stopped one night at the headquarters of the First Cavalry Army, of Shansi, so that I might accept an invitation from General Tsao Chun-sho to inspect his training schools. On my previous trip I had observed some of his troops on the trail, and had been impressed by their soldierly appearance and professional attitude, which were superior to those of the general run of provincial troops. Being pressed for time, I had sent the General a card complimenting him on his achievement. Evidently he remembered.

In appearance General Tsao was far from suggesting the dashing cavalry commander, for he weighed in the neighborhood of two hundred and thirty pounds. Like most heavy men, he was good-natured, and I liked his frank, open-minded attitude.

He candidly admitted that at the beginning of the war his army was not well trained or properly indoctrinated, and it had been severely defeated in

Suiyuan. Retiring into Shansi he had met Ho Lung, and from him had learned the principles of partisan warfare. For the next four months he put his army through an intensive course of training, laying emphasis on the individual self-discipline and ethical philosophy employed by the Eighth Route Army. His army had been transformed from strictly professional soldiers who had no interest outside of pay and emoluments into a well integrated organization with a soul and a consciousness of national purpose.

I inspected his officers' training school and the training center for regiments and brigades. Officers and men were alert, self-respecting, energetic and co-operative. Six months ago these same officers would have been domineering, and the men would have been listless, their faces wearing a hang-dog expression.

The army was now actively participating in operations against the Japanese, using with intelligence the effective measures of guerrilla warfare.

We moved on towards the rendezvous point near the railroad. As we approached we began to overtake pack trains, moving in groups of twenty-five and thirty animals. These trains would cross the lines with us.

A day was spent at the rendezvous waiting for the detachments to assemble—a peculiarly restful day in the home of a peasant woman eighty-eight years old. When we first entered the courtyard we were aware that here was the home of someone who loved beauty, for the yard was a bower of flowers. Presently a little old lady came out to greet us, a knitted shawl about her shoulders. Her frail hands were delicately shaped, her feet had been bound since childhood, and her face was Madonna-like in its serenity. Although she had never before seen a foreigner, she greeted me with a friendliness that made me feel I had known her all my life. She was a garrulous soul and loved to sit on her k'ang, from where she could see her beloved flowers through a window, while she talked endlessly of her children, grand-children, great-grand-children—and of flowers.

With a little time on our hands Wang Yang and I scouted the village to see if we could find food to supplement our regular ration of millet. The people were poor, the houses dingy, and the streets unkempt. Down by the river were two grist mills, with a small canal diverting water to operate their horizontal water-wheels. We canvassed the town, found a few eggs at one place, a handful of wheat flour at another, and then discovered a small garden where we got some tsin tsai, a grass-like vegetable. Returning triumphantly, we turned the result of our labors over to Ching, Liu and Auyang, who prepared a scrumptious meal.

That night we moved three miles further down the valley to the point where the column was being organized for the sally through the lines. Almost immediately we came upon the rear of the column of pack animals. As we made our way past them I counted three hundred and fifty.

Up ahead we found the battalion that would escort us. It had come over from Wu T'ai the preceding day, and the men wore the new green cotton uniform of the Wu T'ai Partisans. The commander was a wisp of a lad, named Li Ho-fei, whom I had met on my first trip. He greeted me like a long-lost brother. Only twenty-two, he was a veteran campaigner, and handled this assignment with ability and celerity.

We would cross between Kwo Hsien and Yuan P'ing, and Mao, the guerrilla leader of this district west of the railroad, had already sent detachments to attack the Japanese garrisons at both those towns, so as to assure that no patrols would be sent to intercept us.

Almost immediately we started to move, darkness having set in. Again, as on previous crossings, the column was divided into advance guard, main body and rear guard, the pack train being at the tail of the main body.

Commander Li was concerned because I was walking, and presently he sent back a small mule to me. The stirrups were set for a man with legs half the length of mine, and the stirrup straps were of raw hide, and had been secured in tight knots. The column was moving, and in the darkness it was not easy to readjust the straps, so I decided to mount and make the best of the situation. I had just reached the saddle, with my knees hugging my chin, when the frisky animal went into a series of jumping-jack bucks. I landed in a heap in the dust of the road —to the hilarious delight of the boys, each of whom by now had done his stint of biting the dust. Walking, I decided, was a more agreeable means of locomotion.

As we approached the Fu T'o river, now shrunk to half its winter size, guns boomed in the distance on our right and left, telling that the Japanese were responding to the guerrilla's bait, for the latter had no artillery. Other than this no sound save the hoofs of the animals broke the silence of the night. By midnight our two-mile-long column was across, and two hours later we were safely bedded down for the night in a valley village east of the river. It was the easiest crossing of the lines I had yet made.

IV

In the morning we climbed to the plateau on which stands Wu T'ai hsien (eastern end of Lake Superior), passing through valleys rich in pear trees. These were in the county of Kwo, home of the finest pears grown in north China. For a penny we could buy four or five.

En route we stopped one night at the headquarters of Tsao Er-lo, commander of this western district of the Wu T'ai area. He had arranged for my passage through the lines in February, and it was he who had supervised this present crossing. He was twenty-six, a native of Shansi, and one of the most active of the guerrilla leaders in this area.

He told of an attack he had led against the Japanese garrison in the walled city of Tai Hsien, on the 14th of April. They carried ladders, and scaled the wails before their presence was discovered. In the fighting they captured the headquarters and carried away 800 grenades and 10,000 rounds of rifle ammunition with a loss of twenty men killed and wounded. The Japanese, he said, lost a captain killed, and ninety-six men killed and wounded.

Food here he said was ample, and consisted of millet, kaoliang and pork.

Tsao provided a fresh patrol to take us to the headquarters of the Border Government (the popular title for the Provisional Government of Shansi, Chahar and Hopei), which was now located in the heart of the Wu T'ai mountains, eighty miles to the northeast. We covered the distance in easy stages.

Life here in this area that was completely surrounded by the Japanese was proceeding smoothly. The people were contented and their spirit was high. Schools were operating in all of the villages, and the people were participating in the functions of government. The village officials were of their own selection, as were the officials of the counties. Taxes were being paid to the provisional government in kind, rather than in cash. The military units no longer secured their provender directly from the people. Each military district had supply depots. Food and supplies came to these depots from the county governments, which in turn received them from the people as payment of taxes. This method removed what had once been a source of friction between the army and the people.

Instead of taking the long circuitous route through the valleys, which I had followed in February, we used a short cut over the higher mountain passes which had been closed in the winter. It meant more climbing, but the magnificent views and the sense of pioneering primeval regions more than compensated for the effort. Towards the end of the third day we descended a barren mountain slope into a refreshingly green pine-ridden valley, and almost immediately came to the picturesque temple village which housed the government.

Nieh Yong-sen, the military commander, and Governor Sung Sao-wen were waiting to greet us, with representative bodies of troops and of various civil organizations. We were lao peng yus (old friends) now, and the reception had the personal quality of a home-coming.

A Guest House had been prepared for our group in a magnificent red, pine-shaded Buddhist temple, and here we devoted the rest of the day to removing the stains of travel and to restoring cleanliness and order to our clothes and kit.

In the evening Nieh came in for a talk. He, too, showed the strain of the activities of the past five months. His lean face was leaner, and there was a sadness about his eyes. Responsibility for the lives of human beings does that to men of feeling.

However, he was even more confident than when I had seen him at Fup'ing, in January. Much had been accomplished in the interim. The Japanese had raided and burned Fup'ing, but several attempts to penetrate the Wu T'ai plateau had been thwarted. The control of the provisional government had been extended to include central Hopei province, and an expeditionary force had actually invaded the regions north and east of Peip'ing, where Japanese control was presumed to be strong.

The progress made in the development of a social, economic and political order designed to enhance the welfare of the people and to increase the effectiveness of their resistance to the invasion was extraordinary. This isolated area had become the test tube for new ideas. Those which seemed to possess merit were given a fair trial. If they worked they were adopted; if not, they were cast out, and others were tried. Although he disclaimed the credit, Nieh's mind and spirit and driving force were at the heart of this policy.

Representative government was the backbone of the political system. During the seven months that the system had been in operation the people had learned sufficiently of the functions of government to be able to select village and county officials. They had also selected the representatives which had met at Fup'ing in January to elect a nine-member political committee to govern the region. Their education was continuing through the many people's organizations, and through the schools that had been set up in every village. Soon they would have the privilege of selecting the officials of the district (which controls ten to fifteen counties) as well.

"How about the economic system, Comrade Nieh?" I asked.

"We have made some progress in this line, too, since you were here," he replied. "We have developed co-operatives, both producers' and consumers', but private enterprise is free to function, and there are many merchants who operate privately. Clothing and munitions factories have been established by the government, and are operated on the co-operative plan. We have co-ordinated agricultural production by causing the people in the various districts to grow the products which the soil is best adapted to produce there. The surpluses are then exchanged so that the people of the entire region may have the benefit of all that the region produces. By encouraging the people to cultivate areas which were not formerly tilled we have increased the productive land within the four railroads by 10,000 acres. We have further increased the areas devoted to food production by prohibiting the growth of poppies for opium, and by limiting the growth of cotton to one-tenth of the tillable soil in any county. Many of these counties formerly grew cotton for export to Japan."

The reference to opium interested me. "Do you mean that opium smoking is prohibited here?" I asked.

"It is prohibited for all under fifty years of age," he replied. "At first we applied the prohibition to everyone. But there are many older people who have had the habit for many years. They cannot be deprived of opium suddenly without dire effects, and we haven't the time or the facilities for curing them in institutions. So the government has taken over the opium supply from the producers, and we ration it out to the addicts. But it is a capital offense for those under fifty to smoke opium."

On my previous trip Governor Sung Sao-wen had outlined plans for the establishment of a government bank. At the time I had thought he was engaging in fantasy, but on the morning following my talk with Nieh, Sung came in and asked if I would like to visit the bank. His face beamed with justifiable pride as he told me of how the feat had been accomplished. Horses were brought and we rode three miles down the valley to the temple where it was located.

Here was a modern guerrilla bank, with tellers, vaults and portable presses for printing the notes.

"The Japanese," he said, "were attempting to accumulate the notes of the three Central Government banks, because they could be used for foreign exchange. When they seized Peip'ing they captured the dies of the Hopei provincial bank, and began printing their own notes. They also established their own Federal Reserve Bank, and used an old Ch'ing dynasty die, which bears a facsimile of Confucius, for printing the notes of that bank. They offered these spurious notes in exchange for the good Chinese notes on the basis of one and a half for one. The people were confused, and they were gradually being cheated. It was to correct these conditions that we decided to set up a bank and issue notes which would be valid only within the region controlled by our government."

Sung paused to show me some of the notes. They were in issues of five yuan (a Chinese dollar, equal at this time to a little less than one American dollar), one yuan, twenty and ten cent denominations. Following the custom prevailing in China, the denomination of each note was printed on one side in Chinese, and on the other in English. The color scheme was brown, blue or pink. Heavy paper was used, and each note bore the legend: "Bank of Shansi, Chahar and Hopei."

"We had the dies cut in Tientsin," continued Sung, with a whimsical smile. "The printing presses also came from cities occupied by the Japanese."

"What is your system for putting these notes into circulation?" I asked.

"We exchange them dollar for dollar for notes of the Central Government banks," he replied. "The latter we place in our vault here."

It was an expedient, but it was working. Later, as I journeyed to the east, I carried some of the notes of this guerrilla bank and found that they were received without question wherever I presented them within the Border region.

Governor Sung showed me some "Salvation" bonds (something on the order of the Liberty bonds sold in the United States during the World War). They were in five, ten and fifty dollar denominations, and were to bear six percent interest, beginning with the termination of the present conflict.

"I'll buy some of these bonds if you can cash American Express Travelers checks," I told him.

Sung looked at Nieh inquiringly. The latter nodded his head. "Certainly," he replied. "We haven't dealt in foreign exchange before, but there is no reason why you shouldn't be the first customer."

The sequel to this story is that I carried the bonds down to Hankow, where they were a great curiosity. When I showed them to Agnes Smedley she came forward with a bright idea— always having in mind schemes for raising money to aid wounded soldiers.

"You give those to me," she said, "and I'll send them to America where they will bring their face value in United States currency. Then we'll have the proceeds turned over to the medical relief fund."

I handed over the bonds, and she fulfilled her promise.

V

There were other things I wanted to know about this youthful government. How was it financed? What was the system of military defense? How had co-operation between landlords and peasants been brought about?

A day or two later Nieh, Sung and Pen Chen, Director of the People's Movement, came over to the Guest House to explain these matters.

"The government has five sources of income," Nieh began. "First, there is a soil tax, then there is a tax on all incomes over one hundred dollars a year. There is a duty on imports and exports, and offices for the collection of these duties are located on the trails which enter the region. The rates vary according to the necessity of the articles. Cigarettes and wine carry a fairly heavy tax. Finally, we derive a fair income from the sale of Salvation bonds.

"The soil tax is twenty-five percent lower than it was before the war. Our total income for the seven months we have been operating aggregates about three million four hundred thousand dollars, while our expenses have been only three millions. This includes the cost of maintaining our army."

"What are the major expenses of the government?" I queried.

Sung replied, "They come under four general headings: Army maintenance, salaries and expenses of government offices, education, and loans for the establishment of factories to manufacture clothing, arms and munitions."

He then explained that salaries were nominal, his own being eighteen dollars a month, while that of magistrates was twelve. Taxes, he said, were based on a graduated scale, determined by the ability of the individual to pay. "Those who have strength contribute strength; those who have money contribute money," he said.

As we talked hsiao kweis brought pears, and stood around to listen to the conversation. The camaraderie here was delightful. An orderly brought Nieh a copy of the daily newspaper, a four sheet mimeograph affair which contained not only local items but a résumé of current developments of the Japanese push towards Hankow, gleaned from the daily radio news letter sent out from Eighth Route Army headquarters.

Continuing with my questions, I asked: "What new developments are there in the People's movement?"

This was in Pen Chen's field, and he replied: "The strength of our resistance, as well as the strength of this government, lies in the people, and we are trying in every way possible to develop the political consciousness of the people. In each village, as in each company of the army, there is a salvation room (sort of a community center) where the people gather to read, sing songs and prepare dramas. One of our problems is the elimination of the element of 'squeeze' (graft) among village and county officials. It takes time for our ethical indoctrination to work, and 'squeeze' has been so prevalent in the past that sometimes even those officials selected by the people stoop to it. Such cases are tried before a people's tribunal in the district concerned. If found guilty, and the amount is over $500, the man is shot; if less than $500 he is imprisoned.

"The commander of the army in each district has orders to aid the farmers in every way possible. Troops are sent to aid in the planting of crops, and in the harvesting. The government provides seed for new crops, and we have a few soil experts who advise the farmers what crops to plant.

"The people respond by co-operating with the troops. They aid in cutting the railroads, cutting and gathering telephone wire, gathering information of the enemy, preventing spies from entering, capturing men who straggle from the enemy's army on the march or in battle, and by providing sleeping accommodations for our troops on the march."

Here Nieh interjected a remark. "I don't believe we have told you," he said, "that we now have a central purchasing bureau which purchases in Japanese-occupied territory those articles which we need, and which we are not able to manufacture here, such as radio equipment, for example. These are provided at cost to our own consumers' co-operatives. Also, Comrade Pen didn't tell you that people in the occupied towns now co-operate with us, and many send us their taxes, though we exercise no control over them."

Nieh then told of some of the engagements that had occurred during the past five months. It was the old story of guerrilla warfare—conducted by swift-moving columns. Lightning moves against small garrisons in which weapons and ammunition were captured, followed by equally quick withdrawals; raids on railway lines, against truck columns, and against the flanks and rear of marching troops. Not a day passed that a battle was not going on somewhere.

The army here in Wu T'ai, he said, was now composed entirely of men who had been recruited and trained within the area. Hsu Hai-tung's brigade of the Eighth Route Army, which I had seen in the winter, had gone south. The village self-defense corps was now used as a training unit, as well as for its regular functions. The work of the corps was directed by a bureau in his headquarters. He did not indicate the number of troops he now had under arms, but I estimated them to number nearly 100,000. The area had been divided into military defense districts, and the commander of each district was responsible for its defense and for conducting offensive operations against Japanese troops which were within or on its borders.

"My mission here," concluded Nieh, "is to build a strong political base in the people so that even if they come under Japanese control they will have hope, and will continue to resist Japanese domination. I also have the mission of attacking the enemy's rear."

He seemed to be performing both missions with marked success.

As the three got up to leave I interrupted them. "One more question, Comrade Nieh. How is it that you have been so successful in getting the co-operation of the landlords?"

They laughed, and Nieh replied: "The Japanese have been our allies in this. The landlords fear they will lose all if the Japanese are victorious. Also, they are Chinese, and they have a pride in their race and nation the same as we have. We explain the basis and the value of co-operation, and we point out that if they reduce land rentals and interest rates they will enjoy better co-operation from the peasants. As a matter of fact, where the landlords have done this, the peasants' societies have made a point of urging their members

Outside a gentle breeze whispered in the pine trees. Could this be war?

VII

Returning the next day, we stopped a few moments at a small village where were thirteen Japanese prisoners. The people smilingly informed us that the Japanese "guests" were doing their lessons. We found them in a sunny courtyard, each seated on a stool behind an improvised table. At one end of the courtyard a Chinese soldier stood before a blackboard talking to them in Japanese. The subject, I was informed, was the basic theory of co-operative societies. They were taking notes, and manifested considerable interest. All appeared to be in good health and well fed, and all were cheerful. Two were officers and the others were enlisted men. There were no guards around, and apparently they were under no severe restraint.

Doctor Bethune was at headquarters when we returned. Tall, thin, with gray hair and mustache, he looked tired. He had made a reputation in Spain by his success in giving blood transfusions on the battle field. I had heard that he was irascible, and if true it was probably due to his boundless energy and desire to get things done. My impression was of a man of great courage and deep conviction.

Although he had brought a large quantity of medical supplies with him, these were already nearly exhausted, and he was concerned with getting more. He gave me a list which I later delivered to the International Red Cross in Hankow.

"I feel that my life mission is here," he told me. "There are twenty thousand wounded in this area, divided among seven hospitals. I intend to visit each hospital and aid in establishing the best method of treatment possible. Then I will organize a field hospital unit which will follow the army during its major operations."

Norman Bethune fulfilled his mission faithfully. Eighteen months later he died in this region, victim of the lack of medical supplies which he was now so concerned in getting for the army.

Nieh and I now discussed routes by which the boys and I could get into Hopei. Only Auyang, Liu and Wang Yang would accompany me from here, for King had decided to remain in Wu T'ai and join the staff of one of the newspapers, of which there were two.

There were several routes to the east, but the shortest was by way of Fup'ing, and we finally settled on this one. It seemed wise now to move from one guerrilla area to another as rapidly as possible, and spend more time inspecting the activities within each area.

Again a mounted patrol escorted us, and on the first of July we mounted and rode off towards the east. It was a wrench to leave this friendly atmosphere, so charged with vital purpose. These men and women were pioneering a new trail for China—perhaps for the West as well. At the bank a crowd was waiting to wave farewell. Another group was outside the training school for government officials. And at the headquarters of the regional government Nieh Yong-sen and Sung Sao-wen came out for a final handclasp. As I write these lines, nearly two years later, they are still there in the Wu T'ai mountains, retaining this strategic region for China, and working out a way of life which, in its political aspects, is close to being a pure democracy, while in its social and economic aspects it approaches the co-operative effort urged by Jesus of Nazareth.

Towards noon we reached the top of the pass over Great Wall Mountain, and paused for a moment to survey the panorama of hills and plains below us. The east side of the mountain drops off sharply for a thousand to two thousand feet before tumbling into a jumble of hills whose eastern extremities taper off into the Hopei plains. Small wonder that the Japanese had not penetrated behind this wall of rock. Even this pass was so narrow and the trail so steep that a squad could exact a terrific toll from an attacking army.

Leading our animals, we descended the tortuous path towards Hopei and Shantung, where Confucius walked with his disciples nearly two thousand years ago as he philosophized: "The wise have no doubts, the virtuous no sorrows, the brave no fears."

CHAPTER IX
THE WAR IN THE CRADLE OF CONFUCIUS

I

THE Border Region of Shansi, Chahar and Hopei had been divided, for purposes of administration, into three administrative districts. The first district comprised that part of Shansi east of the T'ung P'u railroad and north of the Ch'eng T'ai, as well as the portion of Chahar south of the Suiyuan railroad. Western Hopei north of the Ch'eng T'ai railroad was contained in the second district. The third district was Central Hopei, which is considered as the area east of the Peip'ing-Hankow railroad and north of the highway which extends east from Shihchiachwang (where the Ch'eng-T'ai meets the P'ing-Han) to Tsanghsien, on the Tientsin-Pukow line. It is bounded on the north by the railway between Tientsin and Peip'ing. Each district was headed by a governor who was responsible to the regional political committee at Wu T'ai.

East of the Shansi border the drainage is generally towards the east, and while hills abound in Western Hopei, the central and southern parts of the province are vast alluvial plains. How, I wondered, had the Chinese been able to conduct guerrilla operations in flat country where there were no mountains, and where their units were open to attack by enemy aircraft?

After leaving Great Wall Mountain we descended to the village of Lung Chuan Kwan, the walls of which still showed the marks of flames which had destroyed it in 1900. German troops were responsible for this outrage, the people told me, having come here from Peking after that city was captured by the Allies. The air-line distance is one hundred and fifty miles, and I had not realized before that Allied troops went so far afield during that campaign.

Societies of children, women, peasants and merchants came out to greet us as we approached. I had spent a night here on my west-bound journey during the winter, and it was interesting now to observe the progress that had been made in the political development of the people. Nationalistic spirit was high, and each individual seemed to have some specific task which was connected with the work of resisting the invasion. Women were making shoes for the army, and in the late afternoon groups could be seen here and there sewing industriously. Other women were serving with the village self-defense corps, for the young men were in the army, and the older ones were in the fields. The sentry who examined our passports at the entrance to the village was a woman.

The children seemed to be charged with keeping the town clean, among other things, for occasionally I saw one dusting off a street corner with the traditional broom of native brush. But life was not all work; in the mornings there were schools, and in the evenings the people gathered before an old temple to sing songs and listen to speeches, or to hear reports on the progress of the war.

We were getting into a more productive country, and next morning as we moved down to the Sa river valley we passed terraced fields of millet and gardens of cabbage, potatoes, corn and beans. The peasants who worked on these hillsides used a short-handled hoe, and supported themselves by leaning on a short stake with one hand, while hoeing with the other. Later, on the plains, long-handled implements appeared again. A practical people, the Chinese.

Towards evening we reached Fup'ing, but it was not the bustling city I had visited in January. The Japanese had captured the city in March, and half of the buildings had been burned. The population was half its normal size, but those who remained were strong of spirit, and they were rapidly restoring a state of orderliness under the direction of the Magistrate, Tung Wei-hsi. The latter was a youngster only a year or two out of college, whom I had met on my last trip here. This is a young man's war, and in these guerrilla areas, especially, it is the young men who are carrying the burdens of civil and military responsibility.

There was another surprise for me here, for I found that Haldore Hanson, a correspondent for the *Associated Press*, was in town, en route westward. I had known Hanson at Peip'ing where he had arrived in 1934 shortly after graduating from college. Even in those days, when he was trying to get his bearings in the confusing sea of Oriental politics, he exhibited unusual enterprise and initiative, for in addition to his regular job of teaching he was active in local civic affairs, and delved into various aspects of Chinese life. It was not surprising, when, as a journalist, he got out and saw the war at first hand. This present trip made him the first Western journalist to visit the guerrilla areas of Shansi and Hopei.

Hanson had left Peip'ing nearly a month before, and had let his beard grow in the interim. The scraggly red beard was a bit startling, especially to the Chinese, whose faces are usually innocent of hair. We spent most of the night talking, for I had been out of direct communication with the world for two and a half months, and he was able to bring me up to date. In the morning we exchanged patrols and headed in opposite directions, he to emerge at Sian two months later, and I to re-enter free China at Chengchow, after penetrating Shantung province.

Wang Yang was the only one of the boys who smoked. He had admired my pipe, and having two along, I had given him one. Frequent divisions of my tobacco supply with our hospitable hosts along the way had reduced it to the point of exhaustion. For several weeks I had been telling Wang Yang about the fine tobacco grown in the Fup'ing region, which is famous throughout north China. And now we loaded up with a generous supply. It was the long yellow, stringy tobacco, favored by the Chinese peasant, but it was tobacco, and as we rode east from Fup'ing we smoked lustily and exchanged frequent comments on its superior merits.

This road was the one which the Japanese had used when they moved on Fup'ing in March, and hardly a house was standing. At the villages the inhabitants had returned and were making pathetic efforts to rebuild, but many still slept in the open. However, they were favored by the summer weather, and the abundance of vegetables, now in season, assured them of food.

We turned north from the main road, after riding twenty-two miles, and crossed a low mountain, dropping into a fertile valley of rich farm land, where we stopped at the guerrilla headquarters of this area. The commander and his staff had already taken the field to prepare for a co-ordinated drive against all Japanese garrisons along the Peip'ing-Hankow railroad. It was to be launched on the night of the first anniversary of the war, three days hence, and there was a momentous air about the headquarters.

The 4th Regiment of this military district had been charged with the task of putting us through the Japanese lines along the railroad, and the next day we continued east to its headquarters, which was only ten miles from the lines.

Wang Tze-fung commanded the 4th Regiment. He was lean, hollow-cheeked, almost dyspeptic in appearance, but he proved to be a military leader of high order. He was apparently a stickler for details, for affairs in his regiment ran like clockwork. The men were neat and military in appearance, and went about their tasks briskly. There was the same evidence of self-discipline that I had observed in other units trained by the Eighth Route Army, but Wang's attention to detail had produced a superior quality of efficiency that was sometimes lacking in other units.

He explained quietly that we would spend the next day here and leave on the morning of the sixth for a rendezvous point nearer to the railroad. The crossing would take place at night.

That night, after we had settled ourselves on beds that had been improvised by taking doors from their wooden hinges and laying them across wooden horses, Wang came over to tell me the story of how this area had been organized for resistance. It illustrates the manner in which similar areas were organized in these regions which had been penetrated by the Japanese.

"After the victory at P'inghsingkwan last September," he began, "Commander Chu Teh sent a brigade from the 115th Division to Fup'ing to get supplies and to organize the people. A mobilization committee was set up, with Wang P'ing as chairman. For years the people of Hopei have been allowed to have arms in their homes for protection against bandits, and these were now collected and used for the arming of Partisans and the self-defense corps. In a few days the brigade departed to fight the Japanese at Fantze, in Shansi, leaving a battalion to carry on the work at Fup'ing.

"Wang P'ing went around to the various villages and counties organizing mobilization committees and propaganda groups. The old civil administration bad broken down because most of the officials had fled before the invaders. It was necessary to restore order and convince the people that by cooperating they could resist successfully. I aided in this work, devoting most of my attention to the development of a Partisan group which was first designated as the 10th Regiment. In December Nieh Yong-sen established the Shansi-Chahar-Hopei regional government at Fup'ing, and after that the organizational work proceeded more rapidly. This area became the 4th District of Western Hopei, and my regiment became the 4th Regiment."

It sounded very simple, but I could think of a thousand problems which had to be solved in developing this kind of a program. Political administration was only one of these. Imparting the ethical indoctrination to the people must have been difficult. The recruiting, equipping and training of troops presented problems in themselves. And there was the organization of supplies, the development of an information service and, most important, active resistance to foraging columns of Japanese. Yet, today, eight months later, civil administration was functioning smoothly, the people were confident of ultimate victory, and this regiment was a competent military unit, uniformed, well equipped, and exceptionally well trained.

"Has your regiment done much fighting, Comrade Wang?" I asked.

He gave me a tolerant smile. "We are engaged almost daily," he replied. "We whittle away at the enemy along the railroad. On the 26th of February we had quite a battle at Shang Chuan. The enemy moved a thousand troops against Wan Hsien. With their column were eighty-four trucks, twelve tanks, a hundred cavalry and sixteen anti-tank guns. I attacked their flank, near Shang Chuan, with two battalions, and sent one battalion to assault their rear. The Japanese withdrew at daylight, and three trucks were filled with their dead. We estimated that they lost a hundred killed. Our own casualties were fifty-two killed and wounded, including a battalion commander and two company commanders."

II

At daylight on the morning of the 6th of July we started towards the railroad, escorted by a detachment of two dozen cavalrymen. The unit was the most business-like in appearance we had yet seen. Equipment was uniform. Each man's blanket and toilet articles were contained in a blue and white checkered cotton saddle bag, thrown across the seat of the saddle in Chinese fashion. Saddles were of uniform pattern, having been captured from the Japanese. Each man sat his horse like a veteran, his rifle slung from the left elbow, a custom which seemed to be favored by Chinese mounted troops.

The area through which we passed was alive with activity. Soldiers were laying wire to advance command posts, a group of stretcher bearers was moving forward, and here and there detachments of farmers were gathered, equipped with primitive implements with which to tear up rails. All were good humored, and many gave us a friendly hand wave as we passed, but there was no hilarity. The war was a year old and had become a grim business of daily whittling, and of out-smarting the enemy.

Five miles from the railroad we entered a village at a brisk trot, wheeling sharply through the narrow, crooked streets. Suddenly the leader halted and dismounted. It was a signal for all to follow suit. As if by magic, civilians appeared and led the horses down the street at a run. A man grabbed my arm and pulled me through a hole in the wall of an adjacent building. Walking quickly through narrow passageways we emerged into the courtyard of an undertaker where heavy, thick-boarded coffins were stacked around the sides three deep. The three boys were at my heels, and our attendants informed us that we would remain here until sundown.

It had all happened so quickly, and with such an air of mystery, that we were perspiring from the rush and excitement. Auyang had sized up the situation—

"This town is frequently occupied by the Japanese," he explained, "for it is within the occupied railway zone. The people are loyal to us, but there is always a chance that there may be a spy in the village, so when troops come in, they get off the streets as soon as possible."

It was hot in the courtyard and we spent the day lolling about, drinking hot tea, fanning ourselves in an effort to keep cool, and speculating on the adventures that the night might hold. Towards evening we heard massed voices shouting slogans and singing. The attendants informed us that a mass meeting was in progress preparatory to the departure of the men of the town for destructive work along the railroad.

The sun was disappearing in the west when we remounted and rode slowly towards the east. The fields were green with wheat, millet and kaoliang. Off to the north a long black column moved across the fields to the northeast; and to the south there was a similar column. These would be the lao pai hsing going off to cut the railroad. At the frequent villages only women, old men and children were visible. These watched our passing in somber silence. During the past year they had seen many similar columns move to the east, and always there were fewer when they returned. For these people war was shorn of all novelty and glory; it was grim reality, and their lives and homes were at stake.

At one village we stopped to wait for the darkness to thicken. Instantly the people brought out caldrons of steaming hot water and plates of mantou, the dumpling-like steamed bread. An eager group gathered around me, wanting to know my nationality. When I told them, each thrust a thumb upward, in characteristic fashion, and exclaimed, with face beaming: "Mei kuo ting hao (America is a good country)," which was the finest compliment they knew how to pay. Evidently they thought I was a volunteer, for as we departed an old man shouted to me: "Kill a Japanese for me, and bring him back tied to the tail of your horse."

Guns boomed to the north and south as we approached the railroad. The attack on the main towns was in progress. Presently the line of the railroad came into view. Four or five hundred yards to the left a structure loomed against the horizon. The soldier behind me rode alongside. "That is the station," he said. "In a concrete emplacement beside it are forty Japanese soldiers, but they will not come out at night."

Suddenly we broke into a trot, and then a gallop, charging across the railroad and swinging into a tree-shaded lane. Shots rang out from the direction of the station, but we paid no attention to them. From the north the rumble of artillery increased. Reducing our pace to a trot, we jogged along through the night under a sky of matchless blue.

Sometime after midnight we came to a village near the Fu T'o river, that same Fu T'o river I had twice crossed in Shansi, and once before in Western Hopei, now swollen to a good half mile in width. There was no further occasion for haste, and it would be safer to cross in daylight, so we unsaddled the animals and bivouacked under a grove of willows. At daylight we remounted, forded the river, and rode on to Li Ching Chen, where was located the Magistrate of Ting Hsien, his county seat being occupied by the Japanese.

III

We were now in Central Hopei (a hundred miles north of Lake Huron), and a number of changes soon became apparent. The soil was richer, the crops more diversified and the foliage more luxuriant. There was greater wealth among the people, as was evidenced by the increased number of

General Chiang T'ing-wen, Governor of Shensi province, and representative of Generalissimo Chiang Kai-shek in the Northwest.

Admiral Shen-Hung-lei, Governor of Shantung province. Formerly Mayor of Tsingt'ao, in which post he became well known to the officers of the Asiatic fleets of foreign governments.

General Liu Ho-ting, commander of the 39th Army, which fought at Shanghai, and which is now operating in Honan province.

General Tun P'ao-san, Vice-Commander of the North Route Army and commander of the 21st Corps Headquarters.

large houses, better building construction and the number of long-gowned businessmen, intellectuals and landlords. When we prepared to leave for Ankuo the next day we discovered to our amazement that there was also a difference in the mode of transportation. No pack animals were available to carry our tung-hsis (traveling gear). Instead we had to entrust them to a slow-moving springless cart—the type popularly known as the Peking cart.

The Magistrate personally escorted us to Ankuo, a city famed for its production of Chinese herbs and medicines, and only recently retrieved from the Japanese. There we were met by David Hwang, who had been sent by the military commander of Central Hopei, Lu Cheng-tsao,

David Hwang was an old friend. He was short, thick-set, dynamic, and spoke English fluently. His manner was irresistibly friendly, but there was an earnestness about him which was also compelling. He believed fiercely in democracy and in the socialistic economic theory, and for a number of years he had been active in the indoctrination of students in universities of Peip'ing and Tientsin with his convictions. In January I had seen him at Fup'ing, where he directed political education at the military academy. Now he was performing the same function for the Central Hopei government.

"Welcome to Chi-Chung (the ancient Chinese abbreviation for Central Hopei)," he cried, in his vigorous manner. "What do you think of new China?"

I told him I was much impressed, especially by the apparent co-operation between the wealthy classes and the peasants.

"We have made progress here," he replied, more seriously. "But there is still much to be done. The people here are as a whole better educated than those in Shansi. And the cruelty of the Japanese has made the upper classes realize that life under their rule would be a burden, and they are also intelligent enough to see that successful resistance can only be achieved by co-operation of all classes."

Then he pointed out something I had already noted: that the military leaders here were mostly officers from the former Manchurian army of General Wan Fu-lin, while the political leaders were from the Eighth Route Army.

Hwang had brought a motor car to transport us to the headquarters at Jen Chiu, fifty-five miles to the northeast. However, we stopped for the night at Po Yeh to talk to my old friend, Yang Hsu-fang, the former Peip'ing professor whom I had last seen at Liaochow, in Shansi, just before starting the first trip through the Japanese lines.

Here with his wife, he was making plans to open a military and political training school for leaders along the lines of those I had seen in Shansi and Shensi. Classes would commence on the first of August, he said, and already he had a thousand applications, mostly from former university students.

That evening I accompanied him to a meeting of military and political leaders of the district at which the work of recent weeks was discussed and criticised.

No feelings were spared during the critique, which was a healthy sign. The Partisan work along the Tientsin-P'ukow railway, which lay to the east, they felt was poorly coordinated. Something had to be done about it. The technique of protecting surplus food supplies was characterized as imperfect. There was an abundance of food, but the flat character of the country made it difficult to keep it out of the hands of the invaders. A committee was appointed to study ways and means.

Another point brought out was the over-confidence of the people. They had been successful in recent encounters with the Japanese, and this must not lull them into a false sense of security. Vigilance must not be relaxed, and co-operation must be increased.

The final point concerned differences which had arisen between peasants who were members of the Peasants' Society and those who were not. The solution of this problem, the chairman pointed out, lay in perfecting the co-operation of the organized peasants so that the benefits of membership might be more apparent to non-members; but, he added, there must be no friction and no unfriendliness between organized and unorganized peasants. All are brothers working in a common cause.

We drove to Jen Chiu the next day, passing through several industrial cities which had at one time been occupied by the Japanese. Withdrawal had been made necessary by the threat to lines of communication, caused by the increasing strength of Chinese resistance. Everywhere there was great enthusiasm and earnest activity, but it was evident that the doctrines of social equality and individual self-discipline were not as far advanced here as in Shansi. The work of indoctrination here was newer, and there was a scarcity of trained leaders. Nevertheless, it was remarkable that all of this activity was going on within seventy miles of the Japanese bases at Peip'ing and Tientsin, and only twenty miles east of the railroad.

The military headquarters was actually in a village near Jen Chiu, and here Commander Lu Cheng-tsao and the governor of the district of Central Hopei, Li Ken-t'ao, received us with an honor guard of one battalion.

Commander Lu was a quiet, self-effacing man of about forty, who had been a regimental commander in the Manchurian army of Wan Fu-lin at the beginning of the war. He had the erect bearing and self-assurance of the trained officer, and yet there was a thoughtfulness about him, a respect for the dignity of the human being, which inspired confidence.

The governor, Li Ken-t'ao, was a much younger man. He was amiable and well-meaning, but he lacked force of character, and was unprepossessing in appearance. Apparently his was an interim appointment, for in a few weeks he was relieved by General Lu Chung-lin, formerly a distinguished subordinate of Feng Yu-hsiang, who came up from Hankow.

The atmosphere here smacked of the Eighth Route Army. There were hsiao kweis and bodyguards, and there was the same informality and camaraderie. The headquarters was in radio communication with the regional government at Wu T'ai, and there was both radio and wire communication with the defense districts within the Central Hopei area.

Commander Lu and David Hwang came around for a talk that evening, and I learned something of the manner in which this organization had come into being. But first I wanted to know about the results of the attacks which had been made along the railroad on the night we crossed.

"Our forces co-operated with those west of the railroad," said Lu, "in attacking the various Japanese garrisons. Some of the towns were captured and held until enemy re-enforcements arrived. At Tinghsien and Paot'ingfu only the stations were captured. Rails were taken up at various places, and north of Paot'ingfu a bridge was destroyed and train traffic was interrupted for three days. Three trains were wrecked."

The story of the development of resistance here started with the beginning of the Japanese invasion, back in July and August. "I was then commanding the 691st Regiment of the 53d Army," he began. "As the Japanese moved south along the Peip'ing-Hankow railroad, we retired. My regiment fought delaying actions. By the first of October we had reached Chao Hsien, which is nearly two hundred miles south of Peip'ing. We were shifted west to cover the left flank, and suddenly we discovered that we were surrounded. We fought our way out to the east, but by this time my regiment was reduced to a battalion. We were cut off from the rest of the army, and I informed General Wan Fu-lin by radio that we would remain in Hopei and fight guerrilla warfare.

"At Po Yeh some students were organizing the People's Self-Defense Army, and further north a part of the Eighth Route Army had crossed the railroad. Their leaders were in Kaoyang, Li Hsien and Jen Chiu, organizing Partisans and teaching the people how to resist. Representatives from these various groups asked me to assume supreme command so as to co-ordinate activities better. I accepted.

"In December the Japanese captured Kaoyang and other cities in Central Hopei despite our resistance. I realized that we needed more knowledge of guerrilla methods, and I led part of my army to the west of the railroad, where we received instruction from the Eighth Route Army. In January we returned much benefited by the experience, and with a definite plan for the organization of the people and for the formation of Partisans.

"The Eighth Route Army sent me trained political leaders, and I selected officers from my former regiment to organize the new Partisan regiments. When the regional government of Shansi, Chahar and Hopei was organized we accepted membership in order to perfect co-ordination here in the north. Technically this area comes under the First War Zone, which is commanded by General Ch'eng Ch'ien, at Chengchow (Honan), but the distance (350 miles) and the intervening Japanese troops make it impractical for General Ch'eng to exercise jurisdiction."

I asked Lu how he overcame the difficulties of conducting guerrilla operations in a country devoid of hills or mountains.

"It is more difficult," he replied, "especially if the enemy uses mechanized equipment and planes. Fortunately, however, there are many rivers in Hopei, and there is considerable, foliage. We use these features to advantage. And we nearly always operate at night. Our intelligence service provides us promptly with information of all Japanese troop movements, so we are able to attack on our own terms."

He emphasized one point which had also been stressed by Nieh, at Wu T'ai: that the government here is provisional, and that the area is part of China and under the jurisdiction of the Chinese national government. All questions of major policies, he said, are referred to the Central Government at Hankow for approval.

IV

"How would you like to go to Peip'ing?" asked Commander Lu the next morning.

I was startled. "You mean that your men could put me inside the city of Peip'ing without the knowledge of the Japanese?" I queried.

"Exactly. If you can spare three days we'll take you up in a day, give you one day in the city, and bring you back on the third day. The Japanese will never know anything about it."

As an adventure it would be exciting, but as I turned the matter over in my mind I decided that it would simply be a stunt which would serve no useful purpose. My confidence in the ability of these men to fulfill any task they undertook was absolute, but a visit to Peip'ing was no part of my mission, and if by chance I was captured, the notes and maps which were in my possession by courtesy of the Chinese would be extremely useful to the Japanese.

I explained this point of view to Lu, and he grinned appreciatively. Instead, we made a trip to the northern outpost of Pa Hsien, which was only fifty miles from the former capital, and here I saw more captured Japanese equipment, including a grenade projector, an extremely useful weapon for guerrilla operations. It consisted of a rifled tube, eight and a half inches long, with a firing pin that could be moved up and down inside the tube by means of a thumb screw, in order to adjust for range. It weighed about twelve pounds and fired a projectile two inches in diameter by four inches in height, which made it larger than a rifle grenade and smaller than a trench mortar. They demonstrated the weapon and it fired with great accuracy up to six hundred yards. The pattern was German.

The three boys and I held a conference to decide on our future route. Hsiu Shang-ch'ien, who had been in command of the 129th Division when I was at Liaochow in December, was now at Nankung, in Southern Hopei (corresponding to the middle of Lake Huron), organizing that area. We decided to go there first, a distance of a hundred and forty-five miles, and then strike east into Shantung. The following day we got away.

On these trips in the interior I had been extremely careful to guard against dysentery by eating only cooked food, or fruit which I peeled myself, I had also avoided using the hot towels which are always provided at formal Chinese dinners, for trachoma (a virulent eye disease) was prevalent. During the winter my health had been excellent, but now, despite all precautions, I had contracted both dysentery and trachoma. I could deal with the dysentery, but my medical kit was innocent of anything which would counteract trachoma, and there were no doctors here worthy of the name.

The distress was psychological rather than physical, and as we rode south through Central Hopei, my eyes matted with mucus, I had visions of going blind. It was a tremendous relief, therefore, when we arrived at Hokien, to find that a New Zealand nurse was in town. Miss Preece proved to be a

A group of Partisans in Hopei province (behind the Japanese lines). Note that staffs and spears are used in lieu of rifles for training purposes.

A group of women in Western Hopei engaged in sewing shoes for soldiers.

robust, hearty woman who had worked at the local missionary hospital for fifteen years. She laughed when she saw me.

"Trachoma!" she ejaculated. "That's nothing. We all have it sooner or later." And she proceeded to give me a treatment which arrested its development.

But this was just an incident of a trip that was otherwise stimulating. At every town preparations for long years of resistance were going forward. Surpluses of food supplies were being hidden, usually by burying, and the people were receiving the political indoctrination so essential to the cementing of the will-to-endure hardship.

It was watermelon season, and we stopped frequently on these hot days to refresh ourselves. In a country where water was invariably drunk at the boiling point, it was a luxurious experience to be able to cool our palates with ripe melon. There were several varieties, but the most delectable was the san pai (three white), the name being derived from the fact that the skin, seeds and pulp were all white at the ripe stage.

At Anp'ing we crossed the Fu T'o river again. Between there and Shulu I suffered the embarrassing experience of losing most of the front of my pants by fire. I was jogging along, contentedly smoking my pipe, with my mind miles away, when suddenly I became conscious of a burning sensation on my thigh. An ash from my pipe had bobbed into my lap, igniting my khaki shorts. By the time I became aware of the disaster the smoldering fire had eaten a hole the size of my two hands.

There would be a reception at the entrance to Shulu, and obviously I was in no condition to be received. The situation was worsened by the fact that our luggage was on a cart which, on this of all occasions, had preceded us. We put spurs to our horses, all of us in a state of hysterical laughter by now, and five miles down the road we overtook the cart. While the boys and our escort grouped around to protect me from the gaze of curious villagers, I shifted to more presentable attire. But the story was too good to keep, and it preceded me throughout the rest of the trip to the Yellow river.

V

Five days of stiff travel brought us to Nankung. It was good to see Hsiu Shang-ch'ien again. He was as gracious and smiling as when I had seen him at Liaochow, but he was also thinner, and he looked tired.

This was a fruit country, and as we talked, during the two day stay, hsiao kweis brought us peaches, pears and apples. Tun Shao-p'in, Chu Teh's assistant political director, was here on an inspection trip, and he joined in the conversations.

There was a calm assurance here that had been lacking in the Central Hopei area. I tried to analyze the difference and decided that it lay in the quiet self-confidence of the leaders. These men of the Eighth Route Army were sure of themselves. They had thought through the whole problem of social, economic and political relationships during the long years they had fought for existence, and their ideas were definite and clean-cut. Also, they had boundless confidence in their military strategy, and in their ability to apply it.

This area of Southern Hopei (Chi Nan, it was called by the Chinese) lay south of the highway which formed the southern boundary of Central Hopei, and between the Peip'ing-Hankow railroad, on the west, and the Grand Canal, in Shantung, on the east. The southern boundary was a line just north of Ta Ming, where Hopei province narrows to a pan handle, which extends to the Yellow river. The area was about 8,000 square miles, or about the size of the state of Massachusetts.

The Japanese had at one time held a highway across this area from east to west, connecting the two railroads, and consequently the people had suffered heavily. The regular Chinese armies had passed on to the south, as the Japanese advanced, and the people had been left to their own devices. Some became bandits, while others attempted to organize for the protection of specific localities. But they had no basic plan, and their efforts were sporadic.

"It was in December," Hsiu told me, "that representatives from certain towns in this area came to the headquarters of our division at Liaochow (in Shansi, and almost due west of here) and asked for assistance in organizing Partisans. We had our hands full in Shansi at that time, so we sent three trained men, unarmed, to return with them. These were followed a few weeks later by twenty-four men, and in January we sent over four companies. These detachments were able to organize the people in Kulu and Nankung, and to establish a base for us here. In March Sung Jen-chung brought a cavalry regiment over, and he widened the scope of the development. After defeating the Japanese at Shang T'ang P'u, in April, I brought the main force here."

"How did you happen to defeat the Japanese at Shang T'ang P'u?" I asked.

"It was on the 31st of March," he replied, "and a column of about three thousand Japanese was moving through a pass into Shansi with a train of 180 trucks. We struck them suddenly on the flank and killed nearly a thousand. But the best part was that we were able to burn all of the trucks."

I was curious to learn how they dealt with Chinese bandits. "Do you exterminate them?" I asked.

"Not unless they persist in abusing the people after we have explained to them the injury they are doing the Chinese cause," he replied. Then he gave me the conditions which bandits were required to fulfill before they were taken into the Eighth Route Army. They must agree to:

Fight the Japanese until they withdraw from China;

Accept orders from the Eighth Route Army;

Accept political indoctrination and political leaders;

Avoid harming the people;

Provide regular statements of income and expenditures;

Accept the salary schedule of the 8th R.A. (graduated from $1.00 a month for fighters to $5 a month for the commander);

Share the same type of food.

Traitor armies (by which he meant Chinese who had been enlisted in the Japanese puppet armies), he said, must further prove their good faith by killing Japanese troops.

"About five thousand of these traitor troops have come over to us from this area alone," he said, with his slow smile.

"While we are discussing conditions, Comrade Hsiu," I said, "I'd like to know specifically the ten anti-Japanese principles which I understand each Eighth Route Army man is sworn to carry out."

Tun Shao-p'in had been industriously eating fruit while this conversation was going on. Now he leaned back in his chair and took an active part.

"The principles," he said, "are these: To recapture lost territory; develop the collective action of all our military forces; mobilize the people; expel traitors and self-seeking officials from public office, and establish a democratic government; join the Japanese, Korean and Formosan peasants in an anti-Fascist movement; confiscate the property of traitors and use it in the anti-Japanese campaign; improve the welfare of the people; improve the education of the people; detect and arrest all traitors; and, finally, though most important, make the united front an actuality."

As he named the points I mentally checked them with the activities I had been observing in Shansi and Hopei. I had seen concrete instances of the application of each one. The emphasis on the development of the united front had been strong in every locality we had visited since leaving the Yellow river in western Shansi.

The rainy season was beginning, and rain poured down for two days, causing us to delay our progress. However, it provided further opportunities to talk to Hsiu and Tun.

Tun had been a worker before joining the Eighth Route Army. He had spent some time in France and had studied the labor movement there. He was short, chunky and physically tough, and his mind was as keen as mustard.

One afternoon we went over the entire field of international politics, and I was astonished at the extent of his information. One piece of news gave me a shock.

"Last year," he said, "America provided Japan with over half of the war materials she purchased abroad."

"Are you sure about that?" I asked. I knew that American sympathy was preponderantly on the side of China, who was the victim of aggression, and during the eight months I had been in the interior I had taken it for granted, when I had thought about the matter at all, that American people would refuse to sell war materials to an aggressor nation. What sublime innocence!

"Yes," he assured me, "the information came in a press despatch from the United States at the end of the first year of the war."

I was distressed, and said that there must have been a mistake in the despatch. I could not believe that American people would knowingly contribute to the carnage and suffering I had seen here during the past year.

Hsiu Shang-ch'ien came in, and the conversation turned again to the local situation. I asked him about the present condition of the area.

"The Japanese now hold only towns on the railroads and Ta Ming, to the south of us. Banditry in this area has been eliminated, but the areas to the south are not so fortunate. However, there is a good man in charge of the five counties between Ta Ming and the Yellow river. His name is Ting Shu-pen. We have given him some assistance."

He wanted to know how I proposed to get back to Hankow.

"I want to see something of the conditions in Shantung," I replied, "and then I hope to be able to find a route across the Yellow river, and west of Chengchow."

"If you have any difficulty in getting a patrol," he told me, "come back here. I'll get you through, one way or another." I had use for his promise later.

VI

It was late in July when we departed from Nankung for Lintsing

(Lionhead, Ontario, on Georgian Bay), the first large city in Shantung. The road was inundated in many places, but the countryside was green with new crops. There were gardens of beans, corn, kaoliang, millet and sesame, and occasionally I saw patches of cotton. Lintsing was only fifty miles away, and on the second day we approached the city.

When fully a mile away we saw a group of horsemen riding towards us. As it drew near one man spurred out ahead of the rest and charged ahead waving his cap and shouting at the top of his lungs, "Huan yin, ts'an tsan. " And suddenly I recognized him. He was K'ung Ching-teh, the battalion commander with the walk that resembled the glide of a panther, who had put me across the Ch'eng T'ai railroad last January.

He dismounted and we embraced each other warmly. His sensitive, honest face was alight with pleasure, and he held my hand in his in the affectionate manner I had so often observed between intimate friends in the Eighth Route Army.

"What under the sun are you doing here, Comrade K'ung?" I asked.

"I brought my regiment here a few days ago," he replied. Then modestly, "I command the regiment you saw at Kao Lu. Commander Chen Hsi-lien was wounded at the battle of Chang Lo Ch'un, shot through the cheek. He is now vice-commander of the brigade."

I was genuinely glad to see him, both because I had developed a strong liking for him in those days we had marched together, and because I had been apprehensive about my reception in Shantung.

At the entrance to the city I could see a tremendous crowd which was evidently being held behind a rope, thrown across the road. I asked him about it. He grinned.

"I heard from Comrade Hsiu that you were coming. It happens that the Governor of the province, Admiral Shen Hung-lei, is here and I told him about you. He is prepared to welcome you."

We moved towards the city. There had been welcoming delegations at other cities, but none compared with this. When we were still a hundred yards or so away a soldier ran out with a hand full of visiting cards. There must have been fifty, and they were from the governor, various army commanders, and prominent city, county and provincial officials. It was my cue to observe the social amenities.

But there was nothing formal about the reception at the barrier. Doctor Lei, secretary to the Governor, and General Han To-feng, military commander of this district, were the first to greet us. Then came the lesser officials, and behind them, surging frantically between lines of troops which extended along both sides of the road into the city, were hundreds of men, women and children, carrying banners which indicated that they represented students, merchants, workers, peasants, and various other civic groups. Some sang songs, others shouted slogans. It was impossible for me to get the names of the officials in all this bedlam.

Guards shouldered a path through the sea of welcoming faces to a group of rickshas, the first I had seen since leaving Sian three and a half months before. But we might as well have walked, for the streets back into the city continued to be packed with humanity, and it took an hour for us to reach the American Board Mission hospital.

There was a two-fold reason for this enthusiastic reception. It was an opportunity to pay tribute to America, whose stock was high with the people. And it was an opportunity for local officials to focus the enthusiasm of the people on something concrete, as part of the general program for stimulating them to greater effort in the work of resisting the invasion.

The foreign staff was not present at the hospital, and had not been since the invasion, I was told. However, the Governor had directed that we be installed in the home of one of the doctors, and he sent his personal cook over to care for us during our stay.

As soon as I could remove the stains of travel I accompanied Doctor Lei to pay a formal call on the Governor. I found a modest, pleasant-faced man of fifty-seven, whose patrician features and reserved manner bespoke refinement and culture. In slow but understandable English he greeted me warmly, and asked me to sit down. An orderly brought rice wine and cigars.

Admiral Shen Hung-lei had had an unusual career for a Chinese. A native of Hupeh, the province in which Hankow is located, he was first educated in the classics, entered the military academy at Wuchang, and then spent seven years in Japan studying naval tactics. During the World War he was a member of the group of Chinese observers who traveled in Italy, France, Great Britain and the United States. Subsequently he served for ten years as commander-in-chief of the Manchurian naval squadron. But the service for which he is best known abroad was as Mayor of Tsingtao, the principal seaport of Shantung, a post which he held at the beginning of the present conflict. And it was he who executed the orders of the Generalissimo to burn the Japanese factories in Tsingtao before the Japanese occupied the city.

When the former governor, Han Fu-chu, was executed, the preceding January, for disobedience and failure to defend the province, Shen Hung-lei was appointed to succeed him.

After expressing appreciation for the reception and his hospitality, I asked if Lintsing was now his permanent headquarters.

"No," replied the Admiral, flicking the ash from his cigar. "I carry my headquarters in my hip pocket these days. There are 107 counties in Shantung, and these are grouped into twelve administrative districts. I am moving around from one district to another, organizing troops, restoring communications, trying to give the people new confidence and striving to increase the effectiveness of their resistance."

Then he asked about Admiral Yarnell and other officers of our navy. Tsingtao had for years been the summer headquarters of our Asiatic Fleet, and as Mayor he had known the higher ranking officers. He spoke with amusement of the incongruity of an Admiral of the navy conducting a military campaign here in the interior. When I got up to leave he accompanied me to the hospital compound and remained for dinner.

The co-operation of troops south of the Yellow river would be necessary to enable our group to pass through the Japanese lines into free China, and in order to speed up the plans for this last stage of the trip I asked the Governor during dinner what the possibilities were of getting through. He

A children's society in Western Hopei province. They are singing one of the new patriotic songs:"Now is the time for Sacrifice."

A Village Self-Defense Corps in Northern Honan province. Note the ancient spears and cutlasses which these men carry.

thought the chances were slim. It would take days, perhaps weeks, to make the arrangements and in the meantime I could remain here. The prospect would have been alluring but for the feeling that I should return to Hankow now as soon as possible, and so I mentioned that the Eighth Route Army had offered to escort me south if the way was not clear from Shantung. The Governor promised to send a radio to General Ch'eng Ch'ien, at Chengchow, that night.

My diary for the next day contains this opening notation: "Started the day with a breakfast of fruit, cereal, eggs, toast and coffee. What luxury?" I had fared well on the Chinese diet during these months, but we are, after all, creatures of habit, and to find unexpectedly a traditional American breakfast up here in Shantung caused a surge of nostalgia.

A mass meeting was scheduled for the morning, and the boys and I were escorted to a field near the edge of the city by Doctor Lei. Here, grouped in front of a flag-bedecked platform was a crowd that must have numbered ten thousand people. On the platform with the Governor were representatives of the Communist and Kuomintang parties, and of all the civic groups.

The meeting began in Kuomintang fashion with the reading of Doctor Sun's will, followed by three bows by all present to the picture of Doctor Sun, which dominated the platform. It was a huan yin meeting (welcoming), and each representative made a short speech of welcome, ending with a calm, factual talk by the Governor. The crowd was so great that the speakers could be heard by only a fraction of those present, but those in front passed on the gist of each talk to those behind.

It was now my turn, and I made my usual attempt to interpret American policy. But the man who talked in language the people understood and liked was General Han To-feng, who wound up the program. General Han was another of the Feng Yu-hsiang school—a man of the people, and an orator with all the platform tricks of a Billy Sunday. Stepping to the edge of the platform he crouched low, as though to take the people into his confidence. Then in a bellowing voice he described the atrocities of the Japanese and appealed to the patriotism of the people. He pantomimed and gesticulated;

he imitated the traitors who had gone over to the Japanese, shifting his voice to a high, squeaky pitch, and walking across the stage with mincing, deprecatory steps. The people roared with laughter. He ended with an epic description of the valor of the Chinese armies and called on the people to support them. Thunderous applause followed this dramatic appeal, and the meeting broke up with the singing of the national anthem.

VII

General Ch'eng Ch'ien had replied to the Governor's radio by offering me the choice of two routes to the south. One lay directly south across the Yellow river, and thence west into Honan and on to Chengchow. This route was considered perfectly safe, but it was longer and traversed regions that had been flooded by an overflow from the river. The alternative was to go south for a hundred and fifteen miles to P'u Hsien, and then swing west on the north side of the Yellow river, for another hundred and fifty miles to a point roughly north of Chengchow, and from there cross the river. This route lay through country where Chinese resistance was not well organized, and it would be necessary to pass between Japanese garrisons that were only twenty miles apart. But it was shorter, and it would afford an opportunity to sense the spirit of the people in a doubtful region. I selected the latter route.

But nature took a hand again, temporarily. The trachoma had become more active, and a fever that had developed in Hopei became more virulent. Although the foreign staff had left the hospital, a Chinese male nurse was carrying on the work, holding daily office hours and keeping the wards in shipshape order. I sought treatment from him.

"We have a laboratory technician here," he told me. "If you wish, he can test your blood and determine the cause of the fever."

I agreed, and the test showed that I had relapsing fever, a disease somewhat similar to typhus, and transmitted in the same manner—by a louse. It was prevalent in north China, especially in Shansi and Shensi, but this was my first experience with it.

"What's the specific for it?" I asked the technician.

"Salvarsan—one injection," he replied succinctly.

"Can you give it?" I asked.

"Certainly," he replied.

He did the job skillfully, and six hours later the fever left, and has not since returned.

I learned later that this man had been trained by Doctor Ayers in the Baptist Mission hospital at Chengchow.

I had frequent talks with both the Governor and K'ung, the commander of the Eighth Route Army regiment. There was, I could see, some friction between the Kuomintang, as represented by the Governor, and the Eighth Route Army, due to basic differences in the conception of methods to be employed in developing resistance within the province. The Governor was unalterably opposed to the organization of the people, especially along political lines.

"I have no objection," he told me, "to the organization of cultural groups among the people. But the Kuomintang is the governing party, and the people must abide by its dictums."

He went on to say that both political and military authority was vested in the Magistrates and the governors of districts. His plan was to build an army within each county and administrative district which would enable the officials of those districts to deal with the situation.

The Eighth Route Army, on the other hand, took the position that the capacity of the people to resist could reach its highest point only through invoking their co-operation by improving their welfare, teaching them the fundamentals of representative government and indoctrinating them with the spirit of self-sacrifice.

In addition to the regiment here at Lintsing, the Eighth Route Army had two chih tuis (a chih tui is a flexible military unit which may number anywhere from a thousand to ten thousand men, depending on the mission) operating in northeast Shantung. Another unit was in the Taian district, where Confucius was born, and where his body lies today, on T'ai mountain.

These two points of view appeared to be irreconcilable, but here, as in other parts of China, the compulsion of working together in order to defeat a common enemy served to temper the attitudes of the two parties—the Communist and the Kuomintang. In time probably a compromise formula would be worked out.

VIII

After four days, which provided much-needed rest for us all, we moved south to Liaocheng, also on the Grand Canal, and met one of the most interesting men we had seen on the entire trip. He was General Fan Chu-hsien, the Governor of this Administrative District.

Fifty-eight years of age, tall, wiry and bald, he was a man of tremendous energy and intense patriotism. He wore a long beard, which is unusual for a Chinese, and when he talked he had a habit of pulling nervously at the ends of the beard. If the subject happened to be one about which he felt deeply — and he seemed to have strong convictions about almost everything—his animation would become intense, and he would bounce up and down on the edge of his chair.

Fan had seen the war coming, he told me, and as Magistrate of Lin Yi, and more recently here in his present position, he had begun to prepare the people. His early recognition of the value of mass mobilization was responsible for the fact that he now had a hundred thousand guerrillas under his direction. Some, he said, were operating with Tsao Chun, in the Western Hills, outside of Peip'ing. He was liberal minded and believed in representative government, though he was not a communist. Here in his own district he had instituted such reforms as he could, and the people appeared to be giving him their full co-operation.

Shortly after our arrival in Liaocheng I received a note addressed in

English to "The American who just arrived in our city." It was from two Catholic priests, members of the Order of Franciscan Fathers, Andrew Walter Tracy and Hubert Noumier, both from California. They had heard from the Chinese that an American had arrived, but hadn't been able to make out who I was. I was only staying overnight, and General Fan had already arranged for a dinner that night, so the gracious fathers invited me to breakfast. Casting about for a dish that would be essentially American in its association they hit on apple pie, and with this delicious reminder of home I started the trek to the south.

General Fan accompanied us to P'u Hsien, he and his staff riding bicycles, a practice which seemed to delight the people. It developed into a three-day trip, for the General asked me to speak at each hamlet along the way. I was eager to push along rapidly, and cut my talks short, to his manifest disappointment. When we reached P'u Hsien I said to Auyang, who had been interpreting, as usual: "This will be our last talk, so let's make the General happy. We'll give him the works." I talked about everything I could think of, bent on pleasing the General, and interested to see just how long a speech the people would take without walking away. At the end of three hours I stopped from sheer exhaustion of ideas and strength—and the people continued to wait. "That was better," remarked the General mildly.

P'u Hsien was another city which the Japanese had burned before departing. It was near the Yellow river, and troops had been there almost constantly during the Hsuchowfu campaign. The atrocity stories told by the people were beyond belief.

A bicycle patrol accompanied us westward to K'eichow (vicinity of Port Huron, Mich.), in the pan handle of Hopei, which was the headquarters of Ting Shu-pen, of whom Hsiu Shang-ch'ien had spoken. The usual crowd waited at the outskirts of the city as we approached, and as I looked down the line of long-gowned merchants and short-jacketed peasants I spotted a white dress. Was it possible that a foreign woman was in this out-of-the-way place? As I drew nearer I saw that the wearer was unmistakably a Western woman, and—if my instinct wasn't all wrong—an American.

She proved to be Miss Elizabeth Goertz, of Beatrice, Nebraska, a nurse at the local mission hospital of the Mennonite church, and the only foreigner in town. Miss Goertz arranged for our group to stay in one of the empty houses belonging to the mission.

General Ting Shu-pen was one of the few officials I met on this trip who had remained at his post after the Japanese drove through. He had been administrator of five counties in this vicinity before the war, and when the enemy occupied K'eichow he simply moved his headquarters into the country and commenced mobilizing the people. He was a curious combination of liberalism and conservatism. Trained in the old conservative school, he sensed also the value of a contented and co-operative populace.

His manner of receiving me was typical of the man. His chief of staff met me on my arrival, and said the General was waiting to receive me at his office. After settling our luggage the boys and I went to the yamen, where we were received with elaborate ceremony. Eventually we gained the inner sanctum, where the General awaited, tall, pompous and aloof. We conversed formally, sitting stiffly in our chairs. Auyang and I had worked together so long that he knew the extent of my Chinese vocabulary, and consequently did not interpret some of the General's remarks. The chief of staff rebuked him sharply, saying: "Repeat all the General says."

However, that night General Ting came to dinner, and remained until late. Gone was all the stiffness, the pompousness, and the ceremonious attitude. His personality was warm and charming, and his conversation sparkled with wry anecdotes. He spoke of the benefit he had derived from his conversations with Hsiu Shang-ch'ien, and he related with a good deal of elation some of his successful guerrilla activities.

The next morning he sent a company of Partisans to escort us to Pa Li Ying, a distance of twenty-five miles, and there we found a company from the People's Army waiting to accompany us through the Japanese lines to Yuan Wu, ninety miles farther west.

Heavy rains had flooded the Yellow river, and much of the road was under water, making it difficult to get the cart with our luggage through.

Frequently we were stalled for hours at a time.

But the most disconcerting element of this final stage of our trip was the patrol. It was composed of men who had only recently been enlisted, and they were poorly trained and utterly lacking in discipline. After the first day's march their feet began to give out, and by the end of the second day fully half of the company was riding in carts which the men had commandeered from farmers along the way.

The farther we proceeded, the more ominous became the attitude of the people. They had not been indoctrinated with that spirit of nationalism, or of self-sacrifice, which activated the people in the north. The demands of itinerant bands of irregular Chinese soldiery, and frequent visits of Japanese detachments, had combined to break their morale. Between the untrustworthiness of the people and the rank ineptitude of the patrol, the boys and I sometimes wondered if we would succeed in completing the trip.

On the third day we reached the most dangerous part of the journey. The Japanese were both on the Tao-Chi branch railroad, to the north, and at Yentsing, to the south, with less than twenty miles separating the two garrisons. The country was flat, favoring the operations of tanks and motorized columns.

The plan called for passing about eight miles north of Yentsing in the early morning. But the guide, a local civilian, made a mistake (or perhaps it was design) and suddenly we emerged from the shelter of a line of trees to find ourselves within sight of Yentsing, and less than two miles away. There was nothing to do but go on, and taking advantage of folds in the ground we crept ahead, keeping our fingers crossed. A mile beyond we dropped into a sunken road, and got by unseen. At the end of another five miles the patrol decided that it needed a rest, and we stopped at a small village.

It was a blistering hot day in early August, and the men sought the shade of trees and threw themselves on the ground. We were still only five miles from Yentsing, and discipline had been so poor that I decided to make a circuit of the town to determine what security measures had been taken. Not a single outpost had been established, and not a sentry was on guard.

The patrol simply couldn't be bothered.

The boys and I transferred our effects to the one small hill that rose above the town. Here, in case of attack, there would at least be a rallying point which possessed some natural advantage. However, nothing happened, and after an hour's rest the patrol got under way. But we had no feeling of security until we reached Yuan Wu the following day.

IX

The 5th Partisan Group of the First War Zone was at Yuan Wu, and the commander received us with marked cordiality. This unit came under the command of General Ch'eng Ch'ien, and it had done a good job of organizing the people of this rich agricultural region within a radius of twenty-five miles.

General Liu Ho-ting, commander of the 39th Army, we were informed, had arranged to send an escort with a river junk to meet us at the north bank of the Yellow river on the following morning. This would be our last night in the field.

The meeting on the river bank was made according to schedule, and shortly we were sailing across its swollen bosom, now nearly two miles in width. We were elated. The end of this journey which had taken us nearly fifteen hundred miles across north China, and thrice through the Japanese lines, at last was in sight. On the south bank soldiers manning the defense positions helped us ashore, and we were passed successively through the various subordinate headquarters to the brigade command post. Here a truck was waiting to take us to Chengchow (Lansing, Michigan).

Many changes had occurred since I had passed through here in April. The Japanese had captured the Lunghai railroad to a point about thirty miles east of the city, being stopped by the waters which had broken through the Yellow river dykes. General Ch'eng Ch'ien had moved his Zone headquarters to Loyang, eighty miles west, and General Liu Ho-ting, with his 39th

Army, was here. At the Baptist Mission hospital Doctor Ayres was away on vacation, and Doctor Humphrey was in charge.

I called on General Liu to thank him for his courtesies and found a superior type of professional soldier. He had fought well at Shanghai, and was one of the competent young army commanders. In appearance he was slight of build, and his manner was mild and unassuming. With gracious cordiality he informed me that he had already arranged for the transportation of our group. I could go to Hankow the next day, and the boys would go to Sian, where they could entruck for their return to Yenan. But first he wanted to give us a dinner.

The next afternoon we gathered for dinner under the shade trees in Lunghai Park, within a stone's throw of where I had been bombed earlier in the year. It was a delightful affair, with General Lin and his staff extending themselves to make us feel at ease. Everyone was informal and friendly.

For Liu, Auyang, Wang Yang and me it was a last supper. Only those who have traveled together under severe conditions over long distances can understand the tender fellowship which such an association develops. Nationality and race mean nothing. It is the integrity of the human being that counts, and these sterling companions had proved their loyalty, their courage and their integrity on numberless occasions. All were more mellow than when we started, and Wang Yang had changed in these months from an impetuous youth to a man of self-possession and self-abnegation. I, too, was changed, for one cannot live in an atmosphere of self-sacrifice without feeling its power and imbibing some of its spirit.

The dinner had been so timed as to end when my train was due to depart. Together we went to the station. After seeing us to my compartment, General Liu, with fine sensibility, withdrew to the platform, leaving our group together for a final farewell, I distributed to the boys parts of my equipment which I would no longer need, and which would prove useful to them at Yenan. The whistle sounded. With firm handclasps, and with tears in our throats and our eyes, we parted.

On the platform they regained their aplomb sufficiently to sing, and as the train steamed slowly out of the station the words of the refrain came to my ears—words which we had heard so often in these months, from so many thousands of lips:

> "Here we were born and here we were raised,
> Every inch of the soil is ours;
> Whoever tries to take it from us,
> Him will we fight to the end."

CHAPTER X

BLOODY BUT UNBOWED

I

HANKOW was not the same city I had left in April. Physical changes were few, though Japanese bombings had taken their toll, especially in Wuchang and Hanyang. The main difference was in the attitude of the people, the absence of Westerners and the increase in military activity. Hankow was fighting with her back to the wall.

Hsuchowfu had fallen on the 21st of May, some confusion attending the withdrawal of the Chinese army. It was not, however, as great as at Shanghai and Nanking. Most important, from the Chinese viewpoint, was the fact that the invaders had been delayed for another five months, and that the Chinese army was still intact.

Japanese military leaders were not long in determining the next move. Early in June warships were moved up the Yangtze, and preparations pointed to a drive towards Hankow. On the 14th of June Anking, the capital of Anhwei province, which stands on the north bank of the river, fell, and the campaign began.

The westward move was made with three main columns. The northernmost started from Hofei, in northern Anhwei, and headed for Sinyang, two hundred miles to the west, and a hundred miles north of Hankow, on the railroad. The second column followed the north bank of the Yangtze, while the third moved west along the south bank, both of these columns being aided by warships on the river.

For the defense of Wuhan the Chinese armies had been organized into another War Zone, the Ninth, with thirty-eight-year-old General Ch'en Ch'eng in command.

Ch'en Ch'eng had become a favorite with the Generalissimo. He was a native of the Generalissimo's home province, Chekiang, and had served under him since the early days of the Nationalist revolution, as instructor in the Whampoo Military Academy, commander of the artillery corps during the Northern Expedition, and as corps and army commander. Short and wiry, he possessed great energy and driving power, and was devoted to his chief. In some quarters, especially in Communist circles, he was not popular because he was essentially an authoritarian, but as chief of the Political Training department he worked amicably with Chow En-lai, who was vice-chairman.

As the battle for Wuhan (which included Hankow) developed, the resisting forces grew in size until at the end they numbered 148 divisions and over a million men. Japan used ten and a half divisions, with about two hundred and fifty thousand men. The Japanese division comprises twenty thousand men, just double the strength of the corresponding unit in the Chinese army.

But strength in this battle could not be measured in numbers of men and divisions. The Japanese possessed gunboats on the river, strong mechanized equipment on land, and, most important of all, air superiority. The air arm was not used effectively in support of ground forces until the battle was half over. However, when the massed bombing attacks began, China had no alternative but to retire, for whole battalions were blown out of the ground at a time.

This came later, however, and when I arrived in Hankow in August, the Japanese were still more than a hundred miles from the city.

The foreign embassies had moved to Chungking, along with the Ministry of Foreign Affairs. What was of more personal concern to me was the fact that my mail and reserve clothing had gone with our Embassy, for the Ambassador had no way of knowing when or where I might re-appear. For weeks I clogged around Hankow in the outfit I had worn on the trail. But it didn't matter, for under the stress of battle conditions social life in Hankow was most informal.

I established myself in a room at the Lutheran Mission Home this time, for the majority of the remaining journalists were there and it would be easier to keep in touch with the situation. I spent the next two months here, preparing my official report and observing the progress of the battle.

II

In these closing days of the battle of Hankow the foreign colony was reduced to a handful of business men, journalists, consular officers, military observers and the officers and crews of the foreign gunboats. The atmosphere in which we lived was one of gloomy apprehension. The ultimate capitulation of the city was taken for granted; the question was when. It was like waiting for the demise of a friend who had been mortally wounded.

The journalists and the observers were men who had spent years in China, and most of them had met on previous battle fields. It was only natural that in this environment, where we were together for meals, air raids and trips to the front, a close bond of fellowship should grow up among us. We finally organized ourselves under the title of "The Hankow Last Ditchers." In the group were Tillman Durdin, of the *New York Times*, Victor Keene, of the *Herald-Tribune*, Yates McDaniel, of the *Associated Press*, Mac Fisher, of the *United Press*, and my old comrade of the Taierchwang battle, Robert Capa, now covering the war for *Life* magazine. Other members included two news-reel men, Eric Mayell, and George Krainaikov, a New Zealand correspondent named Warren, a young Oxford graduate, George Hogg, Archibald Steele, of the *Chicago Daily News* and Walter Bosshard, a Swiss journalist. News of the battle flowed from the typewriters and cameras of these men to the outside world.

For a time Agnes Smedley was the sole feminine member of the Last Ditchers, but one day another adventurous woman appeared on the scene. She was Freda Utley, an English woman, who came out for the *London News-Chronicle*.

Miss Utley's fame had preceded her, for she had recently written an unusually informative book on Japan's economic set up, entitled *Japan's Feet of Clay*. Data for the book was gathered while she was living in Japan with her husband, the Soviet Trade Commissioner. A short time later her husband became the victim of a purge in Russia, and Miss Utley returned to England completely disillusioned about the Russian system. She was a keen student of Far Eastern politics and economics, and she proved to be a practical humanitarian as well. On her visits to the front she was greatly disturbed by the poor care the wounded were receiving, and she presented facts to Madame Chiang Kai-shek which resulted in drastic corrective action by China's First Lady.

At the American Consulate-General, the Consul General, Paul Josselyn, watched over the interests of American citizens, while Colonel Joseph Stilwell and Captain Frank Dom compiled data for our War Department.

Down on the river the flag of Rear Admiral LeBreton flew at the mainmast of the *U.S.S. Luzon*, which was the flagship of our Yangtze Patrol. The war had scattered his patrol, for some ships were below the boom which the Chinese had placed in the river, while others were above it. Life was pretty dull for these men of our Navy, for the nature of their duties required that they remain on the ships most of the time, and they were denied the diversion of rambling around the countryside, as the correspondents and observers did. Primarily their duty was to be on hand to guard the lives and interests of Americans, if they became endangered. In American fashion, they devised many odd ways of amusing themselves. One was the organization of a select group called the "Yangtze River Rats." Membership went to those of the naval service who had served six months or more on the river. After the Chinese placed a boom across the river, preventing the up-river ships from moving down to Shanghai, a medal was designed and struck off to commemorate service above the boom. It was known as the "Barrier" medal, and any member of the U.S. naval service who served above the boom was entitled to add it to his trophies. It was all in the spirit of good clean fun, and evoked many a laugh in days when smiles were at a premium.

III

Hollington Tong was still directing the office of public relations, and one day he took me over for a visit with the Generalissimo. The meeting had been scheduled for two days before, but the Generalissimo's personal quarters had been hit during a bombing attack, and it had been postponed. That attack, incidentally, was probably the closest Chiang has come to death in this war, despite the fact that he visits the front frequently. One bomb hit the dugout which he and Madame Chiang occupied. Others hit the quarters of his bodyguards, killing several.

The Generalissimo looked worn, and his hair was even grayer than it had been in March, but he was in excellent spirits and full of confidence. He followed the narrative of my travels with interest, and occasionally interjected remarks, or asked questions. I was particularly interested in his reaction to the ideas which Mao Tse-tung had told me were the hope of the Communist Party for the post-war period. "How do they compare with your ideas?" I asked when I had finished. His reply was a succinct "Ch'a pu to," which means "About the same."

On this and subsequent occasions I tried to divine the motives and convictions of this strong man of China. There could be no question of the simplicity of his own life, of the sincerity of his desire to improve the material condition of his people, or of his willingness to sacrifice his life, if need be, for the salvation of his country. Why, then, was he not more vigorous in eliminating inefficiency and selfishness from among subordinates of his own party? Why was he unwilling to permit the mobilization of the people everywhere in the manner that was proving so effective behind the Japanese lines in the north?

My final conclusion was that there are probably three major reasons. In the first place, while the influence of Generalissimo Chiang in China is greater than that of any other man, he is not a dictator, nor does he believe in dictatorship as a policy. He can persuade and coerce up to a certain point, but, especially during the present national emergency, his function is to keep all factions pulling together as a team. And there are many factions even within the Kuomintang Party.

Then, he is a man of profound loyalty. He places great store on the loyalty of subordinates, and he returns it in full measure, sometimes to his disadvantage. There are subordinates in his ranks who were once energetic, liberal and efficient, but who are now simply complacent and conservative. These he is loath to deal with harshly.

Finally, many officials in the Kuomintang entourage were raised in the authoritarian tradition. They believe in the class tradition. They believe that the upper classes are entitled to privileges and perquisites that are denied the great mass of people. And the way to retain them is to retain power. If the people were mobilized, articulate and enjoyed a voice in the direction of their affairs, these selfish officials might lose their positions and their privileges. It takes time to change well established patterns of thought. The Generalissimo is trying to change these thought patterns through persuasion and example, but the process is slow.

In the course of a broadcast to the Chinese people on Easter eve, 1938, he said: "A leader of national revolution must do away with ignorance, corruption, confusion, selfishness and covetousness and then start a new life through the inculcation of a new spirit, which will develop and grow until the emancipation of the whole nation is accomplished." This declaration is indicative of what he is trying to do.

About the war the Generalissimo was confident. He was pitting time, China's manpower, and her vast terrain against Japan's modern military machine and her efforts for a quick victory. During this first phase he had directed his commanders to resist to their utmost when attacked, but when they were compelled to retire they were to retire along a line which he designated. The battles at Shanghai, Hsuchowfu and Hankow were, in fact, delaying actions, designed to afford the time necessary to prepare a base deep in the interior, which the rugged terrain would assist in making impregnable. They also afforded time in which to indoctrinate the people more thoroughly with a spirit of nationalism and the will to resist domination, so that those who might eventually be constrained to live for a time under Japanese rule would continue to work secretly for ultimate victory. This first phase would end when Hankow fell, for China's armies would then be in a central position along the foothills of the great Tibetan plateau, and difficult to dislodge, while Japan's military strength would be dissipated in guarding long lines of communication, and in maintaining positions on the exterior lines of a fifteen-hundred-mile front.

The war would then go into the second, or guerrilla, phase. The problem then would be to prevent Japan from controlling the occupied areas by political means, prevent her from exploiting the natural resources of the country, and make it as difficult as possible for her armies to move supplies along their lines of communication. This would mean blocking the authority of any puppet government which might be formed, and rendering the authority impotent by intensifying the will of the people to resist. It would mean the development of guerrilla operations on a gigantic scale so as to maintain constant pressure against all points vital to the Japanese occupation. By hindering the exploitation of China's rich natural resources, the whole Japanese adventure in China would be made exorbitantly costly.

The concept of this second phase was based, of course, on the conviction that economically China could outlast Japan in a protracted war. The Japanese army was more expensive to maintain, for all supplies, including food, had to be transported from home. The Japanese soldier dislikes the Chinese ration of millet, cabbage, bean curd and beans, and prefers his own rice, fish and beef. Moreover, the Japanese army has been developed and trained along orthodox Western lines, and requires heavy equipage and, the support of artillery and aviation, making it cumbersome on the march and expensive to maintain. Being an inflexible sort of individual, the Japanese finds it difficult to change his ways.

The Chinese army, on the other hand, possessed the advantage of fighting on its own soil, where food is more available and cheap. It was accustomed to swift marches with light equipment; and operating among a friendly populace it could, in guerrilla operations, choose its own time and place for fighting. The people were accustomed to living on a bare subsistence margin, and stimulated by the spiritual urge of defending their own independence, they were prepared to make even greater sacrifices. China lacked the heavy industry so essential to the production of war materials, but she possessed most of the raw materials in abundance. And she possessed something even more important: the moral backing of the liberty-loving nations of the world—which Japan's predatory activities had denied her.

There would have to be a third phase, of course, for guerrilla warfare is not decisive. The third, or counter-offensive phase, would be initiated by the Chinese when Japan, as the result of economic exhaustion at home, or because of the unbearable pressure against her lines of communication in China, or both, was constrained to commence a retrograde movement towards the coast. The counter-offensive would require a trained army of great striking power, and this the Generalissimo already had plans to train in the provinces of the west and southwest, just as he had prepared a base there with lines of communication to Burma, Indo-China and Russia.

All of these plans hinged heavily on China's continued unity. There had been some friction between certain selfish officials in the Kuomintang armies and subordinates of the Eighth Route Army. But I felt then, and I still feel, that mutual confidence obtained between the Generalissimo and the leaders of China's Communist Party. Both had the welfare of China at heart. Both recognized the moral and physical value of an articulate and inspired populace. And both were aiming for representative government. But the minds of bourgeois officials had to be adjusted to this idea gradually. As the crisis increased their resistance to it would lessen.

There is another angle of the Generalissimo's character which needs to be examined. Speculation has been rife as to the sincerity of his belief in Christianity. It has been suggested that his conversion was an astute move to win the support of foreign missionaries, or that it came about in deference to the wishes of his wife, who is a devout Christian. Both of these theses are in contradiction to the Generalissimo's unvarying reputation for honesty.

It is generally known now that when he first proposed marriage, Madame Soong, his present wife's mother, asked that as a pre-requisite he embrace the Christian faith. He is reported to have replied that he would be glad to study it, but that he could not in all honesty profess a faith in which he did not believe in order to gain the woman he loved. This from a man who loved as few men have loved.

No, there is, I am convinced, no doubt about the sincerity of the Generalissimo's conversion. When he was a prisoner at Sian in December, 1936, the only book for which he asked was the *Bible*. When I lunched with him and Madame Chiang, later in my stay here, a minute of silent blessing preceded the meal, and there was no ostentation about it.

It may be that it is the revolutionary aspect of Jesus' life that most interests him, but if this is true he has caught the idea that is the basis of that spirit. This statement, made in one of his public addresses, is significant: "I have long sought to know the source of the revolutionary spirit of Jesus. From whence did it spring? I have come to realize that it came entirely from His spirit of love. Through this spirit of love, He drove from the minds of men all evil thinking and broke up systems of inequality, so that all men might exercise the heaven-given right to enjoy liberty and equality."

I will not attempt to reconcile the Generalissimo's Christian faith with his action in causing the execution of thousands of people of the Communist persuasion during the civil war, except to point out that down through the ages men have placed varying interpretations on Christian doctrines.

There are in America, as well as in other countries, professing Christians who carry on their business relations without regard for either love or compassion, two of the strongest tenets of the Christian faith. There are professing Christians who seem to believe that the capitalistic economic system was anointed by Christ, so violent is their opposition to any who may choose to oppose it. Perhaps Chiang reasoned that communism was an evil which justified the use of unchristian practices to eliminate it. I have known American missionaries who were violent and uncompromising in their denunciation of the Chinese Communist leaders. And yet, I found those same leaders unostentatiously practising Christian doctrines more punctiliously and with greater consistency than many professing Christians of my acquaintance. Ideas sometimes do strange things to the human mind. It is significant, though, that since the Sian experience Chiang Kai-shek has been more mellow and more humanitarian.

The question is sometimes asked whether the Generalissimo will at some time consent to a compromise peace. His record and his public pledges indicate that he will agree to no peace which will infringe upon the sovereignty or the territorial integrity of China.

On December 16, 1937, he asserted to the nation in a radio broadcast: "My position and duty do not admit of evasion of responsibility. As long as I live, I will pursue, to the utmost of my ability, China's determination to resist to the bitter end and secure ultimate victory for the nation. Only by this attainment could I repay the Party, the Government and the people." The tenor of this declaration he has continued to repeat.

IV

Down at the Eighth Route Army office in Hankow I found Chow En-lai, who was maintaining liaison between the Communist Party and the National Government, and serving as vice-chairman of the Political Training Department of the Military Affairs Commission as well. Also there were Yeh Ch'ien-ying, Po Ku and Wang Ming.

Yeh Ch'ien-ying held the post of Chief of Staff of the Eighth Route Army, but he was here as chief of the office, and was frequently consulted by the Generalissimo or his staff on military matters. He was a hearty, explosive individual, invariably good natured, of medium height and stocky. An indefatigable worker, day and night, he nevertheless always had a moment to spare for a chat whenever I dropped in.

Po Ku was one of the political experts of the Party, and in the days before the united front agreement he had been chairman of the North Shensi Soviet. He was young, about thirty-three, tall and gangling, and wore thick glasses. Probably no one knew the doctrines of the Party better than Po Ku, except Mao Tse-tung. His English was excellent, and he was never too busy to explain a thesis or clarify a situation, in his quiet, unemotional manner.

The fourth member of the group, Wang Ming, was essentially a theoretician. He was about thirty years of age, short, and had a pleasing and disarming manner. For a number of years he had been the delegate to the Comintern, and he was exceptionally articulate.

There was no beating about the bush when these men talked. If I went to them for an explanation of a situation they either gave it to me straight out, or they stated very flatly that it was impossible for them to comment on it. Of evasion there was none.

At this time the group was urging on the Generalissimo the adoption of the policy of mobilizing the people in defense of the Wuhan area. They felt that if the measure was adopted, Partisans formed, village self-defense corps established and the people given ethical indoctrination, as in the north, the area might be saved from falling into Japanese hands. Perhaps they were right, but in any event it would have better prepared the people for active co-operation with the government after the capitulation. The Generalissimo may have favored the plan; it was said that he did. But the heavy-weights of the Kuomintang Party, such as Chen Li-fu, the rightist Minister of Education, opposed it, and it was not adopted.

One day Han Ying, the vice-commander of the New Fourth Army, came in from the guerrilla region in Anhwei province, south of the Yangtze. This army had been recently formed around the nucleus of the old Red Army which remained in Kiangsi to cover the retirement of the army when it started the long march in 1934. Han had kept his force together, and continued to resist the Kuomintang forces along the Kiangsi-Fukien border until the autumn of 1937—after the present war with Japan started.

Han was short, shorn of head, and a bundle of closely knit sinew. In conversation he was extremely vital, boring directly into the heart of a subject. Long service as a leader in the field had made him keenly alert and resourceful. As field commander he aptly complemented Yeh T'ing, the commander of the army, who was an older, less active, though equally earnest man.

The New Fourth Army was faced with many difficult problems. It had moved into the area south of Wuhu and Nanking after the Japanese had occupied the Yangtze river ports. The people were discouraged, and had received little attention from the government. Consequently, it took time to get their confidence and to inculcate in them the will-to-endure and the will-to-resist the invasion. Supplies were another problem, for though the national government had authorized the establishment of the army, it was not keen about providing arms and munitions to an organization which was administered in accordance with the doctrines of the Eighth Route Army.

In this respect it apparently suffered a disadvantage that was shared by the Eighth Route Army, for, from what I could gather when traveling through the north, the Eighth Route Army received scant aid from the Central Government. Contrary to the opinion which obtained abroad, it obtained no assistance directly from Soviet Russia. The Russian supplies, which China received on a barter basis, came down the long road from Sinkiang (Turkestan) to Lanchow and Sian, and from those points they were distributed to the various armies, the Eighth Route Army receiving whatever portion the government saw fit to allot.

Both of these armies were paid in accordance with the Central Government pay schedule (ranging from $7 a month for privates to several hundred dollars for the commander), but they disbursed the funds according to their own pay schedule ($1 per month for fighters up to $6 per month for Commander-in-Chief Chu Teh). The difference went into a fund for the purchase of food, medical supplies and for the maintenance of Partisan troops, for which no provision was made by the Central Government.

V

As the days and weeks passed the struggle for Wuhan became more intense. During the summer months both sides had suffered heavily from cholera and malaria. Among Chinese troops as high as sixty percent were incapacitated by disease at one time. With the coming of autumn, illness decreased and the Japanese drive gained momentum. Wounded streamed through Hankow by the thousands, going to hospitals that had been prepared in the west.

Air attacks on the Wuhan area increased, the planes coming in at higher altitudes now, usually bombing at heights of twelve to fifteen thousand feet. Accuracy was much better than it had been at lower altitudes during the Shanghai battle, indicating that a new and improved bomb sight had evidently reached Japanese hands. With the exception of a few anti-aircraft guns, China was powerless to drive off these attacks, for her own small aviation corps had been so badly damaged that it became necessary to reorganize it, and to train new pilots. Russian planes, which had rendered valuable assistance during the spring and summer, were withdrawn, probably due to increasing tension in Europe.

Under these conditions I was somewhat at a loss to understand the attitude of scores of young people of the upper classes in Hankow. They danced and played, gave elaborate cocktail and dinner parties, and were apparently oblivious of the fact that their countrymen were fighting for the nation's existence. The contrast here was striking to one who had just come from the north where the youth, in particular, were making great personal sacrifices and devoting their waking hours to various tasks connected with the program of resistance.

I spoke about it one day to Madame Chiang Kai-shek. "Why is it," I asked, "that a movement has not been started to convince the youth of China that they, too, have a contribution to make to national salvation? It would seem that the very least they could do is to live simple lives."

"That," she replied, "is what the New Life Movement is supposed to do."

And so, I turned to the New Life Movement for the answer to my question.

The New Life Movement was initiated in 1934 as part of a plan for the spiritual mobilization of the nation. Some say that it was the Generalissimo's answer to the ethical indoctrination taught by the Chinese Communists. In any event, it was designed to reduce corruption, advance sanitation and hygiene, induce a higher regard for dignity and neatness in personal appearance, and to provide a spiritual dynamic for the people.

The movement was built around four Chinese characters, representing four ancient virtues: Li, I, Lien and Chih.

Li emphasizes the need for good manners and propriety in human relations; I stresses the duty of the individual, and implies the broader connotation of service; Lien calls for integrity and incorruptibility; and Chih exhorts the individual to develop a feeling of self-respect and to have a "sense of shame" when his deportment has not been correct.

Concomitant with the initiation of the movement Chiang issued a set of eight principles which were designed to serve as a more concrete guide to conduct: "We must rid ourselves of old abuses, and build up a new nation.

"Accept the heavy responsibilities of serving the nation.

"Observe rules, have faith, honesty, and be humble.

"Develop the habit of keeping clothing, food, manner of living, and traveling habits simple, orderly, plain and clean.

"Face hardships willingly, and strive for frugality.

"Seek to acquire adequate knowledge, and develop moral integrity as citizens.

"Act courageously and swiftly.

"Let us act on our promises, or, better, act without promising."

Between the years 1934 and 1937, when the war started, this movement swept the country with tremendous vigor, and adherence to the precepts was closely identified in the minds of the people with nationalism and with moral and spiritual preparation for the test of strength with Japan that all knew must some day come. That it failed to grip the hearts and minds of the rank and file is probably due to the fact that in its application officials placed the greater emphasis on deportment and appearance. Also, it called for no sacrifices from officials and the well-to-do classes which were commensurate with the sacrifices made by the people.

A distinguished foreign official summed up the attitude of many Chinese officials at this time in the remark: "These people are willing to fight—to the last drop of coolie blood." Perhaps this observation was extreme, but it implied the existence of a class consciousness which imposed unequal sacrifices and responsibilities and condoned the unequal distribution of benefits. Small wonder, then, that the children of such men accepted no responsibility for sharing the hardships of the struggle.

VI

At the beginning of the war ninety percent of China's industry had been located along the coastal fringe. The battle at Shanghai and Japanese bombings at Canton and other cities had resulted in its destruction. In the winter of 1937-38 a small group of Chinese and foreigners, which included the writer, Edgar Snow, and the chief factory inspector of the industrial department of the Shanghai Municipal Council, Rewi Alley, met to discuss the situation. Out of this group came the idea of starting for China a guerrilla industry, based on the cooperative system. It would be de-centralized and spread out over the vast interior, so as to reduce its vulnerability from the air. Units would be established as near as possible to the source of supply, iron industries near the iron mines, textile industries in the cotton and wool regions, and so on. Labor would be drawn, as far as possible, from the hundreds of thousands of refugees who had fled to the interior.

The new British Ambassador, Sir Archibald Clark-Kerr, had arrived in Shanghai. Far from being the stodgy, conventional type of British Ambassador, he was hearty, informal and vigorous. He learned of the idea, immediately grasped its potentialities, and, it is said, carried it to the Generalissimo, who authorized the appropriation of five million dollars with which to get the project under way.

I met Sir Archibald when I was in Hankow in March, and while the Industrial Co-operatives were not discussed, I could imagine him playing the part of patron, for he was the rugged, vital, pipe-smoking type of Britisher, with an insatiable curiosity and boundless energy. On the occasion of my first call on him he amazed me by announcing that he had a letter of introduction to me, whereupon he dove into his brief case and produced a letter from Edgar Snow. Such modesty and lack of pomp immediately won my regard.

But the man who became the driving power and genius of the Industrial Co-operatives was Rewi Alley. His position with the Shanghai Municipal Council was a lucrative one, and he had held it for eleven years. But he had a strong social consciousness, and seeing the need for the development of an industrial organization which would support the armies in the field and fill a serious gap in China's internal economy, he gave up his position and offered his services to the Chinese government. They were accepted forthwith.

At this time he was in and out of Hankow, and I came to know him well. Now in his early forties, he had been born in New Zealand, and had served with the Anzacs on various fronts during the four years of the World War, coming out with wounds that kept him in hospitals for many months. In appearance he was short, stocky, tow-headed and red of face. His energy was phenomenal, and was only exceeded by his modesty.

He was endeavoring not only to get the co-operatives started, but to move into the interior the established industries which remained at Hankow. Difficulties were multiple. The industrialists seemed to be divided into three classes. Some were intelligent and co-operative, and saw the advantage of moving early to Chungking, Chengtu, or other suitable sites in the west. Another group consisted of men who were perfectly willing to move, but who failed to comprehend the difficulties and the time required to move machinery by boat and by hand into the interior. They wanted to continue operations at Hankow until the last minute, apparently expecting to be able to pick up suddenly and shift to a new site, where they could continue operations without loss of time. The third group, small in number, comprised those self-centered individuals who apparently cared little whether they operated under Chinese or Japanese jurisdiction, and they deliberately procrastinated and placed obstacles in the way of any attempt to move them. Patience and perseverance eventually won, for the government was itself concerned with the development of an industrial base in Szechuan, Kweichow and Yunnan.

During the months that have elapsed since Hankow fell Alley has traveled far and wide over free China, largely by bicycle, boat and horseback, setting up the industrial co-operative units. Fifteen hundred such units are now in operation, producing textiles, paper, soap, candles, glass, pottery, alcohol, leather goods, matches, flash light batteries, and a hundred other essential items.

The members of each unit participate in the profits in proportion to the degree of skill which they contribute to the productive process, plus their share of the dividends due from the stock they own. Each member must own at least three shares of stock, which he may purchase on the instalment plan, and no member may own more than twenty shares. Regardless of the number of shares he owns, no member is entitled to more than one vote in the councils of the unit. Funds for the establishment of the unit may be borrowed from the revolving fund which was set up by the government appropriation, and which is added to by voluntary contributions from both home and abroad. Loans are paid back, with interest, when the unit starts production. Thus far the products have been absorbed by the home market.

The co-operative idea appeals to the Chinese peasant, and the system has a bright future in China. As the system grows it should be instrumental in raising the standard of living of the workers. Already it has increased their purchasing power, and it is conceivable that as it gains momentum it will become the means by which China will attain, or even surpass, that state of prosperity suggested by the late Prime Minister of the Empire, Li Hung-chang, when, according to popular report, he remarked to a British statesman: "Think what it would mean to the cotton industry if four hundred millions of Chinese coolies were able to increase the length of their shirt tails by five inches."

VII

There were other foreigners who were working for the Chinese government, though for less altruistic reasons than Alley. When the German military mission was recalled, early in July, 1938, four Germans remained.

Most important of these is Captain Walther F. N. Stennes, who had a brilliant war record, was one time prominent in Adolph Hitler's entourage, and who subsequently quarreled with Hitler and was thrown into prison. Released through the successful intercession of his wife, he came to China with his family and became chief of the Generalissimo's personal bodyguards. Of medium height, blond, and in his middle forties, he has an incisive, restless personality. He is more than simply the captain of bodyguards, for his expert military knowledge and his great energy have caused the Generalissimo to rely on him to perform odd tasks requiring skill and technical knowledge such as mining rivers, constructing obstacles and improving the methods of the intelligence service.

Doctor Baerensprung, another veteran of the World War, in which he served as cavalry officer, and later as an aviator, was one of the three quarters of one percent who voted against Hitler in 1933, and his departure from Germany followed shortly. During the years following the war he had become an expert in police affairs, and his function in China for many years was to advise on police matters. A tall, burly man, his rather brusque and aloof manner shielded a warm, friendly personality. After the departure of General von Falkenhausen and the German mission; Baerensprung devoted more of his attention to military matters, becoming one of Stennes' right-hand men.

Another German whose services were of incalculable value was Frank Hoebich, a much younger man than either Stennes or Baerensprung. Hoebich is a fortification engineer. Lean and wiry, and a bit satirical, he was nevertheless devoted to his profession, and performed yeoman work far and wide along the Chinese fronts.

Russian technical experts began to arrive in China after the departure of the German mission. For the most part they were experts in artillery, engineering, communications and transport. Most of them were attached to training centers, or to divisions at the front. Apparently none replaced General von Falkenhausen as adviser in strategy and tactics.

In international affairs, in matters of public relations, and in a thousand other matters W. H. Donald, the Australian whom I had first met at Nanking, continued to be the chief foreign counselor for the Chiangs. Speaking his mind freely, but never presuming to dictate, his judgment was highly valued by the Generalissimo and Madame Chiang, both because he had no personal axe to grind, and because his discretion and his loyalty had been thoroughly tested.

VIII

The army medical service is one of the units which, at this time, had not caught up with the progress made by the rest of the army. In China the medical service has always been sort of a stepchild of the army, care of the wounded being considered secondary to the improvement of combat units. During the Shanghai battle, when wounded poured back from the front in numbers unprecedented for China, the Chinese Red Cross, under the direction of Doctor F. C. Yen, an alumnus of Yale, threw itself into the breech and organized a score of hospitals.

One of the weaknesses of the medical corps was that medical officers in the army had no military standing. Consequently, they were unable to control patients, when they became convalescent, and they could be dictated to by officers of the line. Trained doctors, therefore, were reluctant to make their services available to the government.

Two men were fighting to overcome the handicaps, and to bring order out of chaos. Doctor Hu Lan-sen, who had taken his post-graduate work at Harvard, was Director of the Medical Corps, and handled administration from Hankow. He was an honest, frank and conscientious man of fifty-odd years, who had formerly been with Feng Yu-hsiang's Kuominchun army. But the driving force was provided by young, dynamic Doctor Lu Chi-teh, also a Harvard graduate, and subsequently a graduate of the U.S. Army medical school at Carlisle, Pennsylvania.

Doctor Lu was in charge of medical evacuation, and he spent most of his time in the field establishing dressing stations and field hospitals, and devising ways and means for accelerating the movement of the wounded from the front lines back to the base hospitals.

Co-operating closely with Doctors Hu and Lu was Doctor Robert Lim, for many years a member of the staff of the Rockefeller Foundation hospital at Peip'ing. Lim had been trained at the University of Edinburgh, and during the World War he had served as a medical officer with the British army. This rich experience he now brought to the Chinese Red Cross Medical Relief Commission, which co-operated with the Army Medical Corps in the field and along the line of communications. A tireless organizer, Doctor Lim had at this time (September, 1938) organized curative, nursing, preventive and X-ray teams which were doing effective work in the theater of operations.

Equally important were the training schools he had established for expanding the service and for providing replacements.

IX

General Feng Yu-hsiang was living on the outskirts of Wuchang. I had seen him at Doctor Kung's luncheon, in March, but I wanted an opportunity to make a closer estimate of this man whose career had contained so many startling contradictions. One day I asked Doctor Hu Lan-sen, who was an old friend of his, to make an appointment for me to meet him. General Feng replied that he would be glad to receive me at six o'clock the next morning.

The first ferry from Hankow to Wuchang left at five-forty. I made it, and by dint of rapid walking I reached the General's establishment at the appointed time.

His home was furnished with Spartan severity. With military promptness he entered the room in which I waited—a tall commanding figure in plain, neat Chung San uniform (a five-button affair with standing collar). About his face played a jocular smile—possibly occasioned by the unorthodox calling hour. There was no interpreter, each of us having presumed that the other would have one on hand. But he was tolerant of my Chinese, and for the next hour we covered various angles of the war, he shyly suggesting a word or phrase when I was stumped.

Although over six feet tall and weighing in the vicinity of two hundred and twenty-five pounds, General Feng keeps himself in prime physical condition. An apostle of the simple, frugal life, he is noted in Chinese military annals for the frequency with which he changed sides during the civil wars. After his unsuccessful attempt to overthrow Chiang Kai-shek, in 1930-31, he retired to a temple on the sacred mountain of Confucius, T'ai Shan, where he spent the years until 1937 studying the classics. There are two points concerning which Feng has demonstrated unvarying consistency. One is his love for the common people, and the other is his opposition to

Japanese attempts to violate Chinese sovereignty, the latter dating from the invasion of Manchuria, in 1931.

Back in the early 1920's, when Feng's Kuominchun army was holding forth in the Kalgan-Peip'ing area, he embraced Christianity, thereby earning the sobriquet "Christian General." As in the case of the Generalissimo, doubts have been expressed about his sincerity, but he lives according to Christian principles, and counsels them in his public utterances.

This story of General Feng I heard from an unimpeachable source. Generalissimo Chiang has established the custom of assembling the leaders of the government every Monday morning for the purpose of re-dedicating themselves to the objectives of the nation: the San Min Chu I, or Three Principles of the People, originally enunciated by Doctor Sun Yat-sen, Father of the Revolution (Nationalism, Democracy and Livelihood). At this meeting he, or another of the high leaders, gives a short address.

One Monday morning Feng addressed the meeting on the subject of unity, and he used as a text the verses from the 12th Chapter of First Corinthians relating to unity, with emphasis on the following:

"Yes, God has tempered the body together, with a special dignity for the inferior parts, so that there may be no disunion in the body, but that the various members should have a common concern for one another. Thus, if one member suffers, all the members share its suffering; if one member is honored, all the members share its honor."

After the meeting General Li Chi-sen, one of the Kwangsi leaders, said to Feng: "I didn't know that was in the *Bible*. Where can I get a copy of that book?"

"Just let me take care of that," replied Feng. "I'll see that you get one."

Whereupon he obtained a copy from the local branch of the American Bible Society and presented it to General Li with the latter's name engraved on the cover in gold characters.

Feng is no longer active as a military commander, but his name carries weight with the people, and as Vice-Chairman of the Military Affairs Commission his counsel is of value to the government.

X

On the 25th of September the remaining government offices in Hankow began to close, although no material change had occurred in the military situation which indicated the necessity for an immediate withdrawal. Obviously some decision of moment had been made, though no official would admit it. Eventually I learned through friends in one of the offices that the decision to retire had been reached, the plan being to avoid the confusion which had attended the retirements from Shanghai and Hsuchowfu by withdrawing the troops gradually over a period of four weeks. In the face of relentless aerial attacks the ultimate capitulation of the city was inevitable, and it was considered wise to withdraw the army while it was still intact. The four months time gained by the resistance here had enabled the Generalissimo to build the base and the roads in the west which he had planned in anticipation of such an eventuality.

Hankow was a hive of activity during these last weeks, and there was ample evidence of the sacrifice and suffering which this war had visited upon the people. Refugees who had paused here, hoping against hope that the defenses of the city might hold out, packed up and moved deeper into the interior to undertake the task of again settling themselves in a new environment. Wounded from the remaining hospitals were loaded onto river boats and trains. And there was the last-minute scramble of industrialists and shopkeepers to clear out while there was time. Every mode of transportation was commandeered, and still there was not sufficient to meet the demand.

Throughout these weeks troops marched in various directions from the lines north and south of the Wuhan area. Sixty divisions were sent to the east—towards Nanking and Shanghai—with instructions to carry on relentless guerrilla warfare against the Japanese lines of communication. Other divisions took up positions along the hills to the west, prepared to prevent further penetration of the enemy in that direction.

The evacuation of Hankow was completed on the 25th of October, and on that day Japanese troops marched in. But four days previously a catastrophe had occurred in the south: Canton had been occupied.

The invasion of Canton had been expected for many months, and why more effective provision for its defense was not made is still a mystery. The city had been subjected to the most devastating bombing of any city in China, thousands of lives being lost and millions of dollars' worth of property destroyed. But apparently the military commander, General Yu Hanmou, placed too much reliance on the report that the Japanese would not strike at Canton for fear of antagonizing the British, who occupied near-by Hongkong. But the Munich appeasement had its repercussion in the Far East, and immediately thereafter the Japanese landed at Bias Bay, and drove across the hundred miles to Canton, finding little resistance.

The report that General Yu Han-mou had sold out is not borne out by the facts. If there had been conclusive evidence, or even good circumstantial evidence, that such was the case, Yu Han-mou would have been court-martialed and shot, as Han Fu-chu had been after the Shantung fiasco. It appears that Yu Han-mou's guilt was negligence and culpable inefficiency. When the attack came he was not prepared, and he was faced with two alternatives: either he could resist to the best of his ability, with the prospect of losing both his army and the city; or he could retire his army and simply lose the city. He chose the latter alternative, but when he retired he was careful to retire along the line which had previously been indicated by the Generalissimo, thereby saving himself from the charge of treason.

The first phase of the war had come to an end and China had entered upon the guerrilla phase, determined to wear out her enemy. Eighteen months of war had left her stronger, rather than weaker. The first terrifying shock had been met and absorbed. Both the people and the army knew what to expect now. They were binding their wounds and setting their teeth with grim determination. Battles might be lost, but the final victory would be theirs. Not for nothing had forty millions of refugees and twenty-five thousand university students, with their faculties, trekked hundreds of miles into the interior. Not for nothing had China built thousands of miles of highways to bring the areas of the west into contact with the outside world. These tasks take grit and resourcefulness.

But most important was the fact that people of varying degrees of political complexion and social status were learning how to work together in a common cause. And the longer they worked together, the more they were discovering about each other's basic character, ideals and objectives. Almost unconsciously they were coming to realize that their political goal was the same: democracy.

XI

Before Hankow fell I departed for Chungking, in Szechuan, five hundred miles by air line to the west, having made a rather momentous decision.

For twelve years I had been observing and studying Far Eastern politics, and eight of those years had been spent in China, with frequent trips to Japan. What I had seen had convinced me that the military-naval group which controlled Japan was possessed of an insatiable appetite for power which would inevitably bring that nation to the point where she would one day challenge the United States in the eastern Pacific, unless she were stopped. Eighteen months of observation with the Chinese armies had further convinced me that China possessed the capacity and the willingness to check Japan's will to power if America and the democracies of the West would cease providing Japan with the sinews of war: iron, steel, petroleum.

Government officials cannot speak their minds publicly, especially on matters of international concern, without embarrassing their government. And yet, the diplomatic and military officials of our government who serve abroad are in a position to know what the officials of foreign governments are thinking and doing.

I had already strained the limits of diplomatic good form by bearing public witness to the character of Chinese resistance I had found in north China, but the story had not half been told. I could not do more without reverting to the status of a private citizen. And so I submitted my resignation as an officer of the Marine Corps, and of the Naval Service. A pressing sense of duty had left me no alternative.

CHAPTER XI

SUNRISE IN THE WEST

I

SIX hours of flying, with two intermediate stops, brought me to Chungking, the great trading center of Szechuan province, on the upper reaches of the Yangtze river. Coming from war-torn Hankow, Chungking seemed like a new world, tranquil, green and blissfully soothing, by contrast. Spiraling down through the cloud bank that almost perpetually hangs over the city, we suddenly emerged from the lower rim to find below us the Yangtze and the hodge-podge of buildings that comprises the business section, pinnacled cheek by jowl on the narrow tongue of rock that separates it from the Kialing river, on the north. With motors roaring, our heavy seaplane settled on the surface of the swift-flowing river and taxied to a landing stage.

This was to be the new capital of China—the third which had been occupied by the government since the war commenced. The movement of the government offices here was comparable to moving the capital of the United States from Washington, D.C., to Tulsa, Oklahoma.

The red basin of Szechuan, on the southern edge of which Chungking stands, is markedly different from other sections of China. In Tertiary times, according to geologists, this basin, which embraces an area of seventy-five thousand square miles (about the size of the state of Nebraska) was occupied by a lake, with deposits of red sandstones. Four tributaries of the

Yangtze (giving the province its name of Four Rivers) flow through the basin, and aid in making it one of the most productive regions of China. Surrounded by mountains of the Tibetan plateau, except where the Yangtze has cut a gorge, the climate is humid, the sun seldom shines, and there is rarely a winter frost. Rice, wheat, millet, corn, beans, sugar, hemp and tobacco grow in abundance, and the area supported a pre-war population of forty-four millions of people. Recently constructed roads now link the basin with Kweichow and Yunnan provinces, on the south, and with Shensi and Kansu, on the north.

Chungking would be the new capital of China, and already many of the government offices had moved here, including the Ministry of Foreign Affairs. In a few weeks Japanese planes, from their new base at Hankow, would convert this tranquillity into a living hell, but now all was peaceful.

On the south bank of the Yangtze, where were most of the foreign dwellings, I found the Ambassador in the new Embassy offices which had been established in the compound of the Standard Oil Company. With his customary graciousness he invited me to share the house he was occupying with the Counselor of Embassy, Willys Peck, and a secretary, Sidney Lafoon.

Here I spent a quiet, restful week, basking in this serene and stimulating atmosphere, participating in the after-dinner game of Chinese checkers (which had now supplanted patience poker), and adjusting my perspective of the Far Eastern scene, against the background of a decade of observations.

II

Japanese leaders have attempted to justify the invasion of China on the grounds that they sought economic co-operation and were attempting to stem the spread of communism. The facts do not bear out either contention.

If Japan had desired simply economic co-operation this could have been attained by peaceful means at any time prior to September, 1931, when she raped Manchuria. As a matter of fact, at the beginning of the present conflict China was Japan's best customer, as well as a rich source of raw materials. The pre-war boycotts were not due to a natural antipathy of the Chinese for the Japanese, but were an expression of disapproval of Japan's repeated attempts to violate China's sovereignty.

As for communism, my observations convinced me that the doctrines practised by the Chinese Communists are, in their political aspects, representative government (democracy), in their economic aspect, the co-operative theory, and that only in their social application could they be called communistic, for emphasis is placed on social equality. Japan's attempt to dominate China by military force, rather than restricting the spread of these doctrines, actually accelerated it.

In order to understand Japan's true goals it is necessary to recall that that nation has, for over three hundred years, been dominated by a military clique, with the exception of a few all-too-brief interludes. The first evidence of the desire of her military leaders for military conquest came in 1592, when an ambitious general named Hideyoshi enunciated a flamboyant plan for the conquest of Eastern Asia. Korea was first to be invaded, and this was to be followed successively by the conquest of Manchuria and China. With the Emperor moved to the throne at Peip'ing, Hideyoshi planned to establish his military headquarters at Ningpo, south of where Shanghai now stands, and from there operate for the conquest of southeast Asia, the Philippine Islands, and what is now the Dutch East Indies. Hideyoshi died during the invasion of Korea, and the plan went into temporary eclipse—to be resurrected by the militarists of the twentieth century, with embellishments.

A few years after Hideyoshi's death the Tokugawa Shogunate, a military government which ruled in the name of the Emperor, was established, and Japan entered upon the two hundred and fifty years of isolation, which were broken by Commodore Perry's negotiations. Since the restoration of Meiji the military clique has continued to dominate Japanese policies. The program of expansion by conquest got under way in 1894. Between that date and the beginning of the present war with China Japan had added 710,000 square miles to her original 148,000 square miles.

In 1931 the invasion of Manchuria ushered in the era of aggression that has now gained such terrific momentum in Europe. For Japan it was a trial balloon designed to test the reaction of the Western powers. They remained quiescent, and in 1933 Jehol followed Manchuria into the Japanese maw. Italy took a leaf from Japan's book and moved into Ethiopia, and then came Germany's turn.

It is not, however, simply the steadily mounting conquests of Japan in Asia that is alarming. The menace which must give Americans pause is the mental attitude of the Japanese military and naval officers towards the program of conquest. They are imbued with the concept of divine mission. They have the mission to carry the Japanese brand of culture to the four corners of the earth. And the conquest of China is regarded by them as merely a stepping stone to that end. Hence the desire to *conquer* China, and not simply to enjoy economic cooperation. A Japanese-dominated China would make available the vast reservoir of manpower and of natural resources with which to build an army and a navy which could carry conquest farther afield.

The present struggle between China and Japan cannot be of merely academic interest to the people of the United States. It is a struggle the outcome of which will determine whether Eastern Asia will be ruled by a military autocracy, or whether the budding democracy of China will come into full bloom. If Japan wins then America must look to her defenses, for the desire of the Japanese military-naval clique to crush America is no less intense than the desire of Germany to crush Great Britain. And yet America continues to provide Japan with the war materials with which to establish this hegemony!

What of Japan's military effort in China? After observing the Japanese operations at Shanghai for three months I characterized the army as third rate, as compared with the armies of the Western powers. My observations during the succeeding year served to confirm this appraisal. It is based on inferiority of striking power, poor co-ordination of transport, poor co-ordination of the air force with ground troops, inferiority of weapons, poor direction of artillery fire, and lack of imagination and initiative on the part of leaders. Costly errors have been made, one being the failure to estimate correctly the temper and the capacity for resistance of the Chinese people. As the war progressed the driving power of the army was seriously impaired by the dispersion of forces over a wide area.

Japan needlessly increased the difficulties of her task by the ruthlessness of the methods she employed, which served further to embitter the Chinese people and strengthen their resolve to resist. The attempt to terrorize the populace by unrestricted bombing of open villages and cities failed utterly to accomplish its purpose. The raping, pillaging and burning engaged in by the soldiery was apparently not restrained, and there is evidence to show that in some cases, at least, it was directed. The number of institutions of higher learning which have been bombed has been too great not to have been part of a deliberate plan. And the consistency with which the use of narcotics has been encouraged in the occupied regions can only be interpreted as part of a monstrous plan to undermine Chinese resistance by weakening the moral fiber of the people.

Nevertheless, let no one be so rash as to underestimate the power of the Japanese army. It is a formidable fighting force. Officers and men are courageous, and they are possessed of a loyalty to the Emperor that is almost fanatical in its intensity. They are persistent and determined, and many of the errors they are making in this war will not be repeated. The Imperial General Staff is well trained, and it is almost prescient in its ability to time major moves so as to catch opponents at a disadvantage.

The army has been handicapped by the extent of the war theater—nearly two thousand miles from Mongolia to the border of Indo-China—and by the necessity for maintaining large numbers of troops on the Siberian frontier. Manpower is a problem, for the maximum number of men which Japan could mobilize in an extreme emergency is estimated to be not more than seven million. Her casualties after nearly three years of fighting have aggregated about a million men. Another million are committed to the mainland of Eastern Asia, and large numbers are mobilized at home.

The unqualified fulfillment of Japan's objectives in China is out of the question. Even if organized resistance should break down, the resistance of independent groups would be sufficient to deny control of large sections of the country without military occupation, and this Japan has not the man-power to establish on a large scale. But partial fulfillment of her objectives may be realized if she is willing to pay the price, and if she continues to receive the copper, steel, iron, petroleum and cotton which now flow into her war industries from America. The price would be the doubling, more probably the trebling, of her present military forces in China.

However, even her present stalemated position could not be long maintained without the economic assistance of the United States.

III

China's war aim is to regain her independence, and the united strength of the nation is directed to this end. China's mistakes have been many and serious, but in the main her strategy has been sound. At the beginning of the war her army was not prepared in organization, equipment or training to engage a modern military machine on terms of even moderate equality. Organizational ability is not a strong point with the Chinese, and this deficiency was marked in the early stages of the struggle. A majority of the military units came from the provinces where command appointments were frequently conditioned on political preference. The inefficient had to be weeded out, and the process had to be conducted in a manner which would not injure the sensibilities of the politically powerful. China's unity was of recent origin in 1937, and as the war progressed it was necessary to co-ordinate the efforts of recently antagonistic groups. Perhaps the most serious deficiency was in commanders and staff officers who were trained in the modern technique of war.

However, resourcefulness is a prime characteristic of the Chinese. The determination to resist was almost universal among the people, and with this as an unalterable premise China set out to devise ways and means by which to translate this determination into action. Flesh and blood were pitted against iron and steel at terrific cost, but the invader was compelled to slow down. With the time gained by this sacrifice schools were set up for the training of commanders, staff officers, specialists and technicians. Armies were regrouped and reorganized. The supply system was redesigned to meet demands and conditions, new roads were built, certain reforms were promulgated to improve the welfare and morale of the people, and steps were taken to integrate the internal economy of the nation. While these activities were going on refugees by the millions uprooted themselves from their ancestral homes and migrated to the west, as did schools and colleges throughout the threatened regions.

The Communist Party, recently released from a bitter struggle for existence which had caused its leaders to dig deep into their reservoir of human resources for ways and means by which to preserve themselves, were now able to contribute to the national cause a pattern of life and of resistance to the invasion which were of inestimable value. That the leaders of the two major parties did not see eye to eye on many points, political, social and economic, was no bar to their co-operation in national defense. Fundamentally they were seeking the same end, though by different approaches.

Both Communist and Kuomintang parties subscribe to the objectives set for the nation by the late Doctor Sun Yat-sen, which are embraced in the San Min Chu I, or Three Principles of the People, though they differ somewhat as to the manner of attainment. These principles are summed up in the terms Nationalism, Democracy and the People's Livelihood.

In his essays on Nationalism Doctor Sun observed that China's weakness had been due in large measure to the tradition that placed clan loyalty above loyalty to the state. He did not advocate the weakening of clan loyalty, but urged the intensification of the loyalty of the clan to the state, with the object of building a strong nation around the Chinese race. The Kuomintang continues to stress the idea of clan loyalty to the state, while the Communists contend that individual loyalty to the state should supersede all other loyalties.

Democracy Doctor Sun envisaged as placing political power in the hands of the people, while administrative power was delegated to the government which was chosen by the people. The people were to enjoy the right of suffrage, and to have the power of recall, initiative and referendum. The administrative powers of government he divided into five branches. To the executive, legislative and judicial branches, which are employed in the West, he added the department of civil service examinations and the department of censorship, which had served so well the imperial governments of old China.

In China relief from poverty has been the great national urge. Poverty was so universal, and so extreme, that every man sought to "make a fortune" in order to be free of its chains. And so the third point in Doctor Sun's program, the People's Livelihood, sought to correct this condition. His plan was based largely on state socialism. He advocated using the ideas of Karl Marx as a guide, but employing different methods. "Where there are inequalities of wealth," he said, "Marx's methods can of course be applied; a class war can be started to destroy the inequalities. But in China, where industry is not yet developed, class war and the dictatorship of the proletariat are unnecessary.... In seeking a solution for our livelihood problem, we are not going to propose some impracticable and radical method and then wait until industry is developed. We want a plan which will anticipate dangers and forearm us against emergencies, which will check the growth of large private capital and prevent the social disease of extreme inequality between the rich and the poor.

"We cannot say," he continued, "that the theory of communism is different from our Min-sheng principle (the People's Livelihood). Our Three Principles of the People mean government 'of the people, by the people, and for the people' —that is, a state belonging to all the people, a government controlled by all the people, and rights and benefits for the enjoyment of all the people. If this is true, the people will not only have a communistic share in state production, but they will have a share in everything. When the people share everything in the state, then will we truly reach the goal of the

Min-sheng principle, which is Confucius' hope of a 'great commonwealth.'"

People he divided into three classes: those who know and perceive beforehand; those who know and perceive afterward; and those who do not know and perceive—the discoverers, the promoters and the practical men. "If these three groups," he said, "could use each other and heartily cooperate, human civilization would advance 'a thousand miles a day.'"

On the moral side he put his case in this manner: "Although Nature produces men with varying intelligence and ability, yet the human heart has continued to hope that all men might be equal. This is the highest of moral ideals and mankind should earnestly strive towards it. But how shall we begin? We will better understand by contrasting two philosophies of life — the selfish, which benefits self, and the altruistic, which benefits others.... Those who are concerned with benefiting others are glad to sacrifice themselves. Where this philosophy prevails, intelligent and able men are ever ready to use all their powers for the welfare of others, and religions of love and philanthropic enterprises grow up. But religious power alone is insufficient and philanthropy alone cannot remedy evil. So we must seek a fundamental solution, effect a revolution, overthrow autocracy, lift up democracy, and level inequalities. Hereafter we should harmonize the three types which I have described and given them all equal standing. Everyone should make service, not exploitation, his aim.... In this way, although men now may vary in natural intelligence and ability, yet as moral ideals and the spirit of service prevail, they will certainly become more and more equal. This is the essence of equality."

I have quoted at some length from Doctor Sun's teachings, for they are the guide to the present internal development of China. He planned to realize the Three Principles in three steps: first there was to be the period of military conquest, during which the provincial war-lords would be eliminated and the country united; next would come the period of political tutelage, during which the country would be governed by the Kuomintang Party, which would prepare the people to exercise political power; the final stage would be the period of representative government.

The group which constitutes the present Communist Party rebelled against the government established by the Kuomintang, in 1927, because it felt that Chiang Kai-shek was ignoring Doctor Sun's plan for the development of the People's Livelihood. There were other points of dissension, but this was the important one, and it continues to be a bone of contention.

The Communists also feel that the Kuomintang has unnecessarily protracted the period of political tutelage, and has been dilatory about taking steps to prepare the people for representative government. Continued pressure by the Communists, added to the general change that has taken place in the political situation since the war began, brought about the convocation of the People's Political Council, an advisory body.

At the fifth session of this body, held at Chungking during the first ten days in April, 1940, the council re-affirmed the policy of national united resistance to the Japanese invasion, and submitted the draft of a constitution which provides for the early establishment of representative government. In an address to the Council the Generalissimo stated: "Two years and nine months of war has already changed the entire political situation. The Chinese people have made progress on the one hand, while the government is now more dependent upon the support and cc-operation of the people for pursuing the war of resistance. The necessity, therefore, of putting the Constitution into practice is recognized by all."

As delegates to the People's Political Council come from both the Communist and Kuomintang parties, the words of the Generalissimo and the action of the Council are indicative of the dawn of a new era for war-torn China.

IV

Treason is extremely rare among Chinese, both because loyalty to the nation in times of external aggression also means loyalty to the race, and because the traitor risks almost certain repudiation by his family. And the

Chinese desires above all else to be revered by his children, and his children's children, when he passes on. Every Chinese knows that no son will worship at the shrine of a father who has been a traitor to his country. And so it came as a distinct shock to Chinese, as well as to foreign observers, when Wang Ching-wei, a former Prime Minister of the National Government, accepted the offer of the Japanese to become head of the puppet regime which will attempt to establish control over the occupied regions of China.

It is necessary to know Wang, the man, and his past record, before one can understand how this paradox came about. Wang Ching-wei is fifty-five years of age, cultured, well educated, and possesses great personal charm. He was an early disciple of Doctor Sun Yat-sen, became his chief secretary, and drafted his will when Doctor Sun was on his deathbed. In 1925 he was elected chairman of the National Government, but in 1926 he resigned, after a quarrel with Chiang Kai-shek, and went to Europe. When he returned in 1927 Chiang's right wing government had been set up at Nanking, while the left wing government was still functioning at Hankow. Wang again quarreled with Chiang, and went upriver to Hankow.

In 1930, when Feng Yu-hsiang and Yen Hsi-shan formed the coalition against Chiang Kai-shek, Wang joined the coalition. Here are three specific instances when Wang Ching-wei deserted the National Government, and each suggests that the cause was jealousy of the power of the Generalissimo. Since the death of Doctor Sun, Wang has possessed an insatiable desire to rule China. From a revolutionary with strong radical tendencies he has changed to an unscrupulous opportunist.

On April 1, 1940, he inaugurated at Nanking, with the cooperation of Japan, a puppet government which uses the title of the government which is headed by Chiang Kai-shek, and which continues to function at Chungking, in opposition to Japan. To add to the confusion Wang calls the party which he has organized for the purpose of administering this government, the Kuomintang Party.

This move is Japan's bid for political control of the occupied regions, and it is significant that of the men who have accepted positions in this puppet government Wang Ching-wei is the only one with a national reputation. The only plausible explanation of this repudiation of his country lies in his fantastic ambition for personal power and his bitter antagonism for Chiang Kai-shek.

This government is dependent on the Japanese army for its support. The area which it administers is the area which has been conquered by that army, and includes ninety percent of the nation's railroads, as well as rich natural resources. Most of the foreign interests lie in this region, and Japan is counting heavily on foreign greed to overcome any moral scruples about dealing with a state which has been set up by force of arms, to bring at least financial support to her program.

The fact remains, however, that Japan's control in this region is, for the most part, only along the railroads. The people between these avenues of communication remain loyal to China, and much of the population of the occupied villages and cities is also secretly sympathetic with the Chungking government. And so the success of the puppet regime hinges, as do other aspects of Japan's adventure in China, on the success of Japanese arms.

The Japanese leaders should be experiencing some qualms about the loyalty of Mr. Wang Ching-wei, for a man with his record for deserting causes can hardly be depended on to continue his obeisances to an alien liege if he sees an opportunity to improve his condition elsewhere.

V

It is obvious that the outcome of the struggle between Japan and China will depend in a great degree on forces which are out of the control of both nations. Both nations are dependent on assistance from abroad. What concerns America more vitally is the effect on her that a victory by either side would have.

If Japan wins it will mean a triumph for autocracy. There will be a short-lived demand for American capital, raw materials and those consumers' goods which Japan is not able to produce. But as Japan's industrial empire takes shape these demands will disappear, and Japan will establish a monopoly of all markets and sources of raw materials in the Far East. As her industrial empire grows, Japan's army and navy will expand. If she has not already taken over the Dutch East Indies, French Indo-China and the Philippine Islands, she will do so. Secure in the Western Pacific, she will then turn her eyes towards the east. She is particularly interested in fishing rights in Alaskan coastal waters, and she has a definite interest in Hawaii. The eastern islands of the Marshall group, over which she now has a mandate, are only two thousand miles from Hawaii, which is the extreme operating radius of a modern battle fleet. Her subsequent actions are left to conjecture, but it is well to remember that history has shown that conquerors do not cease conquering until it becomes physically impossible for them to continue.

What if China wins? China is one of the few nations existing today where democratic institutions prevail. Political democracy there is just coming to fruition. A Chinese victory will mean that China will become a base for democratic thought and action in the Orient. The government will most probably be representative, and a form of state socialism will develop. An independent China will demand complete sovereignty, and she will expect to be received by other nations on a basis of equality. The need for foreign capital and technical assistance with which to carry on reconstruction will be great, but such assistance will have to be made on a purely business basis, without the expectation of political commitments or the extension of special privileges.

It is difficult for the West to understand the diastatic effect this conflict has had on the Chinese people, because we of the West cannot visualize easily four hundred and fifty millions of people in the mass, and those who have not traveled there do not realize how primitive are the lives of the vast majority. The necessity to preserve themselves, the movement of forty millions of refugees, and the transfer of the government as well as of educational institutions into west China have combined to raise China's millions out of the ruts of tradition and out of their mental lassitude. This means that

China will be a better integrated and more progressive nation in the future. It means that the people of post-war China will demand and will get a higher standard of living. This will mean more buying power and the creation of wider markets.

By virtue of their proximity, both Japan and Russia will profit by this new state of affairs in China. But the United States, also, is in a favorable position to benefit by them, if we approach the problem with intelligence and in the right spirit. Our men and women who go out to China must be prepared to learn the language, live in the interior with the people, and meet them on a basis of equality, just as they would do if they were going to France, Germany or Great Britain. They must not expect to live an artificial life in foreign concessions, and to extract exorbitant profits from their investments and labors. America enjoys a high place in the regard of the Chinese people, and they will respond magnificently to an honest and unprejudiced approach. Their ways are different from ours, but the reverse is also true. As a people they are intensely human, and, what is more, they have a civilization which antedates ours by several thousand years.

An independent China offers the prospect for the development in our time of that much-talked-of practical Utopia: an equitable political, economic and social order.

VI

The air raid alarm was sounding as the huge Douglas transport plane took off from Chungking for the flight to Kunming. The American pilot turned the ship's nose southwest, and we scudded through the low-hanging clouds, barely clearing the mountain peaks. For the first fifty miles the terraces along the hill and mountain sides were filled with water, indicating that the crop was rice. As we mounted higher the terraces became dry, a sure sign that the crop was millet or wheat. About midway all signs of habitation ceased and we flew over a region of rugged and forbidding mountain ridges, with here and there a torrential stream cascading down a narrow gorge. And then, bit by bit, houses appeared again, and then a village. Suddenly we came out over a green-carpeted valley which widened gradually, and presently a city came into view. The plane descended in a long spiral towards a field lined with planes. We had arrived at Kunming, a little over four hundred miles from our starting point. And the planes we had seen from the air proved to be dummies, constructed of bamboo and matting to deceive the enemy.

Some of the government offices and many universities had moved to Kunming, but of greater interest to me was the aviation training center which was administered from here. A hundred and fifty new pilots had just been graduated—after a year of training under the direction of American instructors.

Remaining only long enough to arrange for transportation to Hanoi (French Indo-China) on the French railroad, and to see the American Consul, Paul Meyer, and his wife, old Peip'ing friends, I embarked on the diesel-operated Michelin. The Michelin runs on hard rubber tires, and the trip to the Indo-Chinese border was without noise or jar. The road itself is like a corkscrew, twisting around the edges of ravines and diving into countless tunnels. At Lao Kai, the border town, a change was made to a steam train, with wagon-lits coaches, for the night run to Hanoi.

Tropical foliage began to appear at Lao Kai, and as we moved south-east along the Red river valley it became more abundant. Shortly after day-light we approached the end of the one-hundred-sixty-mile trip from the border, emerging into a broad delta land where is located the seat of France's colonial government in Indo-China. Here in a semi-tropical setting I found a piece of Paris, set in an Oriental frame. Wide, palm-bordered boulevards led past magnificent administration buildings of the colonial government, verdant parks, elegant residences and imposing-looking hotels, banks and shops of European design, while in the narrow streets of the native quarter, along the periphery, were the picturesque bazaars, their colorful signboards advertising their wares in French and the latinized version of the Tonkinese language. French is evidently a required subject in the schools, for its use seemed to be universal by the natives—at least all understood it.

At this time Hanoi had suddenly become a city of great activity, for with the fall of Hankow and Canton the rail line from the sea at Haiphong to the provinces of Yunnan and Kwangsi, in China, was now one of the three remaining routes into free China, the other two being the road from Burma to Kunming—just completed—and the highway from Russia to China's northwest. Chinese commissions were here to superintend the movement of supplies. Scores of Japanese agents idled in the hotels and sidewalk cafes, keeping tabs on the Chinese activities. And covertly watching both parties were the ever-vigilant agents of the colonial government.

At Haiphong I boarded a coastwise steamer for the two-day trip to Hongkong. My particular purpose in going to Hongkong was to see two other key figures in the Chinese picture: T. V. Soong, and the widow of China's revered revolutionary leader, Madame Sun Yat-sen. No survey of this scene could be complete without them.

As the ship approached the Gibraltar-like island I recalled the impression of it which had been given to me by a British friend, a captain in the Grenadier Guards, years before. He said that when he first saw Hongkong from the deck of his ship his eyes wandered from the busy wharfs to the warehouses, on behind to the banks and business houses, and then part way up the hill to tidy residences of the lesser foreign employees and colonial officials, and finally came to rest at the Governor-General's mansion on the Peak, and he exclaimed to himself: "My God, how British!"

T. V. Soong was in his office in the Bank of Canton. He had grown a little stout since the days when he held the post of Minister of Finance, and he was graver and more mature. But he had lost none of his charm of manner, and the eyes which regarded me speculatively from behind the thick lenses of his spectacles were bright with intelligence and understanding.

"T. V.," as he is popularly known, is regarded as China's financial wizard, and his ability in this field is highly respected by foreign bankers. Brother of Madame Chiang Kai-shek, Madame H. H. Kung and Madame Sun Yat-sen, he was forty-four at this time. He graduated from Harvard in 1915, and then did his graduate work at Columbia. It was he who financed the drive of

Chiang Kai-shek's armies during the northern expedition (1926-28), and when the new government was established at Nanking he became the Minister of Finance. But in 1933 he resigned, after differences with the Generalissimo, and since then he has devoted himself to the affairs of the Bank of China, of which he is Chairman of the Board. However, a man of T. V.'s ability, energy and catholicity of interests could not remain entirely aloof from the national picture in China, and unofficially the government leans heavily on him for advice. His refusal to accept public office in this crisis is puzzling to foreigners, but he probably feels that he can be more useful from his camouflaged position behind the scenes. He is another curious combination of liberalism and conservatism—liberal by instinct, and conservative because of his early inhibitions and environment.

His final words to me reflected the idea I found in most quarters in China with regard to the attitude of the United States towards the war: "We don't expect America to fight for us," he said, "but we don't expect her to aid Japan either. If America will only give Japan less assistance than she is giving now, and if she will give us her moral support and a little financial assistance, we will win this battle for democracy here in eastern Asia."

My last vision of Madame Sun Yat-sen had been of a widow in deep mourning following the body of her distinguished husband to its last resting place in the mausoleum on Purple Mountain, at Nanking, nearly ten years before. Since then she had been seldom in the public eye, preferring to live quietly and simply in retirement, as she endeavored to clarify and interpret the teachings of Doctor Sun. After Chiang Kai-shek swung to the right, in 1927, she took the position that he had violated these teachings, and she refused to have anything to do with the Generalissimo or the Kuomintang government, counting them as traitors to the Three Principles of the People. What, I wondered, was her attitude in this crisis?

One of Madame Sun's secretaries conducted me to the modest apartment where she was living in Hongkong. I sensed something of the spirit of this woman from the severity of the simply furnished room in which I waited. She was allowing herself no luxuries. Presently she entered, and with unaffected sincerity she bade me welcome. Instantly I was at home, for she had the "pu yao k'e ch'i (don't stand on ceremony)" attitude I had met in the Eighth Route Army. But she had something more—a peace of mind, an utter self-assurance which lacked egotism. As we conversed, the reason for this quality became more apparent: she was filled with love for the human being, especially the human being who was unfortunate and down-trodden. She wore no mask, and her face was relaxed, and beautiful in its serenity.

She did not lack for humor, and as I told her of some of my experiences in the north she gleefully interjected interpretations of the reactions of people I described. I had come for tea, but time passed swiftly, and when I rose to go there was still much to be said, so gathering two of her secretaries she suggested that we repair to a Chinese restaurant for dinner.

It was clear that she felt the Kuomintang had not been carrying out the Three Principles of the People, and that the Communist leaders had. Chiang Kai-shek, she believed, had been encouraging loyalty to himself, rather than to the government and the nation. The time had long since passed when representative government should have been established. True, the people were not prepared to exercise the franchise, but no steps had been taken to prepare them. But most serious of all was the failure of the government to apply the principle of the People's Livelihood. Instead it had catered to the Shanghai bankers and ignored the problems of the people, especially the agrarian problem.

She was more hopeful now, however. The war had convinced many self-righteous officials that the strength of the nation lay in the common people. But there was still too much greed, too much selfishness.

She said little of her own work, but I knew that she was putting her heart and soul into the China Defense League, of which she was chairman. Under her guidance it was gathering funds and supplies from abroad with which to organize and equip hospitals, care for the wounded at the front, and relieve the desperate need of refugees. And she saw to it that every dollar was honestly spent. Under her eagle eye there was no diversion of funds to the pockets of unscrupulous officials.

VII

My conversation with Madame Sun Yet-sen was a fitting finale to my months of observation of this great drama. She epitomized the spirit of new China: honest, unselfish, intensely patriotic and tirelessly working for a better, a more equitable way of life.

During the weeks that my ship churned eastward across the Pacific the events of the preceding months became integrated in my mind, falling into place like the pieces of a jig-saw puzzle. The central theme was the preservation of China's independence, but around it swarmed the forces of social, economic and political change which were making it possible to resist the invasion, forces which received their impetus from the central theme and which were also held in check by it.

The central figure in this colossal fermentation of ideas and actions, of striving for opportunity and equality on the one hand, and for the feeding of selfish desires on the other, is Chiang Kai-shek. His experience, his devotion to the nation and his personal integrity have raised him above mere party interests, enabling him to perceive and select for the public benefit the meritorious ideas and practices of all parties. From the Communist Party, and its brilliant, self-effacing leaders, Mao Tse-tung, Chu Teh, Chow En-lai, and others, has come the rich leavening of liberal thought and action, the insistence on recognition of the nobility and rights of the individual, the drive for an equitable social and economic order; from the Kuomintang has come the ability to organize the resources of the nation on a vast scale, using to advantage the instruments and technique of the existing economic system. From it has also come the influx of ideas from the West, scientific knowledge, business methods, Western culture, and technical skill. Military leaders such as General Pai Chung-hsi, Li Chung-jen, Sun Lien-chung and T'ang En-po have improved the organization and efficiency of those armies trained for mobile and positional warfare.

Slowly, but with definite certainty, all of these forces are being woven into a pattern whose dominant note is progress, progress towards the goal of national independence, democracy, and a way of life which will bring economic sufficiency and happiness to all of its four hundred and fifty millions of citizens.

The key to this pattern is the element which alone can be the key to any successful society of human beings: the practice of selflessness by its members and vigilant regard for the rights and feelings of others.

图书在版编目（CIP）数据

中国双星 /（美）卡尔逊（Carlson, E. F.）著.
－北京：外文出版社，2003.12
（中国之光）
ISBN 7-119-03478-2

I.中… II.卡… III.抗日战争－史料－英文
IV.K265.06
中国版本图书馆 CIP 数据核字（2003）第 091233 号

外文出版社网址：
http://www.flp.com.cn
外文出版社电子信箱：
info@flp.com.cn
sales@flp.com.cn

中国之光丛书
中国双星

作　　者（美）卡尔逊（Carlson, E. F.）
责任编辑 蔚文英
封面设计 蔡　荣
印刷监制 冯　浩
出版发行 外文出版社
社　　址 北京市百万庄大街 24 号　**邮政编码** 100037
电　　话（010）68996121 / 68996117（编辑部）
（010）68329514 / 68327211（推广发行部）
印　　刷 三河市汇鑫印务有限公司
开　　本 小 16 开
印　　数 1000 册
版　　次 2003 年第 1 版第 1 次印刷
装　　别 精装
书　　号 ISBN 7-119-03478-2 / Z·678（外）
定　　价 80.00 元

NINGHSIA
SUIYUAN
CHAHAR
JEHOL
Highway to U.S.S.R.
Lanchow
KANSU
SHENSI
SHANSI
HOPEI
SHANTUNG
HONAN
HUPEH
ANHWEI
SZECHUAN
KWEICHOW
HUNAN
KIANGSI
FUKIEN
YUNNAN
KWANGSI
KWANGTUNG
CHINA
Paoto
Hokiu
Tatung
Kalgan
Peiping
Tientsin
Paoteh
Kolan
Wutai
Fuping
Jenchiu
Yulin
Taiyuan
Nankung
Yenan
Lintsing
Yellow R.
Tsinan
Hungtung
Chengchow
Kelchow
Taierhch
Tungkwan
Sian
Such
Sinyang
Nanking
Ichang
Hankow
Anking
Yangtze R.
Chungking
Changsha
Kunming
Canton
Hong Kong
Hanoi
Haiphong
Hainan
FRENCH INDO-CHINA
SOUT
CHINA